Museums and their Visitors

Museums are at a critical moment in their history. In order to ensure survival into the next century, museums and galleries must demonstrate their social relevance and use. This means developing their public service functions through becoming more knowledgeable about the needs of their visitors and more adept at providing enjoyable and worthwhile experiences.

Museums and their Visitors aims to help museums and galleries in this crucial task. It examines the ways in which museums need to develop their communicative functions and, with examples of case-studies, explains how to achieve best practice. The special needs of a number of target audiences including schools, families and people with disabilities are outlined and illustrated by examples of exhibition, education and marketing policies. The book looks in detail at the power of objects to inspire and stimulate and analyses the use of language in museums and galleries.

This is the first book to be written to guide museum and gallery staff in the development of provision for their visitors. It will be of interest to students of museum, heritage and leisure and tourism studies, as well as to international museum professionals.

Eilean Hooper-Greenhill is a Lecturer in Museum Studies at the University of Leicester. She is the author of *Museum and Gallery Education* and *Museums and the Shaping of Knowledge*.

The Heritage: Care–Preservation–Management programme has been designed to serve the needs of the museum and heritage community worldwide. It publishes books and information services for professional museum and heritage workers, and for all the organisations that service the museum community.

Editor-in-chief: Andrew Wheatcroft

Architecture in Conservation: *Managing developments at historic sites*
James Strike

The Development of Costume
Naomi Tarrant

Forward Planning: *A handbook of business, corporate and development planning for museums and galleries*
Edited by Timothy Ambrose and Sue Runyard

Heritage Gardens: *Care, conservation and management*
Sheena Mackellar Goulty

Heritage and Tourism: *in the global village*
Priscilla Boniface and Peter J. Fowler

The Handbook for Museums
Gary Edson and David Dean

The Industrial Heritage: *Managing resources and uses*
Judith Alfrey and Tim Putnam

Museum Basics
Timothy Ambrose and Crispin Paine

Museum Exhibition: *Theory and practice*
David Dean

Museum Security and Protection: *A handbook for cultural heritage institutions*
ICOM and ICMS

Museums 2000: *Politics, people, professionals and profit*
Edited by Patrick J. Boylan

Museums and the Shaping of Knowledge
Eilean Hooper-Greenhill

Museums without Barriers: *A new deal for disabled people*
Fondation de France and ICOM

The Past in Contemporary Society: Then/Now
Peter J. Fowler

The Representation of the Past: *Museums and heritage in the post-modern world*
Kevin Walsh

Towards the Museum of the Future: *New European perspectives*
Edited by Roger Miles and Lauro Zavala

Museums and their Visitors

Eilean Hooper-Greenhill

London and New York

First published 1994
by Routledge
11 New Fetter Lane, London EC4P 4EE

Simultaneously published in the USA and Canada
by Routledge
29 West 35th Street, New York, NY 10001

Typeset in Sabon by Florencetype Ltd, Kewstoke

Printed and bound in Great Britain by Butler & Tanner Ltd, Frome

Printed on acid free paper

British Library Cataloguing in Publication Data
A catalogue record for this book is available from the British Library

Library of Congress Cataloging in Publication Data
ISBN 0–415–06857–6

For my students

Contents

Plates

Figures

Tables

Acknowledgements

This book could not have been written without the generous contributions of a host of colleagues, too numerous to list, from all areas of the museum field, both in the United Kingdom and in the rest of the world. Many have given freely of their time and their ideas and I am sincerely indebted to them. I would also like to pay tribute to many of my students, who, in taking the ideas of the communication courses at the University of Leicester have made them their own and applied them in imaginative and exciting new ways. These ideas, often expressed in essays, have contributed to the development of my own thought.

I would like to thank my colleagues in the Department of Museum Studies, University of Leicester for continued support. Special thanks are due to Jim Roberts for the preparation of the figures.

I gratefully acknowledge the receipt of travel grants from the Establishment Board and the Research Board of the University of Leicester.

Introduction

A new role for museums

In the past decade enormous changes have taken place in museums and galleries across the world. The thrust of the shift is clear – museums are changing from being static storehouses for artefacts into active learning environments for people. This change in function means a radical reorganisation of the whole culture of the museum – staff structures, attitudes and work patterns must all mutate to accommodate new ideas and new approaches. In addition to looking inward to their collections, museums are now looking outward towards their audiences; where in the past collections were researched, now audiences are also being researched; the balance of power in museums is shifting from those who care for objects to include, and often prioritise, those who care for people. The older ideology of conservation must now share its directing role with the newer ideology of collaboration.

This radical shift is an exciting one, and not without its challenges. It means engaging with the complex issue of the relationship between the preservation of objects and their use in education, and it means re-evaluating long-held assumptions. As the Director of the Victoria and Albert Museum in London has put it 'It is important that the museum is not just a passive collection of wonderful objects but a springboard into the community' (Esteve-Coll, 1991: 37). It is now no longer enough to collect as an end in itself; collecting has become the means to an end, that of making connections with people, and making links with their experience.

Once questions are asked about how, with what and to whom museums should make links, the focus of the museum begins to shift from collection to communication. This move towards visitors is understood as the only way forward for the future. For too long, museums have defended the values of scholarship, research and collection *at the expense of* the needs of visitors. The challenge today is to preserve these traditional museum concerns, but to *combine them* with the educational values that focus on how the objects cared for in museums can add to the quality of life for all.

1

What is the use of these objects that are so expensive to keep? Why should society expend scarce resources on maintaining collections? How can artefacts, specimens and objects from distant parts of the globe affect our lives in today's often difficult and complicated world? What is their value to people? If we in museums cannot answer these questions we have no real reason for continuing.

In a climate of changing priorities combined with decreasing resources, the museum must fight its corner alongside other claims to funds. This means an effective and business-like approach to management, a very clear perception of the opportunities for the future, and an ability to explain the social use of museums to anyone who asks. In a competitive situation, it is often the most dynamic and professional presentation of ideas, benefits and opportunities that succeeds in gaining access to resources. To achieve this, museums require clearly identified achievable goals, precise quantifiable knowledge of current projects and successes and an energetic creative approach to problem-solving, with the director backed by a supportive and well-informed governing body and a unified and committed team of trained professional staff who understand and share a common vision for the future.

A new role has had to be found for museums. The museum has become an establishment for learning and enjoyment. This new role can be seen as the continuation and development of an older Victorian vision. The museum is becoming once more the university of the people, and their schoolroom, but in relation to a new interpretation of education, which is understood today as structured discovery within a life-long framework. The reinterpretation of this fundamental museum function is placed on the one hand within the world of education, but on the other, enters a new and rapidly growing world, that of a leisure and tourism industry dedicated to pleasure and consumerism. It is only now in the 1990s with the development of a very varied and professional leisure industry that it is possible to rearticulate a purpose for museums and galleries that can be easily grasped. However, if museums are now clearly placed within the leisure industry, the public sees the form of leisure that museums represent as closely connected to learning, and linked to worthwhile and valuable experiences rather than trivial short-term thrills. It is the educational potential of museums, founded on their unique collections, that gives them their particular market niche within the leisure industry.

In the years to come, the development of this new role for museums will grow, based on the experience of the last thirty years. Useful approaches, including educational processes, methods of display, marketing philosophies and ways of researching and satisfying visitor needs can all now be identified. Much experience is available to inform the dynamic developments required of museums in the next decade. As we approach a new century, museums must grasp hold of those practices and philosophies that will serve to negotiate the route to survival. Museums must become more open, more democratic, more responsive and more professional. A holistic approach to the museum as a medium for communication must replace the fragmented and erratic approaches to their visitors of some museums in the past. The functions of the museum as a communicator must be integrated with the functions of the museum as a storehouse for collections, and the knowledge of collections must be related to and generated by the knowledge of the audience.

The museum as a medium for communication

How can we understand communication in museums? One of the first things to begin to examine is the notion of communication itself. Any process of communication will function as an intended set of messages that can also be read as an unintended set of messages. Museums are engaged in the production of intentioned messages through exhibitions, displays, events, posters, leaflets and other forms of communication. This intentioned process can be analysed through what Georges Mounin (Mounin, 1985; Hooper-Greenhill, 1991b) has called 'the semiology of communication'. Semiology is the science of signs; that is, the analysis of artefacts, symbols, pictures and so on. The semiology of communication analyses the systems used and the methods followed to create an intentioned set of messages. Images, symbols, artefacts and other signs are analysed for their intended messages within a given communicative system.

For example, the designers of the upper floor of the Colour Museum in Bradford have produced a logo that is used as a way of articulating the image of the museum. The logo is like a rainbow, with primary colours. The museum uses this logo on its stationery and at its front door, and uses the colours in the display. The logo acts to introduce the museum through an association of the colours and the mission of the museum (to explore colour). This intentioned sign can be analysed for itself, in terms of its colour, forms and associations and in relation to its use in creating a corporate identity. This is properly the province of the semiology of communication.

An analysis of the display on the upper floor at the Colour Museum from this point of view would discover an excellently consistent labelling system that consists of textual panels with text in two sizes, with images and colour incorporated. The text panels are placed in consistent relationships to the display cases. Colour is used consistently within the cases. Displays can be analysed as communication systems, looking at the physical aspects, including space, text, colour, images and objects; and the intellectual aspects, including the ideas, concepts, levels, associations and meanings.

As socio-cultural institutions, museums, in common with other socio-cultural institutions such as schools, the cinema or the mass media, are susceptible to analysis through the 'semiology of signification'. The semiology of signification analyses messages that are often, but not always, unintentioned. This form of analysis generally searches for the hidden, ideological messages. Ideology is the metaphorical sea within which we swim, the social air that we breathe. It is not possible to live outside ideology; it permeates our existence as social beings. This is not to say that ideology is a seamless unified set of ideas: we live within many layers of ideology, which are often contradictory, which give us the common-sense context for our lives at home, at work, politically, and in relation to the rest of the world (Belsey, 1980). Ideology can be analysed and investigated at each of these levels.

Some analyses of museums and exhibitions from this perspective can be cited (Barthes, 1973; Duncan and Wallach, 1980; Anon., 1980; Duncan, 1991). In applying this form of analysis to the Colour Museum, the following questions would be asked: what are the social messages to be found in the displays at the Colour Museum? What does it say, for example, about the different ethnic groups in Bradford? What view of the family, or of the role of women, do the displays give? As a museum owned by the Society of Dyers and Colourists, whose primary purpose is 'educational', what view of the chemical industry does it give? Does the fact that the museum is placed in the same building as the company that owns it lead to any distortion in its message? What forms of control are exercised by the owners of the museum?

The objectives of the book

Although there is much analysis that is needed in the field of the semiology of signification, *Museums and their Visitors* will concentrate on analysing intentional communicative acts in museums and galleries, while acknowledging that museums and museum processes are part of the world of power and interest and that no communicative act can exist outside its own ideological context.

This book will try, however imperfectly, to draw together a range of ideas and practices of the past decade, and to present them in such a way that they can be of general use. The focus of the book is on making connections with visitors, with an emphasis on the methods of communication rather than on the content of the messages themselves. The analysis of the messages that museums have constructed, do and might construct will be the subject of further work.

Museums and their Visitors begins, in Chapter 1, with a discussion of the imperatives that are pushing us towards the development of new ways of being. The development of the museum as a communicator is explored through the expansion of the museum's educational role, including the emergence of new ways of working with audiences, and the effects of market research. The demands of greater accountability and greater competition from an aggressive leisure industry are also considered.

Chapter 2 looks at how we can analyse communication in museums and galleries. What is communication theory and how is it relevant? Has it been used in museums and if so how and to what effect? The importance of a two-way dynamic relationship between communicators with equal powers is emphasised, and the many ways in which museums communicate with their visitors are outlined.

Chapter 3 explores what we know of museum visitors. Who are they, and where do they come from? Who doesn't visit museums and why? A distinction is drawn between a museum *visitor*, who on the whole is to be found among the displays, using them for educational and leisure purposes, and a museum *user*, who might be found both front of house, but equally, in the stores or research areas of the museum, and who is likely to be using the museum for professional purposes. Museum users include murder investigators, for example, who may check details of maggot growth and development with natural history museum curators in order to determine the date of death of an infested corpse, and makers of historic films who will check object and costume details in history or art museums in order to achieve a period atmosphere. This book focuses on the visitors, rather than the users of museums.

Having established why, how and with whom communicative functions should be developed, the remaining chapters of the book, from Chapter 4 to Chapter 8, offer practical guidance on how to plan and evaluate museum processes with the needs of visitors in mind. The final chapter focuses on the policies and strategies that are necessary in order to do this.

Museums and their Visitors is written for all museum staff, not just those whose job appears to relate to visitors. People working with collections and museum managers and administrators also have a responsibility for the social outcome of their work. Museums and galleries must rise to the challenge of integrating the needs, strengths and delights of their publics into all areas of their work. This holistic approach is absolutely vital to the success of museums.

It is hoped that this book will prove useful to students of museums, whether at the beginning of their studies, or at a time when perhaps study no longer seems necessary. At this time of intensive change in museums throughout the world, a process that can only accelerate as time passes, everyone needs to maintain and upgrade skills and to rethink professional practices. As the world changes around us, we must at least keep up to date. How much better if we could be more proactive, making change happen in a way that celebrates the potentials and joys of museums. It is the writer's hope that this book, based as it is on the experiences of colleagues from many parts of the international museum field, will help to do just that.

1

Forces for change

Museums and galleries throughout the world are at a point of renewal. New forms of museums, new ways of working with objects, new attitudes to exhibitions and above all, new ways of relating to museum publics, are emerging. At the end of the twentieth century, old structures are being replaced to prepare for a new century. Many social institutions are reviewing their roles and potentials, and museums and galleries are among them.

What are the functions of museums likely to be in the twenty-first century? One thing is certain. Museums must develop a clear social function. During the 1990s a new age has dawned, a knowledge-based age that will replace the post-industrial age that has existed for the last hundred and fifty years. As the heavy plant of industrial production is replaced by the micro-circuits of the computer, the emphasis changes from the production of technology to the production of ideas, the pace of knowledge transmission increases, and possibilities for intellectual action multiply. Knowledge races around the world in a micro-second, information is accessed in new ways, and new levels of interconnectivity become possible.

What is the role of the museum within this cultural shift? As electronic media move centre-stage, what is the function of the three-dimensional object? As the importance of knowledge and information grows, how can museums play a genuine part in the production and dissemination of knowledge? How should museums renegotiate and redefine their functions? What is the way forward for the twenty-first century?

During the next decade, the relationship between the museum and its many and diverse publics will become more and more important. And this relationship must focus on genuine and effective use of the museum and its collections. In the past, museum visitors have been content to stroll through the displays and have rarely sought more than a tangential visual experience of objects. Now, there is a clear and consistent demand for a close and active encounter with objects and exhibits. A physical experience using all the senses is called for.

Plate 1 The close examination and handling of a small fragment helps in the seeing and understanding of the archaeological artefacts displayed in the glass cases. These traces enable students at Liverpool University to relate ideas drawn from the objects of the past to their own present and future lives.

Photo: Howard Barlow.

Increasingly this experience is expected by visitors to be of immediate personal relevance with an interaction which is sustainable for several minutes and which results in a clearly identified knowledge gain. When this rapid and explicit benefit is not available, museums are not popular; where displays, discovery centres, responsive exhibits, dramatic performances and interactive videos enable this experience, museums are overwhelmed with appreciative vistors.

How therefore can museums, and perhaps more problematically, art galleries, offer meaningful experiences for their visitors? What conceptual changes are necessary in order for museums to consolidate a powerful new future?

These questions will be answered throughout the course of the book. This chapter will examine a number of forces for change that museums can harness in their development towards becoming relevant institutions for the twenty-first century. Forces for change include an expansion of the museum's traditional educational role, moves towards being more user-centred, and the response in museums to greater accountability and competition.

An expanded role for museum education

The United Kingdom Museums Association asserts in its *National Strategy for Museums* that as an educational resource, museum collections constitute a national asset that has been consistently undervalued (Museums Association, 1991a: 11). It is recommended that museums need to draw the attention of both central and local government to their educational strengths, and that an educational policy should be drawn up and regularly reviewed.

> Museum education is too important to be left to the educators. It needs to imbue everyone who works in museums . . . the policy of any museum should be an education policy . . . education is a key component in every museum's *raison d'être*.
>
> (Pittman 1991: 43)

Nigel Pittman, then Head of the Museums and Galleries Division of the Office of Arts and Libraries (the UK central government body overseeing the work of museums; now subsumed into the Department of National Heritage), here makes very explicit the expansion of museum education. Pointing to the founding purpose of many Victorian museums, Pittman states firmly that museum education today should be understood not merely as the provision of classes for organised educational groups, but should be seen as the shaping force behind a museum's general policies and objectives.

As museums develop into institutions which collect, care for and communicate about objects, so the role of museum education is expanding. Museum staff in general are developing their roles as educators through the new approaches to displays that are being developed, through considering the educational potential of new museum developments and through a heightened awareness of the museum's public. In a great many museums in Britain at the present time, the staff responsible for education are part of the senior management team, contribute to the scheduling and planning of exhibitions and other events, and take responsibility for the management of buildings and staff (Hooper-Greenhill (ed.), 1992). In the development of new relationships with audiences, it is often the education staff who are able to take the lead through their experience with museum visitors.

In Australia and the United States, the concept of the 'audience advocate' has been developed (Duffy, 1989; Hooper-Greenhill, 1991a: 190–3). The 'audience advocate' acts as the person responsible for considering the needs of all sectors of the audience as new projects are developed. The 'audience advocate' researches the actual and potential museum audience, makes links with appropriate experts in order to develop knowledge and understanding of specific target groups (such as those with a particular disability), monitors new exhibitions and other projects, supplies audience-related information to other staff as appropriate and evaluates all aspects of the museum, its exhibitions and educational programmes in relation to visitor requirements.

As this new staff role is introduced to Britain, it has been variously considered within education or marketing departments, or, as at the Science Museum, London, is placed within a new Interpretation Unit, which includes those researching the needs of audiences (audience advocates), education staff, facilitators and enablers working with interactive displays, and a drama team.

In America, a group of museum educators, stimulated by the American Association's 1984 report *Museums for a New Century* (Commission on Museums for a New Century, 1984), formed a task force to consider the development of museum education in American museums and galleries. The initial objectives for the task force were:

- to describe the critical issues in museum education;
- to recommend action that will strengthen and expand the educational role of museums in today's world;
- to outline an on-going role for museums, professional associations and other appropriate organisations in ensuring that the recommendations are carried out.

(Museum Education Roundtable, 1992)

The discussions of the task force quickly moved from the discussion of museum education as a department within a museum to the assessment of education as the mission of the museum. The report of the task force, *Excellence and Equity: Education and the Public Dimension of Museums* (American Association of Museums, 1992), initially proposed that education was *the* primary responsibility of museums, but the report has been accepted by the American Association on the grounds that education is *a* primary reponsibility of museums.

The title of the document *Excellence and Equity* acknowledges both scholarship and public service, expert knowledge and outreach, accountability towards both collections and people. Although perhaps the document (in adopting *a* instead of *the*) did not go far enough for the members of the task force, issues about the balance of objectives and resources in museums and galleries were raised. Where funds, for example, are to be equally distributed between the demands of excellence and of equity, this will generally mean a redistribution of resources towards the provision of a public service, and it is strongly argued that both public provision and expert collection knowledge can and must exist side-by-side (Gurian, 1992).

The report represents an opportunity for museums and galleries to carry out a self-audit to prepare for the social realities of the twenty-first century, in full acknowledgement both of the democratic principle that people of all classes, ages, races and ethnic origins have the right to share the cultural patrimony available to them, and of the fact that museums have an obligation to reflect the nature of society in terms of collecting, the composition of their staff and governing body and their public programming (Swank, 1992).

Museums and the changing needs of schools

While the expansion of the broad educational role of museums and galleries is altering the balance of functions within museums, provision for both formal and informal education within museums is also changing and growing.

Histories have always been contested territories, and the power to define the past is one index of domination. As power and interest groups shift and fluctuate within societies, new approaches to history and the past are developed. The school curriculum frequently makes manifest these new approaches. In many societies today, the museum is part of this shifting of emphasis and perspective, and often takes on new functions in relation to school knowledge. Examples from two countries illustrate this.

As black South Africa struggles towards political power, the political and ideological infrastructure that sustained apartheid is crumbling. In terms of education, vast differences exist in the provision for black and for white children, which include differences in method of teaching, provision of resources and indeed in access to literacy. Some museums are determined to use their collections and resources to raise the standard of black education, and at Grahamstown the education department is staffed by both black and white museum officers, although at the time of appointment of the black officer, this was in fact illegal (Hall, 1992).

Plate 2 The Law Uk Folk Museum, the only village house left in an area of Hong Kong now
covered with skyscrapers. As a unique survival of the farming community, this farm-
house symbolises the simplicity and purity of the past as Hong Kong moves towards a
complex and uncertain future.

Photo: Hong Kong Museum of History, Urban Council, Hong Kong.

A book has been prepared by the museum for teachers which identifies the historical myths that have been perpetuated in South Africa, myths such as: 'Whites and Blacks arrived in South Africa at the same time'; 'Black political ideas were inspired by Whites'; and 'the Homelands correspond to the area historically occupied by each Black "nation" and their fragmentation was the result of tribal wars and disputes' (Owen, 1991). The book makes suggestions about how history might be taught, focusing on historical methodology, and on history as a study of people, families and communities in the past. Teaching through objects is recommended as one way in which myths might be dispelled, and all children from all sections of society might begin to make relationships with the past. Museum objects, used in conjunction with photographs and documents, are seen as having the potential to promote a history relevant to the 'new South Africa'.

Other institutions are also working to shift the balance of access to knowledge and skills. Johannesburg Art Gallery has recently developed the Imbali Teacher Training Project which aims to provide teachers with skills that will enrich their teaching of art within their own communities, which include Soweto, Kwa-Thema and Sebokeng. These practical workshops have grown out of and are sponsored by Women for Peace. The pilot teachers' courses in 1989 focused on line drawing, mask-making and working with oil pastels. The success of these led to further workshops exploring print-making, kite-making and a mural painting project. These are recorded in the gallery's annual reports.

In Hong Kong, a new approach to the teaching of history is focusing on 'Hong Kong Studies'. In a nation which has up until now felt itself to be reaching forward rather than looking backward, but which is soon to experience radical changes in governance, the past has become newly important and has attained the status of something to be valued and cherished (P. Wright, 1992). This has meant an increase of relevance for the museums that hold the key to the past. The Law Uk Folk Museum offers an example.

Chai Wan (literally 'firewood bay') was a part of Hong Kong Island that until the late 1940s consisted of farmland, with several longstanding villages including Law Uk, Lam Uk, Shing Uk and others. The people of the villages were farmers, producing rice, fruit and vegetables which they exchanged with the passing fishermen for fish. In the small communities, a simple way of life existed. The Japanese occupation of 1941 began the process of change in the villages, which accelerated with the arrival of refugees in the 1950s, who settled in squatter huts on the hillsides. Since this time, the old villages have been cleared for redevelopment as Chai Wan has become a highly industrialised area, with the extension of the Mass Transit Railway System, and public housing estates.

The Law Uk Folk Museum is 'the only village house left in the area and now becomes an authentic reminder of the early Hong Kong village house' (Hong Kong Museum of History, 1990: 24). The museum symbolises and represents the past of Hong Kong, and has become one of the sites where local studies can be carried out. Students can consider the difference between the old and the new ways, through the exploration of very different structures for living and working.

Plate 3 The interior of the Law Uk Folk Museum with a single room and a cock-loft above.
Photo: Hong Kong Museum of History, Urban Council, Hong Kong.

The integration of home and work can be observed in the internal rooms of the museum which served as both bedrooms and workrooms, with the roof spaces being used as cock-lofts.

In England and Wales, the introduction of the National Curriculum in 1988, which must by law be implemented in state schools, has opened up many opportunities for museums. The National Curriculum emphasises the use of primary sources in learning and is creating a demand at all levels for resources. The curriculum is enshrined in detailed documents, with specific programmes of study and attainment targets identified for each subject. These documents frequently refer either to the use of museums specifically, or to artefacts, specimens or the real things that museums are well able to provide.

In the National Curriculum for History, for example, at 'Attainment Target 3: the use of historical sources', children at level 2 (juniors) are expected to 'recognise that historical sources can stimulate and help answer questions about the past', and at level 3, 'make deductions from historical sources'. At a later stage, level 6, children are expected to 'compare the usefulness of different historical sources as evidence for a particular enquiry' and at level 10 (older secondary pupils) 'explain the problematic nature of historical evidence, showing an awareness that judgements based on historical sources may well be provisional'. The examples of how these skills might be demonstrated suggest using artefacts from a museum; for example making 'deductions about social groups in Victorian Britain by looking at the clothes people wore' (National Curriculum Council, 1991). Curricula from many other subject areas, such as science and art, also offer enormous and sometimes unexpected opportunities for museums of all sorts (Goodhew, 1989; Copeland, 1991; Pownall and Hutson, 1991).

In part, the relevance of the National Curriculum to museums and galleries reflects the work put into assessing and responding to the curriculum proposals by the Group for Education in Museums. GEM is the professional association for those in museums who work with education. Many of the recommendations made have been adopted by the curriculum working groups, who have in response made more specific references to the use of museums, galleries and sites, and have on occasions inserted references to the values of using objects in learning.

The committee of the Group for Education in Museums coined the acronym DAPOS (documents, artefacts, pictures, oral history and sites) to remind curriculum working-group members to assess their draft syllabuses to make certain that where relevant, these elements were included. This proactive stance by the group has resulted in a very direct relationship between museums and the National Curriculum. This is a major achievement and may well be seen in retrospect as creating one of the most successful ways in which the museums of the late twentieth century can demonstrate their use to society. With these clear opportunities now in place, it behoves museums to reappraise the support they give to schools to ensure that the needs of schools are met as they implement the National Curriculum (Audit Commission, 1991: 6). The methods used by the Group for Education in Museums to forge a strong relationship for museums to the curriculum as it was being written may provide a useful model for museums in other countries.

The Education Reform Act 1988 that introduced the National Curriculum also introduced Local Management of Schools. Where in the past, Local Education Authorities have funded local government or independent museum education posts and costs from their centrally held monies, the devolution of central funds to individual school budgets has raised questions about the funding of museum school services. Currently new structures are being evolved. It is too early at this stage to see how this will work, but already there have been both successes and failures for museums, with some loan services, for example, being closed, but some new education posts being established with funding from other sources. These changes in the management of schools will shortly combine with far more radical local government restructuring and it is impossible at the present time to see what new arrangements for local museums and their educational provision will have been established by the end of the decade.

For museum school services in Britain, therefore, there are both great opportunities at the level of relevance to educational need, but many difficulties at the level of funding and structures.

Museums and family audiences

While links with schools and other educational establishments offer increased opportunities in the field of formal education, new educational opportunities also exist for museums in the field of informal education.

Demographics in many parts of the world indicate that while the number of very young adults is falling as a proportion of the population, the group of 'family-formers' is expanding. Adults between the ages of 25–40, who are likely to be those who are building their families, are an increasing social group.

Recent research in Britain has shown that the family is a very fast-growing section of the museum audience (Middleton, 1991). A similar potential for growth is likely to exist elsewhere. Museums need to be alert to the needs of the family as a target group and should review their exhibitions, events, orientation, cafés, shops and other visitor comforts from this perspective.

Adult family group members often articulate their reasons for being in museums as being in response to the needs of their children. As the Children's Museum of Boston understood twenty years ago, if the interests and needs of children are targeted, all those adults who accompany children as they visit are also attracted. Museums in Britain have been very slow to develop the possibilities of this. Until recently, there have been few exhibitions that targeted the children of family groups, and few exhibitions that targeted families in themselves. Most exhibitions, insofar as this was considered at all, have had adult audiences in mind. Very many adults, however, spend their leisure time with their children, and are very keen to find venues which are both enjoyable and instructive and where a social experience for all will be possible.

Plate 4 At the Barbados Museum, a new gallery opened in May 1992. 'Yesterday's Children' interprets Barbados' social history in ways intended to intrigue and stimulate children. Special events add to the enjoyment of young visitors. A summertime sleepover in July involved roasting fish and breadfruit over a traditional coalpot, and, at midnight, a spooky torchlight tour of the museum. Here the children try on hats from the dressing-up corner of the new gallery.

Photo: Wendy Donova, Education Department, Barbados Museum and Historical Society.

Plate 5 During the sleepover at the Barbados Museum, the education and curatorial staff
worked together in order to enable the best possible experience for the participants. The
African mask, which adds atmosphere and excitement to the torchlight tour, was closely
supervised by the curator.

Photo: Wendy Donova, Education Department, Barbados Museum and Historical Society.

The Barbados Museum and Historical Society opened a new permanent display in May 1992 designed especially for children. In 'Yesterday's Children', the social history of Barbados is interpreted in order to stimulate and intrigue the children of today. The exhibits are arranged at a 10-year-old's eye-level, and there are many opportunities for asking and answering questions. Junior engineers can observe and enjoy the model of the restored sugar factory and the model ships, while budding archaeologists can read history in a cross-section of the earth. Possibilities for direct physical involvement are offered in the Workshop where a potter's wheel can be used, barrel staves can be tightened and wood can be planed. One young visitor commented:

> The whole point of having a museum is to show or exhibit the artefacts recovered from our ancestors, and in a way it gives some identification of who we are and where we came from, our roots and cultures.
>
> (Shanu Babani, aged 13, from the programme of the Opening Ceremony)

The success of science centres demonstrates that they are providing the kind of environment that familes want. The opportunity to handle, to try out, to make, to build and to share this with a range of family and friends in a non-threatening and safe environment without artificial time-constraints is welcomed by families. Many museums are now beginning to provide either family centres, as does the Natural History Museum, London, or exhibitions that offer a range of ways of actively engaging with both objects and ideas.

Two new museums that opened in Britain in the summer of 1992 are Eureka! The Museum for Children, in Halifax, and Snibston Discovery Park in Northwest Leicestershire. Eureka! is quite specifically designed for children, even to the extent of small-scale toilets labelled 'Girls' and 'Boys'. This is attracting large numbers of family and school groups. Snibston Discovery Park is part of the Leicestershire Museums Archives and Records Service, and has been conceived as a venue for a family day out, with ample parking, places to explore, wander about, eat and drink, as well as a small indoor science centre and displays of costume and transport and a remarkable outdoor science playground.

Demographics indicate a further potentially important audience segment, that of older people (Middleton, 1991). With changes in work patterns and an increase in early retirement and part-time work after 55, there is a growing body of relatively wealthy, active people to whom museums and galleries could appeal. Leisure research forecasts suggest that the 1990s will see a move away from a culture dominated by youth towards a culture dominated by the over-fifties. Up until now, this group has been consistently under-represented as part of the museum's audience. It is, however, a group well worth investing in.

Theories of adult learning indicate that at this stage in their lives, people are inclined to enjoy more thoughtful pursuits and to be prepared to make long-term investments in fruitful ventures such as the opportunities offered by museums and galleries (Hiemstra, 1981).

It is clear that in relation to the educational role of museums, the rather narrow function of programme provision for organised groups has in itself expanded, but in addition a much greater awareness is being promoted, of the broader educational function that collections and exhibitions can play in cultural life in general. Education is now felt to be a primary function of all museums, underpinning all museum processess.

One effect of this can be seen in the new approaches that are being developed to enable museums to move closer to their audiences. Stimulated by the often uncomfortable findings of market research, new methods of developing audiences have evolved.

Towards the audience – market research and audience development

In some museums, the concept of marketing is limited to that of publicity, or public relations. Marketing, however, goes further than this. An approach based on publicity is content to transmit information about what is happening, when and where. An approach using genuine marketing methods tries to link these 'products' to the intended target audiences, and asks questions about how appropriate the 'product' is for the 'consumer'.

Museum 'products' are their temporary exhibitions, permanent displays, education and outreach programmes, catalogues and publications and any other experience that the museum can offer. Museum 'consumers' include visitors of all types, but potential visitors and other users are also considered.

One of the tasks of museum marketing is to research the actual and potential audience for the museum, to relate the actual to the potential and to ask why these audiences do not match. Very often the answer will be supplied through market research. Market research focuses on what people think and feel about a particular product or experience, and this kind of work in relation to museums has produced startling results. For the first time, perceptions of museums and galleries from those who feel alienated by them are being collected and made known. This qualitative research, which analyses attitudes and opinions, probes the meaning that either actual or imaginary museum experiences have for people. The perceived irrelevance of museums and galleries to the lives of many people has caused many museums to think very hard indeed about their roles for the future.

Collaborations and partnerships

The introduction of market research into museums in Britain has led to studies of how museums and galleries are perceived by those who visit them and also by those who don't. It has been confirmed that many people who don't visit museums think of them as forbidding, difficult, unchanging and of no immediate relevance (Trevelyan, 1991; Susie Fisher Group, 1990). Those who don't visit museums are unaware of the ways in which many museums have changed, and imagine 'something all fusty, musty, and dusty' (Trevelyan, 1991: 34). Some people feel unrepresented; an Afro-Caribbean in London told some market researchers: 'It would put you off, when every museum you go into, it doesn't have anything to do with you' (Trevelyan, 1991: 47). Many people mistrust museums for being too virtuous; as a white teenager told a market researcher in Croydon: 'You can't say you're off to the museum to your mates, can you?' (Susie Fisher Group, 1990: 17).

These studies of attitudes and perceptions can be linked to surveys of museum visitors, where it is still the case that 'museum visiting in the UK remains primarily a white upper/middle class pastime' (Eckstein and Feist, 1992: 77). Surveys in Europe, Sweden and America demonstrate that similar results have been found in many other countries. Although there are some notable exceptions to this pattern, the persistence of the apparent self-exclusion of broad sections of the population from museums has led many museum workers to an examination of the content and professional processes involved in the production of exhibitions and displays. Market research has confirmed what many museum people have felt worried about for some time.

Museums are now understood as institutions which are concerned with the representation of culture and history. Just as film, television or writing constructs images of the present and the past, so do exhibitions and other museum 'products'. Museums have become self-conscious (at last!) about their power to interpret and represent 'reality' in all its rich variations. This self-consciousness can be observed across the world, and has come about in large part because of the responses (and often extreme resentment) of those being interpreted and represented.

Museums of anthropology, working with objects that have their roots in living cultures, have found that exhibitions of these objects have drawn them into the present-day predicaments of the peoples whose ancestors produced or owned them (Nicholson, 1992). An important example is the exhibition at the Glenbow Museum, Calgary, Canada, called 'The Spirit Sings', which was organised as part of the events connected to the Winter Olympic Games. The objective of the exhibition was to represent Native Canadian culture, presumably for visitors to Canada, and this was planned with minimal involvement on the part of those represented. The exhibition was partly sponsored by a multinational oil company, which was simultaneously engaged in a long-term and bitter dispute over land rights with one of the peoples represented, the Lubicon Lake Cree (G. McManus, 1991; Simpson, 1992a).

Chief Bernard Ominayak wrote to museums around the world who were planning to lend objects to the exhibition, asking them not to do so:

> the Calgary Winter Olympics are being sponsored by basically the same interests which are systematically trying to wipe us out as a people, so that they can steal our aboriginal lands and the valuable gas and oil resources

that our aboriginal lands contain. . . . Display of these artifacts by the Glenbow . . . could only serve to support efforts by these same interests to achieve international respectability and credibility.

(Ominayak, 1987; quoted in G. McManus, 1991: 203–4)

The issues for museums that this exhibition exposes are not limited to Canada. Museum professionals in other parts of the world are also beginning to realise how 'their' displays have been part of a dominant political and ideological force. In South Africa, for example, museum professionals are coping with the fact that artefacts drawn from white groups are to be found in history museums, while those drawn from black or coloured groups have been placed in natural history museums (Hall, 1992). Thus displays on 'Bushmen' and 'Zulus', placed in a mythic timeless static past, are to be found in the Durban Natural History Museum (Wright and Mazel, 1987).

One of the responses in Canada to the experience of 'The Spirit Sings' was the establishment of the Task Force on Museums and First Peoples, which is jointly organised by the Assembly of First Nations and the Canadian Museums Association. In the introduction to the report of the Task Force, *Turning the Page: Forging New Partnerships between Museums and First Peoples*, the National Chief of the Assembly of First Nations writes: 'Out of controversy has come understanding and an opening for constructive dialogue' (Hill and Nicks, 1992). The concept of 'constructive dialogue' and the processes of consultation, discussion, shared perceptions and negotiation which have ensued have become an ideal that many museums wish to share.

Hand-in-hand with the understanding that those whose history and culture is being represented have a right to be part of the construction of that representation has come the development of the idea that effective communication can sometimes only work as a two-way process. Museums have access to a range of communicative methods, some of which are close to the methods of mass communication, and some of which are closer to 'natural' or face-to-face communication. Mass communication can be effective where codes and objectives are shared and understood. Where this is not the case, face-to-face communication, which is capable of reflexivity, immediate modification and the exploration of unfamiliar concepts or ideas, is a more useful tool. With existing museum visitors, therefore, exhibitions, displays, catalogues and video programmes can be very effective. If frequent visitors feel that the museum is of relevance to them (and presumably their frequent visits demonstrate this), then for this group the existing methods of communication are effective.

For those who do not see the museum as part of their lives, more active and personalised methods of communication need to be developed. Many museums are trying to broaden their audiences to include some of those who in the past have not visited, including those from non-managerial social class groups, people with disabilities, a range of ethnic groups and the elderly. Many methods and ideas are being explored to achieve this.

21

One way of developing an audience is through working together with a group to produce an exhibition, a video or a performance. Some museums in Britain have begun to work with a variety of cultural or neighbourhood groups that are unfamiliar with museums. 'Warwickshire Weddings', at St John's House, Warwick, for example, exhibited the costumes and artefacts, and presented the wedding customs, of six different religious groups represented across the county of Warwickshire. These included Hindu, Sikh, Greek Orthodox and Chinese couples. The exhibition was only possible as a result of collaboration with the various groups concerned, who explained their customs (which were unfamiliar to the museum curator), loaned some of their objects and allowed their personal video recordings of the weddings to be used in the exhibition.

Some curators have begun to work with advisory groups for exhibitions. The groups consist of people with specific expertise and knowledge, drawn from within and without the museum. This has been seen as very controversial and time-consuming, but it can be an extremely successful way of testing ideas and opinion, discussing potentially conflictual issues, gathering ideas and suggestions through brainstorming and again, developing audiences through the networks of the advisory group. With this backing, the exhibition team-leader has a strength and a power to carry through the concept of the exhibition that is not forthcoming in other ways. This approach was used in the development of Gallery 33 at Birmingham Museum and Art Gallery, in the development of the new display of some of the ethnology collections (Peirson-Jones, 1992).

As new ways of building partnerships with audiences are found, it is important that they are developed within a climate of support, optimism and management planning. This is sometimes the case, and where the whole museum is working together, resources and opportunities can be maximised with enormous success.

At Walsall Museum, a middle-sized museum in the industrial West Midlands in Britain, the success of the 'People's Show' is due to the commitment to access and audiences that is part of the new ethos of the museum. The 1992 exhibition in Walsall was based on experience built up over three years from an initial exhibition of the collection of American Indian artefacts belonging to a local person. This stimulated the museum staff, looking for ways to involve the local community, to investigate other local collections, and to develop the first 'People's Show'. A rich and unexpected vein was exposed when it was discovered how many people have their own collections of objects that are important and meaningful to them. These ranged from bicycles to stones to plastic frogs; all of which are a source of joy and comfort to the collectors. Tapping into this vein has proved an extraordinary fruitful method of making connections with new audiences. The success of the first exhibition has led to many museums across the Midlands putting on their own 'People's Show', with a mass exhibiting of personal collections taking place. This has resulted in an expansion of the museum's traditional visitor base, and is an excellent basis on which to build more sustained relationships (Hooper-Greenhill, 1992a: 210–15; Pearce, 1992: 78; Windsor, 1992).

The example from Walsall can be contrasted with another example which illustrates how resources can be wasted where the new development is the result of the enthusiasm of one person, and is permitted, but not seen as central to any communicative strategy. The art education officer at the museum worked for a year with an advisory group of teachers to develop ways of using the collections to relate to the new secondary school art curriculum. A small group of six teachers in the first year mounted a small exhibition (in a non-public space at the museum) of the work done by students on the pilot projects, and from this recruited a group of fifteen teachers for the second year of the project. The recruitment of the second group depended on the successful experience and the word of mouth recommendation of the first.

At the opening of the exhibition (held in a public gallery) of the work done by students of the second group, the entire museum was filled by an enormous crowd of proud and happy parents and other family members, many of whom were not regular museum visitors. The museum is surrounded by a very cosmopolitan population, with a large Asian community, and substantial groups of Afro-Caribbeans, Ukranians, Irish and Poles. All of these groups have children who attend the city schools. Very few of the adults are museum visitors. The education project succeeded in attracting this vast new constituency to the museum.

This one project, then, over two years of very hard work for the education officer, succeeded in building two new audiences: first, a small, committed, vociferous and influential group of teachers, which had the potential to expand through word of mouth; and a very large loose-knit group of families, many of whom were not regular visitors, but all of whom, for a while at least, were predisposed to approve of, enjoy and support the museum.

This project operated through the work of one education staff member, supported by a small team which included many non-museum people, and the curator of art and of decorative art. The receptions were funded by the museum, with some small amounts of sponsorship from elsewhere.

However, the project came about because of the conviction of one member of staff. Management support for the project was, at best, luke-warm, and at worse, discouraging. In many ways, this is typical of many museum projects that come about in a policy vacuum. It was not part of a museum-wide audience development strategy, and consequently there was no attempt to recruit the families to the museum on a more permanent basis, either by securing their names and addresses, or by considering how the initial interest could be sustained.

The development of new audiences through projects, consultations and collaborations is not in itself difficult. It is time-consuming, and requires skills of empathy and networking, but on the whole, most groups and individuals are open to approaches from the museum, and are happy to be involved. A climate of good will does exist. However, this good will and initial enthusiasm for involvement is completely wasted, not to say abused, if the involvement does not stem from genuine commitment on the part of the museum. If the initial establishment of relationships and mobilisation of good will is not supported through agreed policies and strategies, it is likely to be abandoned and will not then be easily rekindled.

A planned, resourced and sustained approach to the development and recruitment of new audiences should be part of forward planning and will relate to the work of all concerned with communication, including educators, exhibition organisers and marketing officers.

The introduction of marketing staff into British museums

Museums in Britain and other European countries have, over the last five years, become far more aware of the need to pay attention to their actual and potential visitors. Marketing methods and marketing strategies have become part of the work of the modern museum. The introduction of marketing as a concept has not always been easy in museums, and it has been argued that the wholesale adoption of marketing approaches designed for other institutional contexts is not helpful to museums (Bradford, 1991). None the less, suitable approaches have begun to emerge and there is now a growing body both of literature and good practice (Baker, 1990; Bott, 1990; Susie Fisher Group, 1990; Foster, 1988; Hull, 1990; James, 1991; MacDonald, 1990a; Trevelyan, 1991; Wright, 1990).

The development of museum marketing has been encouraged by central government as part of the ideology of 'plural funding'. In a context of reducing state support for museums and galleries it has become vital to find strategies to attract other possible sources of funds, whether these come from industry through sponsorship or corporate hospitality, from the public through visitor spend or from partnerships with voluntary bodies.

In many museums the need to move away from the so-called 'culture of dependency' has been greeted with dismay at both a pragmatic and a moral level. For many smaller museums, opportunities to attract non-governmental funds are limited, especially in comparison with some of the larger national museums and art galleries, which have the benefit of many attractive features such as central major city locations, prestigious collections, hospitality potential and wealthy patrons. Many museum staff in Britain, especially those in the public sector, are passionately committed to free entry to museums, and feel that well-supported museums are one index of a healthy and civilised society. There is some evidence that the public share this view, but research on this is by no means clear-cut.

Whatever the moral or ideological position, this conflict over funding has formed part of the context for the introduction of marketing to museums in Britain, as in other places. Many people have therefore resisted the demands of marketing because of their personal attitudes to plural funding and lack of state support. However, it is not helpful to equate the strategies of marketing in museums with approval for government policies towards museums. Marketing is about 'listening to our public and helping them understand who we are, what

24

we do and why museums could be important and relevant to them' (Hull, 1990: 7). At its best, marketing should be concerned with gathering information on perceptions of the museum and its work, relaying this information to colleagues, working as a team to decide on promotional policies and developing and implementing promotional strategies. It is the task of marketing to develop and promote the image of the museum. Problems arise when strategies that have been developed to sell products for profit are introduced into an institution where commercial values are generally less important than a range of other values drawn from scholarship, education and community relevance. It is important that people from marketing backgrounds are fully incorporated into the culture of the museum and that they are made aware of museum philosophies. It is equally important that museum staff should understand the benefits that the development of marketing methods can offer to the museum (Bott, 1990; Hull, 1990).

There are currently approximately forty full-time marketing and development officers in museums in Britain. A recent poll carried out by the United Kingdom Museums and Galleries Commission investigated the working context for these new members of museum staff. The survey found that more support staff were required for marketing, but, more worryingly, that most marketing officers felt that they would benefit from clearer instructions from their directors (Runyard and Anderson, 1992). More inter-departmental contact and communication within museums and galleries were felt to be necessary, with the marketing staff stating that they were willing to share information and experience with their colleagues.

If marketing staff are feeling isolated and under-used, this is a tremendous waste of expertise, perhaps symptomatic of the persistence of out-moded attitudes. It is of vital importance that the marketing staff, who are in constant contact with the public, take their place as essential team-members within the museum. They are among those members of staff that operate at the interface of museum and public, and it is their work that will ensure the success of the work of curators and other museum professionals.

Museums and galleries are encouraged to appoint marketing managers, and where the scale of the museum is too small to permit this, one suggestion is for museums to share a post. It is also recommended that Area Museum Councils, which exist at a regional level to work with and support regional museums, should consider the appointment of marketing advisers for museums on the model of the Scottish Museums Council (Museums and Galleries Commission, 1991: 114). Some city museums have access to marketing expertise as part of a local team, and this can be very useful, although conflicting demands may mean that the museum is at the end of a long list of commitments. However, marketing across a number of local institutions (museums, libraries, parks) can open the museum up to new audiences. The development of a marketing plan should be one of the more important action plans to arise from the museum's forward plan (Museums and Galleries Commission, 1991: 61; Ambrose and Runyard, 1991; Koe, 1991).

The British Museums and Galleries Commission's marketing scheme, which began in 1988, has given grants totalling some £335,000 to enable museums to employ marketing consultants for short periods. Some of those which received the grants found that the consultants enabled their staff to think more clearly about the objectives of the museum, and made them realise how much should be discovered about both the actual and the potential audience before beginning a major marketing project. The importance of marketing the museum to the museum governors and council members was also emphasised: 'Getting the marketing right to our paymasters may make all the difference to our survival' (Bott, 1990: 5).

Marketing is at the present time more or less accepted by museums and galleries in Britain, although the evidence suggests that there is ample scope for better use of marketing methods and better integration of marketing philosophies (Runyard, forthcoming).

An American example

Marketing methods were introduced to museums in North America at about the same period as in Britain (Fronville, 1985; Adams and Boatright, 1986; Robinson, 1983). The conflict noted earlier between the values of profit-led marketing and the values of museums can also be observed here (Ames, 1989; Addison,1986). However, by 1983, Colonial Williamsburg in Virginia, USA, was spending a million dollars on advertising, while by 1986 the Philadelphia Museum of Art had established a five-year marketing plan, and the Museum of Fine Art in Boston was using marketing surveys, print and broadcasting advertisements and special promotions to broaden its attendance (Danilov, 1986).

Some museums have embraced marketing philosophies and approaches with great enthusiasm. In 1984, the Denver Children's Museum published a handbook entitled *Non-profit Piggy Goes to Market*, which describes how the museum was raising £600,000 per year through using marketing as 'a new way of thinking about how a non-profit organisation can be managed and financed' (Simons, Miller and Lengsfelder, 1984). The introduction describes how the museum, opened in 1972 by a group of parents and educators, began to be organised as if it were a business in 1976, and was generating 95 per cent of its income by 1981, replacing the ebb and flow of grant money on which the museum existed previously by a steady stream of earned income. 'Marketing' is defined as: *matching* the museum's assets and capabilities with a corporation's needs; *producing* a product that will meet those needs; and *selling* the product to the corporation at a price that includes a profit for the museum.

The handbook describes the way the museum operates and gives examples of both successes and failures. One success was the development of an activity book for children on money and the economy. This was sold for $65,000 to a financial institution which wanted to promote its image in local communities, and inform the public about its services. Fifty thousand copies of the activity book cost $55,000 to produce. The museum made $10,000. Failures are also instructive: the art-work for an airline activity book was sold to the airline for a one-time fee of $5,000. The airline already had extensive printing facilities, which enabled production in the first place, but also enabled the airline to run off more booklets whenever they were required. The airline gives away 80,000 of the activity books each year. A licensing agreement that provided residual income each time the book was reprinted should have been negotiated by the museum.

It might be argued that the work of the Denver Children's Museum is reduced to commercial practices. However, the success of partnerships with businesses is based on the quality of the museum's products (exhibitions and educational programmes) and on the fact that the museum staff are recognised as expert educators (Simons, Miller and Lengsfelder, 1984: 11). It is perhaps easier for a museum that is not based on collections to adapt its products to the researched needs of potential business partners, and it is undoubtedly easier to develop specifically focused management approaches where the needs of the audience do not have to be balanced with the needs of the collections. None the less, the handbook presents a fascinating example of a museum that has interpreted and adapted marketing techniques and strategies to its own purposes.

Increased accountability

At a time when both local and central governments are reviewing expenditure, the issue of value for money becomes acute. Where cost-effectiveness is questioned, one of the most obvious ways in which to demonstrate value is through well-established relationships with audiences. This, if well demonstrated, is far more readily understandable than much of the rest of the museum's work, which is very unfamiliar to most people.

In Britain, there has been little information on appropriate standards and levels of public service and few standards have been specified (Museums and Galleries Commission, 1991: 56). However, this state of affairs is changing extremely rapidly, and new standards are being drawn up. Recent work on performance measurement is beginning to address some of the issues that are important in assessing the success of audience relationships. A number of agencies have become involved, including the Department of National Heritage, the Museums Association and the Audit Commission. The Museums and Galleries Commission has produced guidelines on caring for museum visitors and on provision for people with disabilities. New planning procedures in museums now include planning for people (Lord and Lord, 1991). Interesting and useful work is being carried out in North America (Ames, 1991), and the Ontario Ministry of Culture and Communications in Canada has produced a broad range of policies to guide its community museums. In South Africa, detailed guidelines for museum communication policy and practice have been produced (Southern African Museums Association, 1989).

A Museums Association working party on performance indicators in the UK recently stated that

> the review of performance through the qualitative and quantitative measurements of outputs and inputs should be an integral part of the management process as a means of maximising all available resources. The performance of a museum should be assessed in the three key areas of curation, communication and operation.

Communication is defined as 'the presentation of the collections to the public through education, exhibition, information and public services. It is also the outreach of the museum to the community' (Walden, 1991: 27).

The areas for the assessment of museum communication are outlined in the 'Guidelines on performance measurement', published in the annual *Museums Yearbook* (Museums Association, 1991b: 442–5). It is suggested that all museums produce a written *communications statement* commensurate with the museum's aims and resources. Basic methods of measurement are suggested for exhibitions, education, enquiries, access and publication. The measurement of 'enquiries' for example, includes specifying the number of enquiries dealt with each year, the percentage successfully dealt with, the percentage answered using standard replies, the number of new standard replies produced. In many ways these suggestions remain at first draft and will benefit from the development that will ensue from further work.

The Road to Wigan Pier? recommends some simple quantifiable indicators for measuring the success of basic objectives. For example, if the objective is 'support for scholarship and education', measures would include: 'number of organised school vists', 'number of teacher and pupil packs distributed', 'number of requests from scholars for access to the collection' and 'number of publications produced' (Audit Commission, 1991: 47–8).

The *Report on the Development of Performance Indicators for the National Museums and Galleries* (Office of Arts and Libraries, 1991) identified two areas of relevance. These are *access and use* and *quality of service and visitor care*. The report recommended that the national museums should carry out two visitor surveys per year (Office of Arts and Libraries, 1991: para. 320), with questions on visitor motivation, expectations and experience. From this, it is suggested that information can be gathered on the percentage of visitors who are satisfied with the displays. This suggestion has been taken up by the Department of National Heritage, who have commissioned the National Audit Office to conduct a review of the quality of service in five representative national museums. This review highlights marketing policies and strategies and customer care.

Stimulated by this investigation, the Museums and Galleries Commission has developed guidelines on customer care, *Quality of Service in Museums and Galleries* (Museums and Galleries Commission, 1993). This customer care policy is a comprehensive document which suggests guidelines in the areas of access, marketing, display and education, training, on-site care, safety, and monitoring and evaluation. The guidelines for museums are set in relation to the wider leisure industry, and are seen as the first step on the road to encouraging museums to consider their standards for visitors in the same way as other leisure venues might.

In Canada, a comprehensive set of policies and guidelines in relation to visitors and other areas of museum work, *Museum Notes*, has been developed by the Ontario Ministry of Culture and Communications. These are written for the (generally small) community museums that are administered at provincial level, and have a particular force as they are taken into account when grant applications are received by the ministry. The policies include those for exhibitions, interpretation, education, the disabled visitor, museum research, collections management and conservation (Ontario Ministry of Culture and Communications, 1985; Ontario Ministry of Citizenship and Culture, 1985 and n. d.).

An interesting range of detailed and searching performance indicators for American museums has been suggested by Peter Ames (Ames, 1991). Indicators that relate to the effectiveness of the communicative roles of the museum appear throughout the range, which covers access/admission/security, fundraising, human resources, marketing/ancillary services, programme (exhibits, collection, education) and finance/facilities.

In the section on access/admission/security, for example, we find the suggestion to review this year's total attendance figure against the average attendance of the previous three years, along with measures examining the level of attendance of minority groups in relation to the total attendance, and the number of hours per week of 'low-income accessibility'. These measures presuppose museum entry charges, but do suggest a basic concern for a broad audience and offer a realistic way of assessing level of performance. Fundraising is treated as a distinct museum function and given an entire set of indicators, amongst which we find the total membership of individuals or families measured against the total annual attendance. An equivalent in Britain would be to measure the membership of the museum Friends organisation against the total attendance figures. The fact that in Britain this would seem to be a rather pointless exercise because most Friends groups are small and some museums have none, demonstrates some aspects of the very different attitudes to visitors in the two countries.

The analysis of human resources includes a review of the proportion of volunteer staff in relation to paid staff (seen as a good measure of community involvement), and an assessment of numbers of volunteer services staff in relation to the numbers of volunteers. The number of advanced degrees and rate of publication of the full-time staff is measured. In the section on marketing, the visitor spend per head is assessed, as is the efficiency of marketing, through the comparison of the marketing budget with the total income from admissions. The effectiveness of publicity is assessed by looking at the number of free media exposures against the total publicity budget.

In the section called 'programme', which includes exhibits, collection and education, a range of measures appear. It is interesting to see these three functions placed and measured together. The use of collections is measured through the number of objects on display or used in an educational programme, compared with the number of objects in the collection. The commitment to evaluation is measured by the number of evaluations carried out in relation to the number of programmes (educational events, exhibitions) offered. To count as 'carried out', the evaluation should involve at least 200 responses, the process and conclusions should be in writing and the results of the evaluation should have been responded to by the 'programme administrator' (Ames, 1991: 6). It is suggested that an evaluation should be carried out every seven to ten programmes.

The commitment to education is measured by relating the education staff payroll to the total staff payroll, with a recommendation that this should be at 10 per cent of the total. The financial self-reliance of education through grants, fees and other sources should be running at at least 70 per cent. The operating cost per visitor is measured by examining the total operating expenses against the total attendance.

Many of these performance measures will strike a discordant note for many museum workers. They are not currently in use in America, where Ames found (in 1990) no performance indicators in use. However, the professionalism of any museum that could demonstrate such self-knowledge would be impressive. These measures are suggestions only, and are of course related to the American context, but they provide a useful guide to the kind of management information that would greatly facilitate and demonstrate improved museum communication. As accountability increases, more museums will find themselves moving towards these ways of thinking.

Greater competition

Museums and galleries can be reviewed in relation to the world of education and scholarship, but can equally be placed in the world of leisure and tourism. Many local museums in Britain at the present time are managed through the leisure departments of local government and are therefore in direct competition with other leisure venues. The UK national museums, although managed by independent boards of Trustees, find many of their visitors made up of tourists or of people on holiday. The links to the leisure industry are very strong, although museums and galleries are more than leisure institutions. In fact, it is their educational potential, their vital base in scholarship, that makes up part of their leisure attraction.

It has been pointed out that although visits to museums and galleries in Britain have been growing in the last decade, the growth has been slower for museums and galleries than for historic houses, gardens, wildlife parks and amusement parks (Middleton, 1990: 18). In addition, figures fell during the depression of 1980–2, and fell again during the depression of 1989–91. Looking further into the figures, it is clear that overall the average attendance per museum fell over the last decade and has been dropping steadily, with an annual average per museum reporting of 72,000 in 1978 to 48,000 in 1988 (Middleton, 1990: 18). The apparent discrepancy between an overall rise in visits to museums and a fall in average attendance figures per museum is explained by the increase in numbers of museums. The same (or slightly more) numbers of visitors are being shared around an increasing number of venues. The use of average figures per museum disguises the fact that some museums have had enormous drops in visitation, generally because of the introduction of entrance charges. Those London museums that introduced entrance charges in the late 1980s saw their visitor figures drop by 40 per cent (Spalding, 1991: 169).

The lesson to be drawn from this is that greater efforts will be needed in the future than in the past to maintain current visitor numbers. The most up-to-date information confirms that museums are competing for shares in a relatively static market (Eckstein and Feist, 1992: 73).

The principal competition for museums lies with the overall leisure industry. This was the case during the 1980s and will grow during the 1990s (Middleton, 1991: 154). Greater and greater efforts are being made by a range of leisure venues to gain the time and the money of families and other people interested in spending leisure time outside the home. Themed environments, often on a large scale, offering a range of experiences that include shopping, entertainment and food, are enticing and attractive places to visit that are often easier for people to feel comfortable with and to enjoy than are many museums or galleries.

One example is 'Cadbury World: the Chocolate Experience', at Bournville near Birmingham. A small section of the large chocolate factory has been given over to the development of a 'visitor experience' where an exhibition tells the story of chocolate, a vast range of Cadbury products are on sale at substantially reduced prices and an enormous choice of food and drink is on offer.

On entering the exhibition, visitors are given a free bar of chocolate, and there are frequent opportunities to taste more as the exhibition moves from the use of cocoa beans by the Mayan Indians in a Central American rainforest, through the Aztecs, the discovery of South America by Christopher Columbus, the subsequent importation of chocolate to Europe and eventually to England. The story is told in the exhibition through environments and sets depicting key moments of the story, and in the accompanying souvenir brochure through text, contemporary images and words from significant figures.

The story continues with the establishment of chocolate houses in eighteenth-century London, and tells us of the beginnings of the Cadbury enterprise in a small shop in Birmingham, which in time developed into the large factory (where we are) built by the Quaker family on an extensive rural site which included model houses in a garden village, schools and recreational spaces for

31

the employees. The experience of the exhibition is concluded by a walk through an area where a number of chocolate-making techniques are demonstrated (and can be tasted), using equipment used at the beginning of the century. The story is brought up to the present time by showing how some of the familiar and spectacular advertisements for Cadbury's Milk Tray are produced.

The content of the exhibition is very close to that of many museum exhibitions, with a good well-researched story, and much interesting historical, geographical and social detail. A range of communicative methods (which include reconstructions of a rain forest, an Aztec environment, eighteenth-century period rooms and workshops, figures, images, video, maps and diagrams), varied at appropriate moments, are professionally designed and installed. The souvenir brochure, presented looking like a bar of chocolate, offers fascinating additional information. This enterprise is phenomenally successful, with long queues whenever it is open, and visitors, representing a broad range of social groups, from all over Britain.

Why is 'Cadbury World' successful where some museums fail? How does 'Cadbury World' manage to attract a much broader span of visitors than many museums? The exhibition experience is very close to that of many museum exhibitions (except of course for the free chocolate), but depends more on a range of environmental experiences rather than on an experience of collections. The free chocolate performs a number of functions: it is comforting and induces a feeling of well-being and optimism at the start of the exhibition; the taste, smell and touch of mass-produced wrapped bars, rather bitter proto-chocolate drinks, and warm freshly produced chocolate squares all stimulate the senses; and during an hour-long exhibition visit, it is offered at points of rest or change. Opportunities to sit down during the exhibition are more frequent than in most museum exhibitions (although still not enough), with, for example, the section on the eighteenth-century family told in a small darkened auditorium, with the audience seated, and the action moving with light and sound across three room-sets with figures. The exhibition is too long and attempts to cover too much, but there is rarely a surfeit of text, and much of the display is very imaginative. People spend at least an hour in the exhibition.

On leaving the exhibition, the visitor arrives in the shop where chocolate can be bought at reduced prices; access to the shop is only possible after the exhibition. The standard of amenities is very high indeed, with excellent toilets, and food and drink to cater for all tastes presented in small 'shops', each with a different emphasis, a familiar idea from many large main-line stations. The experience is well-managed and very easy. Although the exhibition has some intellectual depth, and is too long for most people, there does not seem to be any sense of inadequacy or failure if parts are skimmed. The exhibition 'gives' (with the free chocolate) more than it 'takes' (in mental effort) from the visitor. Visitors emerge feeling they have definitely had value for money.

Many museums can offer very similar 'products'. But 'Cadbury World' is in large part successful precisely because it is not a 'museum'. Many museums suffer from the image of the museum as 'worthy but dull' (Audit Commission,

1991: 6). Many museums also suffer because they are seen as 'educational'. This connotation is unproductive for those who were not successful at school. The museum has the challenge of presenting itself as 'worthy, *and* fun'.

Many people who have not visited museums recently still think of museums and galleries as intimidating and boring. Once this view is changed through the experience of visiting a lively, active modern museum, it is clear that museums could be more successful than 'Cadbury World' and similar ventures. 'Cadbury World' is a one-off experience, with the exhibition being capable of sustaining possibly two visits, but certainly not more. Most museum displays can be visited again and again, with different things to see on each occasion. This is particularly true for object-based displays, although more difficult where environments and model figures are used. The 'Cadbury World' exhibition with its environments is entirely constructed, with a few replicas and some mannequin figures. Although this is cleverly done, museum collections represent very special opportunities that reconstructions cannot replace.

'Cadbury World' is very small and limited in size. To cope with the success of the venture, a new display area has been opened at some distance away across the car park. Here, real objects such as parts of machinery, photographs and ephemera are displayed. This display falls very short indeed of museum standards, and is clearly an emergency measure designed to cope with the numbers. Many museums consist of large, and often very large, amounts of space, and can accommodate numbers of people fairly easily. Display quality, although not always of the same standard across all the spaces of the museums, is usually of at least an acceptable standard, and very often, museums offer a number of high-quality displays that deal with a number of themes and use a number of approaches to communicate. This enables a depth and choice of experience which is not possible in pre-packaged themed and restricted environments.

It would be difficult to offer free chocolate in most museums, but the lessons concerning use of the senses, and both physical and psychological comfort are good ones. The opportunity to handle unusual and interesting artefacts in comfortable and relaxing surroundings, with the possibility of refreshments when required (in different easily accessible spaces), is a very strong attraction for many people.

Conclusion

If genuine links can be made with audiences, and if comfortable and valuable experiences can be made available, people will come to museums in the numbers and with the enthusiasm with which they visit places like 'Cadbury World'. In some museums, this is already the case. Two exhibitions from city museums in the Midlands in Britain may serve as examples. Eight hundred people attended the opening of the exhibition 'Who are the Coventry Kids?' in April 1992, and nearly a thousand people went to the opening of 'People's

Show' in Walsall in May 1992. In both these cases the social span of visitors was broader than we have come to expect of museum visitors. In both, a huge amount of work had been done prior to the opening to develop the audience, in contrast to many museum exhibitions which are developed with no contact with the intended audience. In Coventry, for example, the curator organising the exhibition 'Who are the Coventry Kids?' talked to over seventy city groups to explore the concept and meaning of this local expression, and used a thousand questionnaires to encourage people to take part in the exhibition process and to feel that the exhibition was of importance to them.

This chapter has examined a number of forces that are influencing museums as they move closer to their audiences. We have seen how the educational potential of the museum is expanding and how new methods of working with audiences are being developed, partly because of the results of market research, and partly because of the convictions of museum people that museums can and should have a broader social relevance. We have seen how standards of professionalism and methods of performance measurement are being developed in the field of museum communication.

The shift towards audiences does represent a very radical departure from museum thinking in the past. It is also fair to say that it is only one of the areas that museum managers must develop and support. However, because the change from an internal to an external emphasis is so great, and yet so vital to survival, the quality of thinking and planning to develop this side of museum work must be of the best. In the past the museum curator acted as the definer of the museum message, with content and mode of communication chosen because he or she felt that it was right. The effectiveness of the exhibition in relation to the reception of the message was not in question. Now we understand that this is no longer justifiable, and that people must find museums interesting and useful in order for them to survive.

Museums must communicate or die. For communication to occur, both the sender and the receiver of the message must share the same concepts, even the same passions. The task for museums and galleries is to find ways of arousing and instilling passions and ways of exploring ideas that people will find illuminating, using the collections of the museum, and the curiosity and experience of actual and potential visitors.

2

Communication in theory and practice

Museums and mass communication

In recent years many writers have emphasised the communicative nature of museums. Robert Lumley argues that 'the notion of the museum as a collection for scholarly use has been largely replaced by the idea of the museum as a means of communication' (Lumley, 1988: 15). Hodge and D'Souza see the two roles as complementary:

> Museums are not only protectors but also communicators. . . . A museum display is an exercise in one branch of the mass media, requiring a special kind of understanding of the processes of communication, namely the nature of mass communication systems.
>
> (Hodge and D'Souza, 1979: 146)

Mass communication systems are unnatural forms of communication, in that they operate at a distance and often in the absence of one of the two parties necessary before communication can take place. It is difficult therefore, to be sure that the process has worked. Has the message really been understood? In 'natural' communication, which we can visualise as a face-to-face conversation between two people from a common background, the main message of the communication is interpreted through this common background. Shared experience enables the message to be decoded. The words that might be used are supported by many other channels of communication, such as gesture, facial expresssion, emphasis. Any point of misunderstanding can be verified by asking a question and by repetition or restatement. In a face-to-face conversation, there is a possibility of the message being modified by either party and being reshaped as ideas are exchanged. In natural communication, and particularly in a domestic situation where two people know each other very well, ideas are often exchanged in fits and starts, with frequent repetitions and clarifications. Often two conversations are carried on at once, or ideas are conveyed through a series of grunts and gestures, with perhaps a drink acting as mediation. The shared domestic environment makes this erratic and unelaborated transfer of ideas comprehensible to the two people concerned. In natural communication, then, we find the following features: interpretation through shared experience, modification or development of the message in the light of response, and many supporting methods of communicating. Natural communication has the potential to be direct, responsive and equal.

With mass communication situations, things are very different. Let's take television as an example. Here, at the moment of communication, one party to the communicative act is present (perhaps sitting at home in the evening), while the other (the team who prepared the programme) is absent. The transmitter (the team) must rely on their skill to produce a message that the receiver (sitting at home) will be interested in hearing. The message is one-way, with no chance of immediate feedback. If the message is not clear, there can be no clarification. There are few supporting channels, although the comment in newspaper listings might be seen as one source of extra information. If the message is boring, unenjoyable or unpleasant, the remedy is simple; the television is turned off. Mass communication is one-way (indirect), impossible to modify (unresponsive) and takes place in the absence of one of the partners (unequal).

In order to succeed in communicating through television, considerable research is undertaken, both into ways of putting the message across and into audience response (Alvarado, Gutch and Wollen, 1987). This research includes preliminary (front-end) research into what is likely to succeed, and summative research into the effects of the programmes on the audience. Those programmes that are not successful are quickly identified through audience ratings, and are axed. Successful programmes are repeated or developed. Market research is seen as a vital tool, and as an integral part of the communication process.

In museums, there are many of the features common to most forms of mass communication, but in addition there are opportunities for face-to-face communication. The museum is fortunate in that it has a variety of methods of communication at its disposal, and in museums this modifies the starkness of the mass communication situation. Traditional museum methods are now being modified to take account of visitor needs, and practices are changing, but in the past the experience of displays and exhibitions has shared the characteristic features of the experience of mass communications. One of the parties involved (the visitor/viewer) has been present, while the other (the exhibition team) has been absent. There have been few opportunities to modify the message of the display according to the response of the visitor. There has been no certainty that visitors would share the background of the museum communicator, although visitor surveys, in demonstrating the middle and upper-middle social class groupings of most visitors, probably illustrate that visitors are self-selected on this basis.

Those displays that demonstrated the features of mass communication were prone to a range of problems. These included a failure to transmit the intended messages, a distortion of communication and an inability to involve the visitor. These problems of communication, understood and explored at an empirical level in a range of forward-looking museums, have led to the shifts we can now observe, where methods of mounting displays are changing to take account of the needs of visitors and to provide opportunities for sharing and involvement through handling, activity sessions and through collaborative exhibitions.

In addition to display methods which are close to the methods of mass communication, museums also have the opportunity to exploit natural communication, through talks, guided tours, meet-the-curator sessions, demonstrations, handling sessions, enquiries, discussion groups and social events. It is also true that the mass media themselves provide other opportunities for museums to make connections with people: using television itself, either in advertising or as part of an exhibition or event; through the use of videos, as an aspect of the interpretation of displays, as souvenirs to take home, or as outreach into the community; through newspaper and magazine advertising or articles; through posters, leaflets and flyers; and through publishing at all levels. The communicative methods of museums are extremely varied and this is surely one of the great advantages that museums have over many of the other institutions of the mass media. The 'communication mix' will become a vital concept in the next decade as museums and galleries develop policies and strategies for museum communication.

Mass communication, as we have seen, is likely to be prone to miscommunication, and this is as common in museums as elsewhere (Hodge and D'Souza, 1979). The two most common problems with museum displays concern saying things which were not intended, and not saying what was intended. For museum workers, it is important to try to understand as well as possible the communication process itself, both in general and in museums. There is room for considerable theoretical development in museum communication methods. Most branches of the mass media now have extensive texts on methods, but in museums this is only just beginning. There is a need for new methods of communication to be tried out, evaluated and published.

In addition to developing knowledge and expertise in the techniques of museum communication, it is at least as important to try to understand people and how they react to museums. Again, work has begun in this area, and we will consider some of it later, but more is needed. Visitor surveys have been fairly common since the 1960s in Britain, but have tended to remain at the level of counting who comes, and how. Information has remained at the demographic level, and it is only very recently that more qualitative research has begun. Research into visitors is as important as research into communication methods. Indeed, the one cannot exist without the other. As we need to know more about how people respond to particular displays or events in order to evaluate and develop new techniques, so we will need to research attitudes to museums, opinions on a range of methods, feelings about a variety of different experiences and so on. In the same way as the mass media researches its audiences to evaluate reaction to its products, so we will need to research the audiences of the museum to discover whether an exhibition, a poster, a café or an event has been successful.

The communication process

An act of communication is one that aims to produce an effect on another person or persons. If this intention is absent, the act tends to be expressive rather than communicative (Morgan and Welton, 1986). Any study of communication, therefore, can logically assume a desire to influence, and can assess the strength and nature of this.

Plates 6 & 7 Communication is a two-way process. Interaction is much easier to achieve in a face-to-face 'natural' situation than in an exhibition. Here for example, the little girl from Northam First School, Southampton, is listening intently to a former pupil of the school, Harry Triggs, as he recounts his memories of his schooling. The challenge is to find ways of stimulating this level of attention to displays and exhibits.

Photo: Southampton City Heritage.

In museum exhibitions there is frequently a subjective element – the exhibition can be, and has been, seen as an act of expression on the part of the curator. Expressive acts, such as works of art, or exhibitions that are very largely the subjective work of a curator, can and sometimes do, communicate effectively. They will communicate with those people who share the same subjectivity, the same interests, the same modes of expression. If, however, a broader audience for communication is looked for, an awareness of the mechanics and psychology of communication can help.

The understanding of the process of communication has evolved from the development of a simple model to something more complex (McQuail, 1975). The initial simple description of the process of communication was based on the idea of one person sending a message to another, perhaps over the telephone, or through the post. The process involved a communicator, a receiver and a relationship between them. Several elements were required: an intention on the part of the communicator; the subject of the message; a common language; some shared experience; and, to demonstrate that something had in fact been communicated, some activity or change as a result of the process. Described like this, it seems very unproblematic. A simple diagram expresses this process well (see Fig. 1).

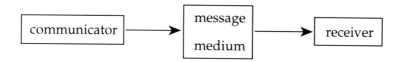

Figure 1 A simple communications model

This simple model was elaborated slightly by Shannon and Weaver (see Fig. 2) (McQuail and Windahl, 1993: 17). Distinctions were made at the beginning of the process between the source and the transmitter, and at the end of the process between the receiver and the destination. Also introduced was the idea of 'noise', which is anything external (or sometimes internal) to the process that might interrupt the transfer of information.

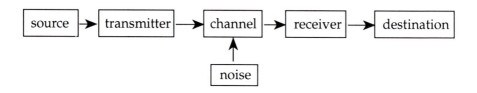

Figure 2 The Shannon and Weaver communications model

The Shannon and Weaver model has been applied to various forms of communication (McQuail, 1975) (see Fig. 3).

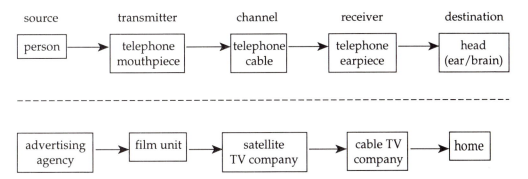

Figure 3   The application of the Shannon and Weaver model to a mechanical process and a process involving agencies working together

The application of the Shannon and Weaver model works both with a mechanical process (that of a telephonic message), and in the case of agencies working together. In the first instance the source is the person making the call, the transmitter is the telephone mouthpiece, the channel is the telephone cable, the receiver is the telephone earpiece, and the final destination is the head or the brain of the person receiving the call. In the case of agencies working together, the source is the advertising agency, who hires the transmitter (the film unit) to make an advertisement broadcast through the channel (the satellite TV company) to the receiver (the cable TV company) into the destination (the home).

The model can be applied to a museum exhibition. It is possible to describe the exhibition team as the source, the exhibition as the transmitter, with objects, texts and events as the channel of communication, the visitors' heads as the receivers, with the visitors' understanding as the final destination (see Fig. 4). In this instance the 'noise' which interferes with the message might include anything from crowds to visitor fatigue, or workmen in the gallery next door. Internal sources of noise might include confusing signals such as poor graphics, or inappropriate use of colour (Duffy, 1989).

The value of models such as the Shannon and Weaver model is the preliminary separation of a complex process into a series of elements. Each of these elements can be analysed as a unit, which is sometimes a useful way of beginning to penetrate a difficult and multi-layered event, such as the development of an exhibition or an event.

However, there are problems with simple models of communication, such as the Shannon and Weaver model. One very basic problem is that this model suggests that communication is the simple transfer of a message from one part to another. Communication is, of course, far more than this.

41

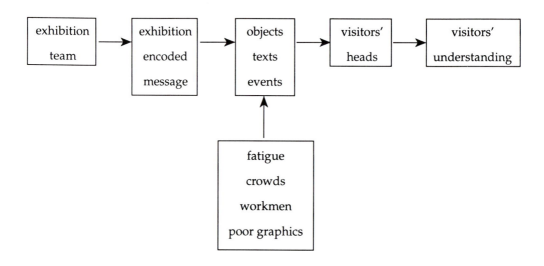

Figure 4 The Shannon and Weaver model applied to exhibitions

Two other ways of thinking about communication are as 'networks of contacts', or as 'hierarchised chains' (see Figs 5 and 6).

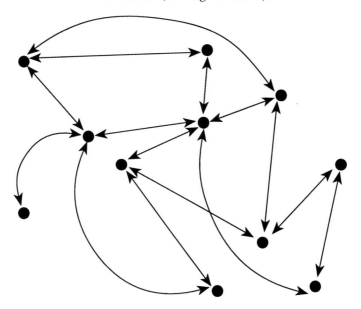

Figure 5 Alternative models of communication: a network of contacts

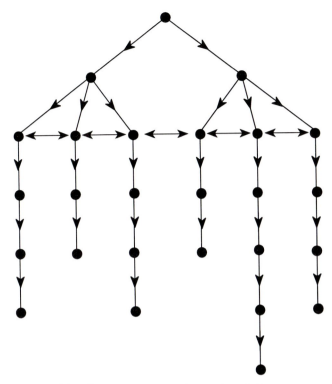

Figure 6 Alternative models of communication: hierarchised chains

The idea of communication as a network of contacts works well in relation to the forms of communication that are sometimes to be found in families, or in informal groups. Messages are passed by word of mouth, letter, phone-call – non-hierarchically, in a free-flowing and mobile way. Any part of the network might contact any other part as required, and communication is relatively open and equal between parties. Power relations emerge from this network according to a multitude of factors, but are not enshrined within the structure itself.

Hierarchised chains describes a form of communication that is often to be found in formal institutions, including traditional large museums. It is premised on power and authority, with communication flowing from the top down, but not from the bottom up. The communication links are very closely delineated, and in fact *prevent* a great deal of communication taking place. In museums with a staff structure based on a director, two deputies and a number of departments, probably mostly based on divisions of the collections, such as archaeology, natural history, fine art, social history, with possibly an education and/or design department tacked on the end, this form of communication structure is all too familiar. In such museums, there is little communication between departments at the lower levels, and that communication which takes place between department heads generally operates as a form of defence of territory.

This rigid and authoritarian power structure is seen by modern management theorists as wasteful and lacking in cost-effectiveness. Industry is now moving towards flatter structures that are more flexible and democratic, that assign more power to branches, that are organised as units each with its own autonomy and network, and where a range of relationships to the work task are possible (Handy, 1990).

The simple communications model, therefore, can be seen as only one way in which communication can be conceived. There are many other ways in which the process can be understood.

The simple communications model has been criticised because it makes a number of assumptions that are not always appropriate. The model proposes a wholly linear view of communication, one that begins with a source which also defines the meaning of the communicative act. The receiver is conceived as cognitively passive, and contributing nothing to the process. The role of the receiver is simply to receive. If this reception does not occur, the communicative process must be deemed to have failed.

Here, the concept of feedback enters the process. In order to test the system, we must see whether the message has been understood. If it has not been understood, then the message must be modified to make understanding more likely (see Fig. 7).

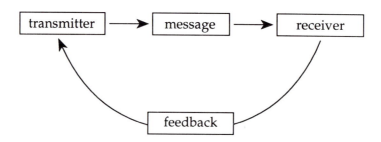

Figure 7 The simple communications model with feedback loop

If (as it will) feedback indicates difficulties with the reception of the message, so it is successively modified until it may well become fragmented out of all recognition (see Fig. 8).

Once a feedback loop is introduced into the process, the message is likely to change. It is likely to change because any linear process of communication cannot be certain of speaking the language of the receiver, or even of having anything to say that is of interest to the receiver. In the absence of coercive power, the message may simply be ignored. Once the receiver is brought into the process to play a more active role, the whole process changes and begins to break up. The linearity of the process is altered. The meaning of the message is no longer defined only by the sender, but also by the receiver. The work of making meaning begins to be shared between the two parties. The greater this sharing process, the more likely effective communication is to take place. The logical outcome of this process is to consult the receiver before any messages are sent, to try out a variety of messages to see which are appropriate and interesting.

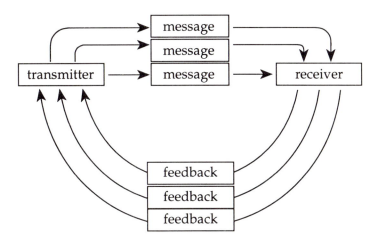

Figure 8 Successive feedback loops progressively alter the original message, and eventually change the process from linear to circular

This preliminary research can be carried out in relation to the content of the message, but might also usefully be carried out in relation to the medium through which the message is to be carried. Which is the most appropriate channel for which audience? What channels are the audiences used to? Which do they find difficult? Which do they enjoy? When a match can be made between the audience (the receiver), and both the content of the message, and the nature of the medium, then a communicative process may be begun.

What is interesting in the above discussion is the amount of work that is required *before* the communicative process can start. It is now recognised that it is not enough to make a decision to communicate a message and to put the receivers on stand-by to receive it. If the receivers are not predisposed to appreciate the message, to find it relevant and to make it their own, then it is likely that no initial contact will be made at all. This explains the preliminary or piloting work that is carried out by television and advertising companies in the very early stages of a product, and it is clear that there are lessons here for museums and galleries.

Communications models in museums

The simple communications model was introduced to the museum world in North America by Cameron in the late 1960s, and this stimulated a debate (Cameron, 1968; Knez and Wright, 1970; Miles, 1989). The focus of the debate was whether objects were the most important aspect of a museum's communication system, or whether objects were merely one form of communication. The debate seems a little sterile today, but it is instructive to note the uses and adaptions of the simple model of communication and to notice the concentration on the medium, and on how messages are transmitted.

Cameron used the model virtually intact, but suggested that, in a museum, there are many transmitters, many media and many receivers. The prime medium used is that of objects ('real things') (see Fig. 9).

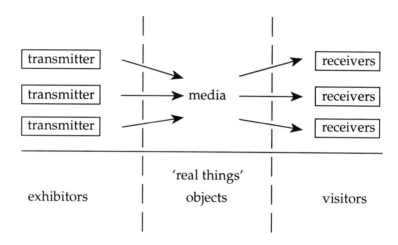

Figure 9 The use of a simple communications model by Cameron (1968)

Knez and Wright agreed with Cameron that the museum was, among other things, a communication system, and also agreed that a professional museum officer (whether curator, exhibit designer or educationalist) was the 'transmitter', and that the 'receivers' were the visitors. However, Cameron's emphasis on objects as the medium of museum communication was challenged by Knez and Wright (1970), who proposed that a distinction could be drawn between those museums, such as science museums, that relied on verbal symbols (written or spoken words) as of primary importance in exhibitions, and those such as art museums, where objects were more important.

Knez and Wright proposed that putting across ideas (intellectual cognition) was the primary function of museum communication, at least in science museums, and their suggestions led to the following modifications in the basic communications model (see Fig. 10).

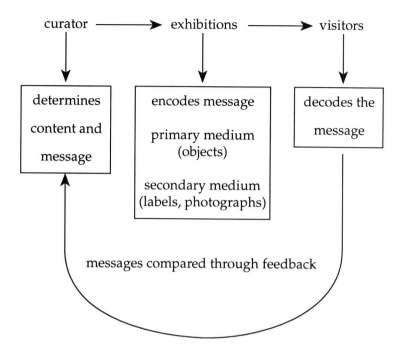

curator ⟶ exhibitions ⟶ visitors

| determines content and message | encodes message | decodes the message |

primary medium (objects)

secondary medium (labels, photographs)

messages compared through feedback

Figure 10 The communications model (particularly applicable to science museums) as suggested by Knez and Wright (1970)

However the media for exhibitions is understood, and however this might vary with different types of museum, the basic linear 'hypodermic' model, able to 'inject' the receivers with ideas remains (Morley, 1980: 1). The model (and the writers) assumed that the audience was passive and merely reactive, and there was no acknowledgement of the fact that audiences actively interpret their experiences of museums in the light of many individual and social factors, including their backgrounds, cultural assumptions, levels of knowledge and personal agenda for the museum visit.

The influence of this model of communication on approaches to exhibition production is discussed by Miles (1985) who points out how this linear understanding of the communication process is mirrored in the linear process of making exhibitions (see Fig. 11).

Miles has described museums as 'disabling institutions' when they produce exhibitions using this model. The model is based on people working independently in separate departments (curatorial, design, education), with no team-work and little co-ordination. The work of one department is finished before the work of another begins. Change is difficult and painful and leads to inter-departmental or interpersonal friction.

In this model the curators, as exhibition-generators, play the role of power-broker. They define the content and the message according to their own point of view, without taking into account the views of the other departments or of the audience. Designers are expected to attend to packaging the ideas of the curator and are treated as functionaries and technicians rather than as communications professionals. The educator is brought into the process at far too late a stage to contribute to planning, and is forced into a remedial role, making the best of a bad job once the exhibition has opened, (re)interpreting it for those people who take part in events or activities. The absence of feedback from the audience means that any improvement is based on intuition or trial and error, and evaluation is impossible. The absence of preliminary audience-related research makes a communicative act unlikely.

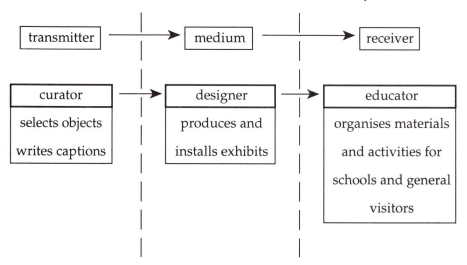

Figure 11 The simple communications model adapted as a way of understanding the exhibition process. The move from curator to designer to educator takes place in time

Miles proposes a very different approach to exhibition production which is much more flexible and makes use of extensive research at all stages of the process, including market research before the process begins, trialling of exhibits during production and summative evaluation after the exhibition opens (Miles 1985). Miles also includes reference to the concurrent development of the literature that is written to accompany the exhibition (which might include catalogues, handlists and teachers' packs), and the design of educational activities related to the exhibition (see Fig. 12).

The simple communications model is here superseded by a vastly more complex and reflexive system, one which begins to reflect the various activities and their interrelationships in the production of exhibitions. The incorporation of research and evaluation into the processes of development and production enables the design of exhibitions, and their related literature and educational activities, that has some relationship to the proposed audiences.

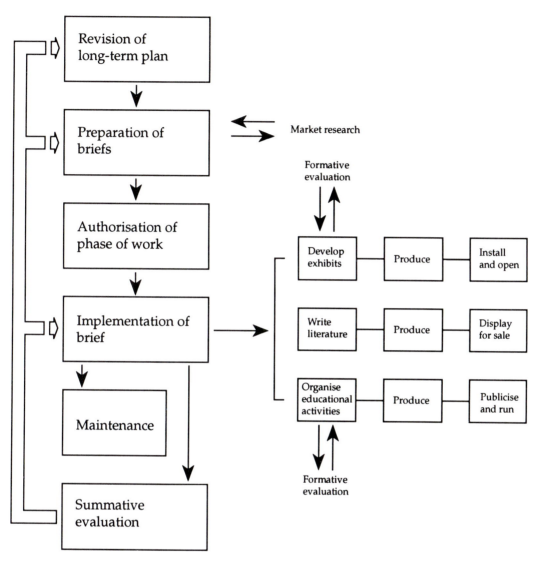

Figure 12 Activities involved in planning, designing and producing exhibitions, from Miles (1985)

The simple communications model has been discussed in relation to the production of exhibitions, and on the whole, this is how it has been deployed in the literature. And although rarely overtly articulated in internal museum debates, the linearity of the information flow, the definition of the message, the attitude to visitors and the position of power for the curator/transmitter, can still be recognised in the exhibition process in many museums. Indeed it can be recognised in much more than this. Many of the attitudes to museum audiences that can still be found in museums can be traced back to the idea that visitors are passive receivers of those worthwhile experiences that are prepared for them by the museum transmitters.

In many museums there is still no understanding of the nature of the communication process, of the fact that it is a shared process, and that if two parties are not involved, the process may not occur at all. Very many exhibitions are still mounted and demounted at great cost, with visitors having little or nothing to do with them, to the extent in some museums of not even bothering to visit. All too few museums are involved in dialogue with their audiences, at whatever level, and all too few directors understand more than the rhetoric of the importance of effective museum communication for survival, let alone development, in the next decade.

A holistic approach to museum communication

The simple communications model has already been given much to answer for, but there is still one more aspect that we must address. One of the effects of the use of the simple communications model as it has been used in the literature is to reduce discussion of museum communication to discussion of exhibitions. It is all too easy for the notion of museum communication to become subsumed into the production of exhibitions. This is of course an important method of making connections with people, but museums are fortunate enough to have a whole battery of other methods. In addition to formal methods of communication, many other aspects of the museum need to be considered (see Fig. 13).

In considering a holistic approach to museum communication we should be aware of museum-wide elements, those aspects of the operation of the institution that impinge either on the museum's image, or on the general experience of the visit. These include the museum's buildings, both internal and external features; the attitudes and activities of the museum staff, including the director and the whole range of staff; the general atmosphere in the institution, which will owe much to management styles and staff morale; and the attention given to comfort, orientation and the general guiding of visitors through the experience of the museum.

Museums communicate on-site through a range of methods which includes exhibitions of many different types, functions, sizes and approaches to interpretation. The balance between, for example, a costly, short-term, popular blockbuster appealing to tourists and expected to raise money, and a small-scale exhibition of perhaps the work of a local adult education group, needs to be carefully considered. Different audiences need different provisions, and thought should be given as to how different types of exhibition or display can be used to attract different sections of the public.

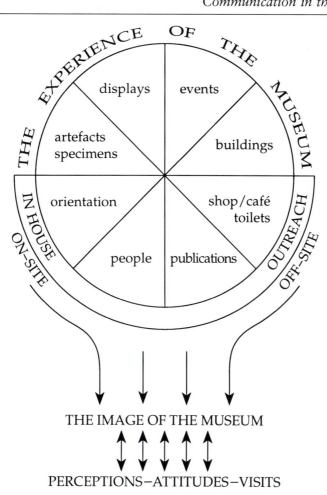

Figure 13 The entire experience of the museum contributes to the image of the museum. The image of the museum affects the perceptions and attitudes of people, and will affect whether or not they decide to visit the museum

Acitivities, events and educational programmes are generally designed to match the needs of particular audiences, and a vast range of approaches can be found in museums and galleries, including the use of actors or demonstrators; talks, lectures and tours; films or concerts; opportunities for handling or involvement with the collections; chances to try out practical skills such as dancing, drawing or weaving; invitations to view the stores or the conservation laboratories and so on.

Many museums have extremely well-organised shops where a range of goods are sold, the main criteria being one of relationship to collections. Many museums have taken the opportunity to develop specialist shops in tune with their missions; the Science Museum, London, for example has an excellent specialist science bookshop. The shop is an opportunity to make the museum's scholarly work available through catalogues of the permanent collections,

51

temporary exhibition catalogues, books and monographs. Postcards, information packs, calendars, notebooks, pencils and other small items can often be found alongside replicas of some of the collections. Some museums, and Ironbridge Gorge Museum is an example, have developed sophisticated and very successful mail-order systems.

In addition to communicating with visitors to the museum on-site, museums use a variety of means to communicate to people outside the building. These include the establishment of connections with the local and national media; the building up of secure supporting networks among the local, and sometimes national, business, educational and cultural communities; and the use of a variety of marketing techniques, such as research, mailing and advertising. In addition, some museums have very lively and comprehensive outreach programmes, where activities and events are organised by the museum but take place in a community venue such as a shopping centre, a school, a day centre for the elderly or a hospital (Beevers *et al.*, 1988; O'Neill, 1990, 1991; Hemmings, 1992; Plant, 1992). Some museums have established mobile museums that carry collections and events to housing estates, school play-grounds, fairs or pop concerts. Some museums have collections of loan objects that are available to schools and other institutions.

The role of the museum as a communicator is enormously varied. It can include communicating information in a clear and effective way, perhaps through a leaflet or telephone answer service; enabling a learning experience related to the demands of school curricula, with a role-playing session for a small group of school children; promoting enjoyment and fun, possibly through manipulating interactive technology; and facilitating reminiscence and mental activity in the old and frail through the provision of suitable objects as stimulus.

Communication is one of the primary functions of museums and galleries. As such, it relates closely to the other main functions of the museum, the collection, conservation and management of artefacts and specimens, and the management of the whole institution. The priorities and policies for communication should be considered when decisions are taken in the other two main areas of museum work, just as communicators must consider management directives and conservation constraints when developing communicative approaches. For example, the use of objects should be considered before a decision to acquire is finalised. What is the object's value for teaching, for exhibiting, for handling or for promotional purposes? If it has no use in any of these areas, how will it contribute to the knowledge-base of the museum, and can research work carried out on it realistically be disseminated to a broad audience? If the object can satisfy none of these requirements, is it really justifiable to collect it?

When museum managers are making decisions over budgets, funds should be set aside to carry out research into visitors, their needs and their responses. There is little point in approving exhibition budgets without including ways of measuring the relevance and success of the exhibition. A little market research, some preliminary front-end analysis and attention to the lessons of earlier summative evaluation is likely to prevent expensive mistakes.

Communication can be considered from a number of different points of view. It impinges on all the activities of the museum, and for a good proportion of them, its success is of vital importance. Up until now, in many museums, communication has been left to chance. Communicative activities have certainly happened, but often in isolation from each other, even when in the same museum. Education for schools and adults, exhibitions for whoever cares to come and advertising through leaflets and posters have all been organised in a communication policy vacuum. A framework of institutional commitment has not often supported and inspired these activities. Many happen because of the enthusiasm of one individual, and without the help and co-operation required across the institution. This is clearly wasteful and frustrating.

Very few museums have coherent and well-managed communication policies. Some have exhibition policies and some are now producing education policies. A few marketing strategies are emerging. A few audience development plans are being introduced. But how do these relate to each other? Are they informed by the objectives of the museum? And once the plans or policies are written, what are their chances of being implemented? If strong links to a variety of publics including the governing body, visitors, new audiences, schools, the media and industry are required to sustain the museum in its work, then the communicative functions of the museum will need to be better understood, and better managed.

3

Who goes to museums?

Museums and galleries have been concerned to know who their visitors are for some years. But why do we need to know who visits museums? And is it enough to know who visitors are? What else is there to know? Why bother anyway? How can we find out?

There are a number of reasons why museum workers need to be aware of the patterns of use of museums and galleries. These include the continued justification of a public service, the demonstration of a professional approach to management, the development of knowledge and expertise and the improvement of performance.

First, museums are a public service, and it is important to be aware of how the service is taken up. A public service will not be maintained if it is not used. How are museums used? Which sections of the public benefit from museums and which do not? Why, and what are the implications? Visiting the displays is an obvious use of museums, but there are others that should also be considered, monitored and documented, and encouraged: the numbers of enquiries about objects received and answered, the numbers of photographs of items from the collection supplied, the range of researchers and scholars that use the collections and the expertise of the staff for information, the extent of corporate hire and so on. All these are also indications of the use and value of museums and galleries as a public service. They are on the whole, much broader and more varied than most of the public, or the governors and funders of museums, would think.

Second, information about the uses of the institution in relation to resources is vital to demonstrate managerial competence. Museum staff will not be perceived as professionals by government, colleagues in other areas of leisure or educational work or other business colleagues, unless detailed knowledge of the operation of the museum can be called upon when required. No business can succeed if its managers do not know who wants its products or services.

Third, in the present climate of accountability, it is sensible for museums and galleries to begin to develop some in-house knowledge and expertise by carrying out research, even if on a small scale, into the perceived use and value of the institution. This experience will be useful as standards for museums are developed. One example is in relation to the development of standards of visitor satisfaction and customer care, where the existence in museums of an understanding of how to measure the experiences of visitors would aid the development of realistic and useful performance indicators. Ignorance on the part of museum workers of the procedures for discovering what visitors enjoy, how they respond to the museum, why they have come and so on, may lead to the imposition of unrealistic and unhelpful demands.

In addition, in using the concepts of 'visitor satisfaction' and 'customer care' (Museums and Galleries Commission, 1992), the measurement of the use of the museum tends to become limited to the activities and perceptions of visitors, whereas the use of museums is in fact much wider than this. If judgements are to be made about the public effectiveness of the museum following the measurement of 'visitor' satisfaction (and it is possible that levels of funding may be determined by this), then it will become vital to be alert to 'use' as a broad category, rather than 'visit', which although extremely important, is a narrower concept.

Finally, it is important for all staff to know what level of success is being achieved. Both quantitative and qualitative information should be used by managers on a regular basis to monitor successes and failures and to improve targeting of provision.

What do we need to know? We have discussed the idea of the 'use' of the museum as a broad category. It is of great importance to gather information about 'use', which would include details of a whole range of public functions that are generally not very visible, such as the use of the museum for work-experience for school and college students, the use of the museum as a place to volunteer, the museum as a location for film, the provision of archive material for the press and so on. The invisible and behind-the-scenes character of much of this public provision makes it all the more important to monitor and document.

In this chapter, however, we will concentrate on the idea of the 'visit'. Knowledge about patterns of museum and gallery visiting operates both at a general level, in relation to the museum's role in society, and at a specific level, in relation to particular institutions. Both types of information are necessary.

It is important for museum professionals to have a broad understanding of the social functions of museums and galleries. What proportion, and which sections, of the population visit museums? Does this vary in relation to different types of museum? What image do people have of museums, and what expectations do they have when visiting? Why do some people feel that museums are not for them? Knowledge of the general level and structure of patterns of museum and gallery visiting will give a measure against which to assess achievements in individual insitutions.

At a specific level, museum workers need to know who comes to their own institution. How does this pattern relate to the broad general pattern of museum visits? Do we attract a more or less élite public; more or fewer school

55

groups; are visitors more or less pleased with their visits to my institution than to others? Although these kinds of comparisons are extremely difficult to make, as we shall see, the questions deserve to be asked.

The pattern of visitors to any museum or gallery should be compared with the pattern of the population in its catchment area. This geographical area can be identified and elaborated in relation to obvious geographical characteristics; so, for example, with museums in a city with approximately 250,000 inhabitants, we might have a first-level catchment area to include the city, a second-level area to include the immediate region and then a third-level very diffuse area outside this region. The demographic pattern of visitors to the city-centre museums could be usefully compared to the demographic composition of the population of the city and the county. The match with a local population is particularly necessary for a community museum; perhaps of less immediate need for a national museum.

How can we find out?

There is now considerable information available about the patterns of use of museums and galleries by visitors. From this we can assemble a sketchy outline, but it is not easy to build up a reliable composite picture of a national or international pattern of visiting. Some of the work which has been done is contradictory, and much of it addresses specific issues related to the objectives of a particular piece of research. There are several approaches to research which may be used, each of which tends to yield specific types of data, which can make comparison difficult. Sources of information on museum visiting include academic research, government statistics, research from the leisure industry and research generated from within the museum, gallery and arts community.

A great deal of research on visitor patterns has been carried out in the United States. Much of this is most usefully collated and discussed by Falk and Dierking in their book *The Museum Experience* (1992) which discusses museums from the point of view of visitors, and draws on a large reservoir of research studies that have mainly been produced in the last twenty years. The funding arrangements of American museums, which tend to rely heavily on grants for specific projects, have encouraged attention to the evaluation of these projects. The responses of participants in educational programmes, the attention paid to exhibits, perceptions of a range of types of museum and memories of museum visits have been comprehensively analysed. Some of these studies have been published in journals such as *Curator, Journal of Museum Education* (originally called *Roundtable Reports* and renamed in 1985) or the more recent *International Laboratory of Visitor Studies (ILVS) Review: A Journal of Visitor Behaviour*; some of the research has a more tenuous existence as conference papers. *The Art Museum as Educator* (Newsom and Silver, 1978) and *Museum Visitor Evaluation: New Tool for Management* (Loomis, 1987) are key texts with relevance for all museums. The two anthologies drawn from the Journal of Museum Education, *Museum Education*

Anthology, Perspectives on Informal Learning: a Decade of Roundtable Reports, 1973–1983 (Museum Education Roundtable, 1984) and *Patterns in Practice* (Museum Education Roundtable, 1992), are also essential reading. Harris (1990) offers a review of the history of visitor research in America.

In Canada, the development of a national museums policy in 1971 led to a very interesting and comprehensive survey on museum use published as *The Museum and the Canadian Public* (Dixon, Courtney and Bailey, 1974). The exemplary methods used, including questionnaires and focus groups, are discussed in the appendices. Attention to the needs of visitors once in the museum is discussed in the Royal Ontario Museum's *Communicating with the Museum Visitor: Guidelines for Planning* (Royal Ontario Museum, 1976) and in subsequent publications.

There has been considerable research into the patterns of museum and gallery use in some parts of Europe, notably in Holland, and some centres for study, such as Paris, France and Karlsruhe, Germany, can be identified. Little of this work is available in English. The Swedish travelling exhibitions, Rikstutstallningar, carried out a fascinating study of visitors to their exhibitions in the 1970s which is still of value (Arnell, Hammer and Nylof, 1980).

In Britain, some interesting pieces of academic research have been carried out in recent years. Two will be introduced here to illustrate the breadth of different approaches that may be adopted when considering the use of museums and galleries. Placed within different theoretical perspectives, both have been published and are easily available. Each yields useful material.

Merriman's approach is drawn from sociological paradigms (Merriman, 1989, 1991): it tackles some first principles relating to the social functions of museums. Merriman's basic contention is that although museums are seen and see themselves as educational institutions, access for all has not been achieved. This idea in itself is not revolutionary, but the value of Merriman's work is that he wishes to go further than mere documentation of this fact. He seeks to explain it by analysing the symbolic power of museums, using the work of Pierre Bourdieu. A large-scale survey was carried out in 1985 to examine attitudes to the past, to archaeology and history and to museums. Attitudes and perceptions were then analysed in relation to status, education and other social variables. Bourdieu's work has been concerned with the reproduction of social relations, and specifically, the reproduction of power and domination. Through the analysis of social phenomena such as education systems and cultural systems (including museums) he demonstrates the interrelationships of economic and symbolic power. Merriman uses Bourdieu's work as a starting point for the construction of an explanation for the patterns of museum visiting, analysed in the context of hierarchical social structures.

McManus takes a different approach. In some ways her focus is narrower, limited to the investigation of how people learn in science museums. Her research is based on psychological methods and approaches, with an attention to the way individuals behave within particular environments. McManus observed and documented the reactions of groups and individuals in the displays of the Natural History Museum, London (previously known as the British Museum (Natural History) or BM(NH)) and in other science museums (Lucas, McManus and Thomas, 1986; McManus, 1987, 1988, 1989, 1990, 1991).

In Britain, the work of government departments and bodies is sometimes very useful in tracking down information. Although much of the data is too general to be of use, some is vital, and often forms the basis for reporting in the national media. For example, the *General Household Survey* is produced annually: in the 1979 edition, the subject of Chapter 7 was leisure. Of more use in recent years has been *Cultural Trends*, produced four times per year. In *Cultural Trends*, 8, 1990, the first twenty-four pages were concerned with museums, and gave useful information on funding, costs and other management issues. In *Cultural Trends*, 12, 1991 (Eckstein and Feist, 1992) one section focused on attendance at museums and galleries.

The Office of Public Censuses and Surveys has carried out a number of surveys on behalf of specific national institutions during the last ten years (for example, Heady, 1984; Harvey, 1987). These vary in interest and quality. The Policy Studies Institute, a government think-tank, published *The Economic Importance of the Arts in Britain* in 1989 (Myerscough, 1988). The aim of this report was to demonstrate how the arts, in a changing policy framework, contributed to the economic life of the nation. Research was conducted in three contrasting areas of Britain, and this included the investigation of audiences for the arts, including museums and galleries.

The leisure industry in Britain regularly produces information which is useful, but mainly limited to tourist statistics, such as numbers of visitors to specific sites. Now and then more detailed work is produced, such as the English Tourist Board's *Visitors to Museums Survey 1982* (English Tourist Board, 1982). *Sightseeing in the UK, 1990* places the statistics for museums and galleries in the context of visits to other places (British Tourist Authority, 1991). The Henley Centre for Leisure Forecasting, a private business supported by subscribers, produces a time-use survey for the leisure industry four times per year. These look at what people do in their leisure time, and generally include a few details about museums and galleries.

Two detailed reports have emerged recently. *Museum Funding and Services – the Visitor's Perspective* (Touche Ross, 1989) reports the results of a national opinion poll of 2,800 museum visitors and their attitudes towards museum funding, including entry fees. Details include information on visiting patterns and visitor perceptions. *New Visions for independent Museums* (Middleton, 1990), a comprehensive review of the issues faced by independent museums in the UK, is based on the best available information on museum visiting, including references to many of the sources listed above.

A final source of information is the research that is carried out by or on behalf of the museum or arts community. The major arts community bodies in Britain, including the Arts Council and the Regional Arts Boards, are all to a greater or lesser extent generators of research. Although most of it is concerned with the arts in general, this includes art galleries and sometimes museums.

The Arts Council commissions research for their clients on a regular basis, with recent reports including *Target Group Index 1990/1* (Arts Council, 1991a), *Galleries and Museums Research Digest* (Millward Brown/Arts Council, 1991) and *RSGB Omnibus Arts Survey, Report on a Survey of Arts and Cultural Activities in GB* (Arts Council, 1991b) prepared by Research Surveys of Great Britain (RSGB).

Greater London Arts produced two useful reports in 1990: *Arts in London: a Survey of Attitudes of Users and Non-users* (Greater London Arts, 1990a) and *Arts in London: a Qualitative Research Study* (Greater London Arts, 1990b). Both of these were carried out by Mass Observation, and used market research methods to talk to people to ascertain how they felt and what participation in the arts meant to them.

Museums UK: the Findings of the Museums Data-base Project (Prince and Higgins-McLoughlin, 1987) gathered useful data about museums and their collections, but was less concerned about their use. However, *Museums UK* pointed out that museum visitor surveys have been increasing in frequency since the early 1980s, and were likely to become a basic tool for planning.

Museums in Great Britain began to survey their visitors during the 1960s, rather later than museums in North America (Merriman, 1991: 42). Merriman lists and discusses some of the early British surveys, many of which were published in the *Museums Journal*. Many of the early surveys were limited to one-off studies. An important suite of surveys were those carried out at the Natural History Museum, listed in Miles and Tout (1991).

Interesting recent approaches include large-scale detailed surveys of the use of museums by the population of a defined area, such as *The Findings of the 1991–1992 Study of the Perception and Use of Leicestershire Museums, Arts and Records Service*, recently carried out by Prince Research Consultants Limited (Prince and Higgins, 1992), and fairly small-scale reports on the visitors to a specific site such as *The Wordsworth Museum Visitor Survey 1991*, a report prepared for Dove Cottage, the museum of the Wordsworth Trust, by the Tourism Research Group of the Department of Geography at the University of Exeter, UK (University of Exeter, 1992). Many museums are using surveys such as these as management tools to aid in monitoring change or in forward planning. The Dove Cottage survey, for example, showed that the pattern of visitors had remained relatively constant comparing 1990 to 1991, although visitors from the London area had fallen slightly. The report also pointed out that 80.2 per cent of the museum's visitors came by car and used the Dove Cottage car park. There are implications in both of these bits of information for forward planning. It is not always easy to use museum visitor surveys for research purposes as they are generally regarded as internal management tools and are not therefore published, but many museums will release details if asked.

Recently, museum visitor research has followed a new direction. With an increasing professional concern for democracy and access, it has become clear that talking to *visitors* does not help in discovering what it is about museums that keeps some people away. The only way to discover this is to go and ask them. Some research has therefore focused on the attitudes and perceptions of people who fall into one of the many groups that are unlikely to visit museums. This generates qualitative as opposed to quantitative data.

Bringing History and the Arts to a New Audience: Qualitative Research for the London Borough of Croydon (Susie Fisher Group, 1990) is an example of this new approach. Carried out by a market research company, the report discusses how focus group interviews were held with people who agreed that they 'wouldn't be seen dead in a museum'. The research objectives are concerned with discovering attitudes and perceptions, digging down to people's personal meanings and interpretations of experience. The findings of the research are reported using (some of) the words of participants rather than tables full of figures. This research is being used to inform the development of a new museum in Croydon. A second example is *'Dingy Places with Different Kinds of Bits': an Attitudes Survey of London Museums amongst Non-visitors* (Trevelyan, 1991). The London Museums Consultative Committee, a London-wide body representing the interests of all museums in London, having seen the work done by Mass Observation for Greater London Arts, and the market research methods used by the Susie Fisher Group in Croyden, commissioned Mass Observation to carry out rather similar research with a London-wide museum application.

The range of material for research into the use of museums is wide and is seldom gathered in one place. It is often difficult to use as different parameters for the research are used, which makes comparison problematic. For many people it is very trying to make sense out of figures as relatively raw data. However, for all the reasons discussed above, it is important to try to develop some kind of a picture of museum and gallery visits.

What do we know?

In Britain, museums and galleries attract a mass audience. Estimations of numbers of visits include 72.8 million in 1984–5, between 75–8 million in 1989 (Middleton, 1991: 153; Myerscough, 1991: 16) and 74 million in 1990 (Eckstein and Feist,1992: 70). It is likely that the museum and gallery market is Britain's largest sightseeing draw: of the visits in 1989 it is probable that visits from overseas tourists accounted for some 20 per cent, approximately 15 million visits. School party visits are estimated at 5 million, with visits made by British adults accounting for the remaining 55–7 million visits (Middleton, 1991: 153). The number of visits to museums and galleries made by overseas tourists appears relatively constant for 1990 (Eckstein and Feist, 1992: 70).

Seven museums (British Museum, National Gallery, Tate Gallery London, Natural History Museum, Royal Academy, Science Museum, Glasgow Museum and Art Gallery) were among the thirty-nine tourist attractions with more than one million visits in 1990 (Eckstein and Feist, 1992: 70). The British Museum attracted 5,410,000 visits in 1991, the National Gallery 4,300,000 and the Science Museum 2,525,000. Very large attendances are the exception for museums, with *Sightseeing in the UK* pointing out that 83 per cent of museums attracted annual attendances of 50,000 or less in 1990, 15 per cent recorded between 50,000 and 500,000, and only 2 per cent achieved more than 500,000 (British Tourist Authority, 1991). Birmingham Museum and Art Gallery attracted 559,000 visits in 1990, and the Castle Museum Nottingham 632,000. The average attendance at the 1,547 museums surveyed by the British Tourist Authority was 48,000, the same as in 1988 (Eckstein and Feist, 1992: 70).

Middleton (1990: 23) estimates that around 29 per cent of British adults (13 million people out of a population of 45 million) visited a museum at least once in 1989. If this is the case, they visited a museum on an average of four visits each. However, opinions differ as to what proportion of the British public visits museums. Merriman (1991: 48) suggests that between 47 per cent and 58 per cent of British adults visit museums at least once a year, and he reminds us that this figure is close to the figures of some other researchers. Time Use Surveys from the Henley Centre Leisure Futures suggests a figure of 47 per cent for Britain, and this figure remains more or less constant over their regular quarterly surveys.

The Canadian museum survey (Dixon, Courtney and Bailey, 1974) suggests that more than half the Canadian public (55–60 per cent) visited Canadian museums; and an American survey carried out by the National Research Centre for the Arts estimates 56 per cent of the public visit a history museum at least once a year, with slightly fewer people visiting art galleries and science museums.

The English Tourist Board survey of 1982 proposed that 24 per cent of the adult public visited a museum at least once during the preceding year, while the Touche Ross report (1989) suggests that 44 per cent of the adult population have visited a museum in the last two years, considerably more than the 25 per cent which have visited an art gallery. The *RSGB Omnibus Arts Survey* (Arts Council, 1991b) suggests that 32 per cent of British adults were museum visitors and 18 per cent were gallery visitors (see Table 3), with 10 per cent visiting photography galleries or exhibitions. This survey also points out that once all types of exhibitions and museums are considered together, 48 per cent of the population visit 'nowadays'. 'Nowadays' is a market research term which is taken to mean 'at the present time'. It is likely that had people been asked if they had visited a museum, gallery or exhibition within the last two years, this percentage would have been considerably higher.

Many researchers do not include visitors under 16 in their surveys, but where they have been included, they very often make up the largest group of visitors, for example making up half of the museum audience in Ipswich and a quarter in Glasgow (Myerscough, 1988).

The figures overall are very confusing, and it is difficult to form a complete picture of what proportion of the population visits museums on a regular basis. The discrepancies may be due to a number of factors, such as whether the definition of a museum includes art galleries, how the public perceive this distinction, how the surveys are carried out, what system of weighting is used to adjust the figures and and what period of time is covered by the questions asked. However, in terms of numbers, the RSGB findings are interesting and encouraging (Arts Council, 1991b).

Reviews of a range of surveys enable the identification of the general characteristics of museum visitors (Merriman, 1991: 42–56). Students and higher-status socio-economic groups tend to be over-represented in proportion to their numbers in the population in general, while lower-status groups, the retired, the unemployed and people with disabilities tend to be under-represented. Museum visitors tend to be educated beyond the minimum school-leaving age, or are still in full-time education. Museum and gallery visiting is less likely among older people. Middleton's research (1990) shows the pattern of visiting museums, compared with demographic patterns in general (see Table 1), while the 1991 *Target Group Index* research (Arts Council, 1991a) shows how art galleries attract an even more exclusive audience than museums (see Table 2). The Research Surveys of Great Britain survey makes a direct comparison between museums and art galleries (see Table 3).

Table 1 Museum visiting by British adults in 1989

All adults	G B population (millions)	% visiting museums
All	45.1	29
Male	21.7	30
Female	23.4	27
Age		
15–24	8.7	29
25–34	8.1	31
35–44	7.7	36
45–54	6.1	30
55–64	5.8	28
65+	8.7	20
Class		
A/B	8.3	43
C1	10.3	34
C2	12.7	24
D	7.8	21
E	6.0	18

Source: Middleton (1991) and published in Eckstein and Feist (1992).

Table 2 Attendances at art galleries or art exhibitions in Britain

	% currently attending art galleries	% going more than once per year
All adults	21.4	9.2
Men	21.0	9.1
Women	21.8	9.4
Age		
15–19	25.2	9.5
20–24	22.4	9.8
25–34	23.3	10.1
35–44	25.9	9.9
45–54	22.5	9.2
55–64	20.7	10.7
65+	13.3	6.7
Social grade		
AB	41.4	20.4
C1	26.9	11.8
C2	15.0	5.3
DE	11.3	4.3
Terminal education age		
14 or under	8.4	4.1
15	12.7	4.6
16	16.6	5.7
17/18	27.7	11.8
19 or over	49.4	25.4
Still studying	38.1	16.5

Source: *Target Group Index, 1990/1* and published in Eckstein and Feist (1992).

All the tables confirm that museum visiting decreases with age. As people grow older, their interests tend to be more home-centred, but this tends not to happen until some years after retirement, whereas the tables show this process beginning in museums at a much earlier stage. More thought for the needs of this group, and more directly targeted provision would increase visits. This is particularly important as the elderly as a percentage of the population is expanding and it is likely that British society is moving away from a culture dominated by youth to a culture dominated by the over-fifties. The growth will be in the group aged 45–59. An extra 1.5 million people will be entering this age-group during the next decade, while there will be no change in the group aged 60–79 (Middleton 1991: 140–1). People aged 45–59 are active, energetic, have generally completed or nearly completed their child-focused years, and have more time and often more money to spend on themselves. Those reaching this age-group during the next few years are those who were born after theSecond World War, and who were young during the 1960s. Their expectations are far higher than those who were born and grew up during harsher and more austere times. They are a prime target for museums and galleries during the next few years.

Table 3 Attendances at museums and art exhibitions and galleries

	% visiting museums	% visiting art exhibitions/galleries
All adults	32	18
Men	34	17
Women	30	19
Age		
16–19	31	18
20–24	33	18
25–34	35	15
35–44	40	20
45–54	36	21
55–64	29	20
65+	22	14
Social grade		
AB	51	35
C1	39	23
C2	29	11
D	24	9
E	17	11

Source: *RSGB Omnibus Arts Survey* and published in Eckstein and Feist (1992).

The largest group visiting museums is in the 25–44 age-range (with a bulge in the 35–44 age-group) and by implication this is likely to consist of people with children. This is not the case with art galleries and art exhibitions, where visits are more evenly spread throughout adulthood, with a possible increase after the family has grown up. This is interesting as it suggests that where museums are seen as suitable for young children, art galleries are not. Art galleries are not generally targeting the family audience in the design of their displays, and as long as this continues it is unlikely that art galleries will attract a much larger proportion of leisure or tourist visits. The *RSGB Omnibus Arts Survey* (Arts Council, 1991b) suggests that while 32 per cent of all adults visit museums, only 18 per cent visit art galleries. The Touche Ross survey indicated that 44 per cent of the population had visited a museum during the last two years, while 25 per cent had visited an art gallery (and 35 per cent had visited a National Trust property or stately home) (Touche Ross, 1989: 14). However, the growth of the over-fifties age-group presents opportunities for art galleries.

The group of adults of young family age is also expanding as a percentage of the population, with an extra 1.1 million entering the age-group 30–44 during the next decade. The family visitor has already become one of the more important targets for museums and this will become increasingly important during the next decade.

Although most museum visitor surveys do not include young people under the age of 16 (presumably because they are not expected to know what they think or do!), this group represents a further point of growth. While the group currently aged 15–29 years is expected to decrease by about two million in the next decade, those currently in the age-group 5–14 will expand by about one million (Middleton, 1991: 140). Targeting children in families directly, and targeting schools will become important marketing strategies. The combination of the growth in numbers of family-formers and the growth in numbers of young children means that the small group consisting of adults and children visiting together will become perhaps the most important group to plan for in considering displays, events, comfort facilities and literature.

The level of education is a very important variable in indicating whether an individual is likely to become a museum visitor. The more highly educated someone is, the more a museum or gallery visit becomes likely. This has been confirmed by research in many other countries (Dixon, Courtney and Bailey, 1974: 30; Arnell, Hammer and Nylof, 1980). It is clear from the tables that museums appeal more to the higher social classes (social classes ABC1). It is also the case that visiting museums is less popular among Asian and Afro-Caribbean ethnic groups. As *Cultural Trends*, 1991 states baldly: 'museum visiting in the UK remains primarily a white upper/middle class pastime' (Eckstein and Feist, 1992: 77).

It is easy to under-emphasise the appeal of museums to a wide public. Even if the rather pessimistic figure of 29 per cent of the adult population is taken as a guide to the proportion of the public visiting museums in Britain, and this is agreed by both Middleton (1991) and Myerscough (1991), museums and galleries would appear to reach a broader cross-section of the population than many other cultural institutions. In Glasgow, for example, 30 per cent of the museum audience is made up of people from social classes C2D and E, and in Merseyside the proportion of lower status groups is 47 per cent. These figures are considerably higher than those for theatre and concert audiences (see Tables 4 and 5) (Myerscough, 1991: 20). Middleton (1990: 23) suggests that one in five of museum visitors is on average from social classes D and E. The market for museums and galleries is also younger than for theatres and concerts.

Table 4 Social class of visitors to museums in the three regions of study

	Glasgow	Merseyside	Ipswich
ABC1	70%	53%	67%
C2DE	30%	47%	33%

Source: Myerscough (1988).

Table 5 Social class of visitors to theatres and concerts in the three regions of study

	Glasgow	Merseyside	Ipswich
ABC1	80%	73%	67%
C2DE	20%	26%	33%

Source: Myerscough (1988).

The market for museums and galleries varies with different types of museums. Art galleries tend to attract more female than male visitors, and more highly educated visitors; science and transport museums attract more men than women, and visitors tend to be less highly educated.

In Canada, there is evidence that open-air museums attract a broader cross-section of the public than other types of museums, and that art galleries attract the least democratic audience (Dixon, Courtney and Bailey, 1974).

It is likely that, of visitors to museums in general, approximately one-third are very infrequent, while of the others, possibly a further third are regular users, going perhaps three or four times per year or more (Middleton, 1990: 23). The Touche Ross survey stated that of the museum visitors interviewed, just under half had been to a museum three or more times in the past year, and one-third had made their previous museum visit in the past month (Touche Ross, 1989: 15).

In relation to repeat visits, surveys of the patterns of visiting for individual museums reveal very individual patterns. At the National Portrait Gallery in Trafalgar Square, for example, an area popular with overseas and home tourists, but also with a large and consistent day-time population, the following pattern was found in 1985: of the UK visitors, 43 per cent were first-time visitors, and 57 per cent were returning visitors; of the overseas visitors, 71 per cent were first-time visitors and 29 per cent were returning visitors (Harvey, 1987: 8). In contrast, frequent visitors (those who had been three times or more) to Dove Cottage and the Wordsworth Museum in the Lake District during 1991, for example, consisted of only 0.5 per cent of the visitors. People who were visiting the museum for the first time during the same year formed 86 per cent of visitors (University of Exeter, 1992).

The Leicestershire survey found that there was a core of relatively frequent visitors, with rather different characteristics from those who visited less frequently (Prince and Higgins, 1992: 98). Those who described themselves as frequent visitors tended to belong to a group described by the researchers as IPT-A (Index of Population Type – A). This group in general consists of professionals, managers and white-collar workers who occupy secure and high-salaried jobs, and have been educated to a high level. Frequent museum visitors from this group were aged between 35 and 54, and were likely to have also joined a group concerned with conservation or heritage. Self-defining infrequent visitors came from IPT-C, a group that as a whole consisted of manual workers in industrial jobs, where take-home pay might well be high, but where job security was low. The education level of this group was typically low and, interestingly, those visiting the museums were in the age-group 16–34. They tended not to have joined any related society.

Why do people visit museums? From the tables above it is clear that social class and educational background are important determinants. Socialisation, family habits and attitudes, interests related to collections and exhibitions, all play their part in disposing people to make visits. When asked why, many people give rather general answers, but themes do emerge. The Touche Ross survey found that an overwhelming majority of their interviewees in a national poll considered that museums should be both educational and entertaining. The main reason for visiting was interest in the displays or the collections, cited by one-third of the respondents. The second most popular reason for making a visit was as an entertainment or as part of a holiday (Touche Ross, 1989: 16). Very few of those interviewed as part of the national poll visited museums in connection with their studies. Average visit length seems to be about one hour, although it tends to be longer when paid for through entry charges. Interactive exhibits were regarded as being the most popular type of exhibit, especially among younger respondents, while older people tended to prefer what they knew, static exhibits (Touche Ross, 1989: 2). More than three-quarters of museum visitors thought that more should be done to promote exhibitions and events. Facilities such as seating, toilets, cloakrooms, signage and floor-plans received some criticism (Touche Ross, 1989).

Those people who did not visit museums were cited by Touche Ross (1989: 15) as giving not enough time as one of the main reasons, and this reason also appears in more qualitative accounts (Trevelyan, 1991: 24; Susie Fisher Group, 1990: 44). However, the qualitative accounts also reveal other attitudes, including a feeling that museums are for people with education and specific interests, and people who want to learn. One of the major reasons why some people don't visit museums and galleries is because of bad experiences in the past. Many people still see museums as they were at that time, and think that museums are austere, forbidding, dusty, empty, church-like and remote (Trevelyan, 1991: 34–6). The research for Croydon revealed deep-seated psychological barriers relating to participation in the arts: 'Arty people are hypocrites, do-gooders'; 'Black artists? Our country's culture shouldn't be changed for them'; 'They should fund hospitals, not the Arts'. Many people revealed fears of being shown to be ignorant, of feeling self-indulgent, of neglecting more important basic chores, of looking ridiculous, of being treated as in need of charity (Susie Fisher Group, 1990: 44–6). These barriers are very real, and not always easy to break down, although many of the recommendations in the report are very sensible. The suggestions made for the museum and arts centre at Croydon recommended a complex of small related experiences, rather like a small shopping centre. Opportunities for eating, drinking, sitting and watching offer a non-threatening and welcoming first-level experience of the centre, with arts and crafts workshops, video and object-based displays, exhibitions on the past and the future easily accessible for a more in-depth exploration.

It is very clear that museums are competing for customers in a relatively static market. The average number of visitors per museum reporting has steadily declined during the last decade from 72,000 in 1978, falling to 61,000 in 1982, 51,000 in 1986 and 48,000 in 1988. The average number of visitors per museum remained at 48,000 in 1990. During the period from 1978, museums reporting data to the English Tourist Board rose from 716 to 1,222. Museums surveyed by *Sightseeing in the UK* in 1990 numbered 1,547 (British Tourist Authority, 1991). In part, the fall in the average number of visitors per museum is accounted for by the growth in number of museums. In part too, the average figure is distorted by the accommodation of huge visitor losses at those national museums that have introduced charges – for example, admissions at the Natural History Museum were 47 per cent lower in 1991 than in 1981, and at the Science Museum were 53 per cent lower (Eckstein and Feist, 1992: 73). However, it would appear that it is not going to be easy to sustain visitor numbers, particularly in a period of recession.

Visitor research is an essential management information tool. It should include both qualitative and quantitive research, and be carried out as part of a systematic and planned programme. In the past, museums and galleries have seen this as expensive and time-consuming, but as museums strive to get closer to their audiences, the need to know first who they are, and second, what they think, will become more and more imperative.

4

Research and evaluation

Research and evaluation are often confused. When is a piece of research an 'evaluation' and when it is something else? Evaluation as a concept has been used in museums as a blanket expression to refer to investigation and analysis carried out before, during and after a process, which has until recently often tended to be the exhibition process. Thus 'evaluation' might refer to work that is exploratory in nature and open-ended in its focus, such as for example general attitudes to themes for exhibitions, but might equally refer to work carried out to test detailed specific ideas, such as words and images for text panels.

Korn has suggested that 'evaluation' is the systematic collection of data and information about the characteristics, activities and outcomes of an exhibition or public programme (educational or leisure session, event) that is useful in making decisions about the programme's continuation or improvement. 'Research', on the other hand, involves the generation of new knowledge and the exploration of hypotheses, which, while not necessarily providing immediately useful information, does offer material for the development of theories (Korn, 1989: 221). Both processes use the same methodologies: questionnaires, interviews, focus groups and observations, and, although Korn's definitions are useful, in practice it is sometimes difficult to separate the two concepts. The major difference is in the objective of the work, in that evaluation is driven by the need for information for specific action in the short term, while research is stimulated by the need to know more for professional or personal awareness and for the development of conceptual frameworks (Munley, 1992).

Munley (1986) has identified five purposes for what she calls 'museum audience studies'. These are: *justification* of the value of the institution itself, or of its exhibitions or public programmes; *information-gathering* to aid in long-term planning; assistance in the *formulation* of new exhibitions or programmes; *assessment* of the effectiveness of existing exhibitions and programmes; and increased general understanding of how people use museums through the process of research and the *construction of theories*. The first two reasons, justification and information-gathering, require marketing and demographic studies; the next two, formulation and assessment of programmes, require evaluation work; and the last reason, that of developing a general under-standing of the use of museums, requires on-going research (Korn, 1989).

Munley's five categories represent a logical and coherent framework for the understanding and development of audience research and evaluation within museums and galleries. It is extremely rare that any museum or gallery has such a well-thought-out approach to audience research, and very unusual therefore that any one piece of research or evaluation can be placed within such a context. In many museums, very little research is carried out at all; in some, some of the processes identified by Munley might be in place from time to time, as circumstances demand. It is helpful therefore to see the nature and extent of a structured framework.

In the last chapter we looked at a range of pieces of research that related to the development of a general picture of the use of museums. Some of these had been carried out by museums and some by other agencies. Most of the work was discussed in the context of three of Munley's categories: the justification of the value of the institution, information-gathering for long-term planning and an increased general understanding of museum use. This chapter will examine the work that may be undertaken to justify the value of specific exhibitions or public programmes, and methods used in the formulation and assessment of exhibitions and programmes. We will begin by tracing the development of exhibit evaluation in Britain, review some of the types of evaluation that can be undertaken and conclude by considering the origins and uses of the two major theoretical approaches to evaluation.

In common with many museums across the world, neither research nor evaluation has been embraced with great enthusiasm by museums and galleries in Britain. Many museum workers have failed to see the relevance of research-ing or evaluating their products, and have viewed these ideas with distrust, as something which at best is time-wasting, and at worst, demonstrates a lack of professionalism, skills and abilities. Where more far-sighted curators, educators or designers have wished to carry out research or evaluation, it has sometimes been difficult to persuade the museum's governing body of the need to produce the necessary funds.

Evaluation studies are relatively well-established in the United States, where project funding often requires an assessment of work done in order to demonstrate value for money and the success of the project to the funder. Evaluation is also familiar in museums and science centres that depend on interactive exhibits, where it is part of the development process of the exhibit. Where science centres have a strong position in the museum field, as in India or some parts of South America, the relevance of evaluation studies for other types of museums is more in evidence.

Where work has been done in Britain, the result of research has suggested important modifications and improvements to original intentions and plans (MacDonald, n.d.). In one or two instances, research and evaluation have been built into a project from the beginning, and the development of the project has been fully informed by continuing research. Examples are Gallery 33 at Birmingham Museum and Art Gallery (Peirson-Jones, 1992), the Natural History Centre (Greenwood, Phillips and Wallace, 1989), and the Interactive Technology Centre (Harlen, Van der Waal and Russell, 1986) both at the National Museums and Galleries on Merseyside. The success of those projects on Merseyside that have been based on thorough and on-going empirical research, and consistent trialling and evaluation of exhibits, has led to this research-based exhibit development process being used in many other areas of the work of the museum (Rees, 1990).

As some of the more innovative and exciting museum projects of recent years are seen to have been based on research and evaluation, so professional interest in the methods used is growing. Methods are also changing, to reflect improved understanding of the nature of museum and gallery communication and visitor motivation.

Early approaches to evaluation in Britain

The development of the theory and practice of evaluation in Britain acts as an interesting case-study. As it has been mainly limited to the work of one group of people working in one museum and has been thoroughly documented it is possible to trace the evolution of the ideas that lay behind the practical methods that were employed. Both the ideas and the methods have changed as time has passed and work has demonstrated the strengths and weaknesses of different approaches. An examination of this process of trial and error is useful and instructive for those who are considering embarking on a similar journey of discovery. As all museums begin to move closer to their visitors and to develop new ways of discovering and responding to their needs, lessons from the pioneers are of value.

The Natural History Museum in London was the early pioneer in the field of exhibit evaluation in Britain (Miles, 1986a, 1986b, 1988; Miles and Tout, 1991). In the early 1970s the museum drew up long-term plans for the development of the permanent galleries. The galleries were to be educational in approach, and the exhibitions were to be designed with educational principles firmly in mind. A further aim was to develop a systematic approach to the design of exhibitions, a museum technology.

The educational principles used were drawn from educational technology and programmed learning, in part based on the experience of designing distance-learning materials for the Open University, but also informed by work that had been carried out in the United States (Alt, 1977; Shettel, 1973; Screven, 1969, 1976). Educational technology works with a specific focus on the materials to be produced and pays much less attention to the needs of the learner. 'It is not possible to consider individuals even if we limit ourselves to the serious learner. Our predictions must concern populations of visitors' (Miles and Tout, 1979: 215). Evaluation of the effectiveness of the museum technology was built into the project from the beginning.

71

By the end of the 1970s a theory of exhibition design was presented (Miles and Tout, 1979). Based on the precepts of programmed learning, the following principles for effective exhibits were proposed: exhibitions should have explicitly stated objectives; the order in which material was to be learnt should be carefully considered and carried through to the exhibits; the material was to be arranged in steps of appropriate size; provision was to be made for various levels of ability, knowledge and interest; opportunities were to be offered for visitors to respond actively to the exhibit and to obtain some feedback. Exhibitions were to be designed so that the emphasis was on the concepts to be communicated rather than on objects *per se*, and exhibitions were to be presented in such a way that both the intellectual and the physical structures were made very plain to the exhibition visitor. It was assumed that exhibitions (at least in science museums) were a teaching medium and that visitors would be disposed to learn if the design of the exhibition was appropriate and skilful in enabling learning. As exhibitions were designed, this general theory was applied to specific cases (Miles, 1986b).

The main methods of evaluation used in the early days were interviews and observations (Miles, 1982: 159). Large-scale visitor surveys were used on an annual basis to research the nature of the audience and the opinions of visitors to the new displays and to the museum itself (Alt, 1980, 1983). The new displays were subject to much criticism at the time, but the research demonstrated that although most of the visitors to the museum did not have a scientific background, they found the new displays 'thought-provoking', 'made learning easy' and made 'the subject seem exciting' (Griggs, 1990).

Observation studies entailed watching visitors using the galleries, tracking the routes taken, looking at where stops were made, and measuring how long these stops lasted. These are difficult observations to make, and it is convenient if a gallery overhangs the exhibition to enable the tracking to take place unobserved. Observations can be made, however, of both 'cued' and 'non-cued' visitors, although some would argue that once a visitor is made aware that they are the subject of a tracking study ('cued'), their behaviour necessarily changes (Lucas, McManus and Thomas, 1986).

In the early observation studies at the Natural History Museum in London, two measures based on American research were used to assess the effectiveness of exhibits – 'attracting power' and 'holding power' (Griggs, 1984: 415, Miles; 1982: 159). 'Attracting power' is measured by expressing the number of people stopping at an exhibit in relation to the number visiting the exhibition as a whole. A display case where nearly everyone stopped would be successful on these terms. 'Holding power' is measured by noting the length of time that people remain at the exhibit. If the display case where nearly everyone stopped only attracted them for a few seconds this exhibit would not demonstrate much 'holding power'.

These methods used at the Natural History Museum were based in part on theories of exhibit evaluation that had been developed in America (Weiss and Boutourline,1963; Parsons, 1965). This American approach was grounded in behaviourist psychology, with an emphasis on studying how people behaved in specific environments. The evaluation of exhibitions was built around the development of behavioural objectives, that is, the study and measurement of the behaviour of visitors in relation to specific quantifiable targets. Two main methods were used to measure visitor behaviour, observation and pen and paper tests. Interviews of visitors were also sometimes carried out. The first of these main methods, observation, was the study of what visitors did in exhibition galleries, with an (apparently) objective and distanced observer watching activities, movements and routes taken through the museum spaces. Movements were coded onto plans of the galleries. The success or failure of exhibits was judged from these tracking studies and observations, mainly in terms of attracting and holding power.

The second measure of exhibition success used pre-visit and post-visit pen and paper tests to assess what the visitor had learnt. This method assumed that the exhibition had set out to 'teach' something specific, and entailed the development of specific behavioural goals for visitors. 'Goal-referenced evaluation', therefore, consisted of measuring the success of the exhibition against specific stated objectives.

Screven (1986) gives us an example of a typical exhibition goal statement: 'To improve the general public's sensitivity to the influence of Greek pottery on Roman pottery design.' This is the type of objective that any exhibition developer might come up with. However, in order to assess performance in relation to such an objective, the objective would need to be restated in such a way that performance, or behaviour, could be measured.

> Given six pairs of colour slides of pottery, presented one slide at a time, each pair showing one Greek and one Roman piece, the visitor will correctly identify the Greek (or Roman) example in five out of six pairs.

The objective restated in this way specifies what the visitor does (identifies pottery), the conditions under which it is done (looking at slides), and the acceptable performance level for success (five out of six).

There are specific problems with this approach to evaluating exhibitions. Visitors are, on the whole, observed rather than talked to. Observation might indicate where people stop, but cannot show why the stops occur. What is it about the exhibit (or is it something else?) that caused people to stop? Unless researchers ask visitors why they stopped, or listen very closely to what people are saying to each other while they stop, it is impossible to answer this question. Assumptions are made about the success of the exhibit based on very limited evidence.

The attention through pen and paper tests to knowledge gain is often focused in a very specific and limited way, and suggests that only the prescribed way of relating to the exhibition counts as appropriate, which is clearly unreasonable. Visitors are assumed to be passive and mechanistic, and able to be manipulated by the exhibition rather than purposeful in their use of exhibitions according to their own agendas. The focus on specific limited objectives ignores both the complexity of the learning process, and the specific characteristics of visitors. In addition, the learning objectives are considered in relation to cognitive gains only and ignore affective or emotional aspects (Griggs, 1984; Prince, 1984: 426; Roberts, 1990).

The exhibition team at the Natural History Museum rejected the use of behavioural objectives, and developed the less prescriptive concept of 'teaching points'. However, their reliance on exhibitions based on theories of educational technology led to a greater attention to the structuring of the material to be learnt (the exhibition) rather than to the motivations or interests of the visitor. Attention to the principles of communication that informed the emerging theory of exhibition design led to a lack of attention, as the theory was tried out in practice and exhibitions were built, to the perceptions of visitors.

Once exhibitions began to emerge, the responses of visitors could be explored (Miles, 1986b). Gradually the attention to the exhibition structure was balanced by an attention to the needs and responses of visitors (Miles and Tout, 1991). Both are, of course, necessary. Research, at the Natural History Museum and elsewhere, has revealed the importance of the social aspects of museum visiting (McManus, 1987, 1988, 1989), and the power of museums to change perceptions and attitudes rather than instil facts (Pond, 1983, 1984, 1985). The work of McManus, who developed ways of listening very closely to visitors as they stopped at exhibits, has been seminal in demonstrating the agendas that visitors bring with them to museums, but also the willingness that exists to 'talk' to the exhibit developer through interaction with the exhibit text (McManus, 1990). At the Natural History Museum, the experience of the whole gallery is now considered, rather than the success of individual exhibits, and attention is paid to the affective as well as the cognitive aspects of the museum experience (Miles and Tout, 1991).

The original approach to evaluation at the Natural History Museum was to build the exhibition, observe how it worked and then to use the results to revise the poor exhibits and to inform future work (Miles and Tout, 1991). This presented a problem. Any change that was required once the exhibition was mounted and opened, such as redesigning a display case that was being ignored, or repositioning it to make it more accessible, was bound to be costly both in terms of funding and in relation to the emotional investments of the exhibition developers and designers. Evaluation needed to be moved from the end of the exhibition process to a much earlier stage and needed, in fact, to be completely integrated into the process (Miles, 1985).

Front-end, formative and summative evaluation

Evaluation can take place at three main stages of the exhibition process, but these do, of course, overlap (Griggs, 1992). Front-end analysis is carried out at the beginning of the development of the ideas for the exhibition; formative evaluation tests ideas and exhibits while in production; and summative evaluation examines what has been achieved at the end of the process. Front-end analysis, also sometimes called preliminary research, could be as simple as the testing of the titles for an exhibition, or might be as complex as a research study of visitor attitudes to the theme of an exhibition. Formative analysis generally consists of testing mock-ups of display panels or texts, or, in the case of exhibits in a science centre, trying out the various designs that might be possible for one of the exhibits. Summative evaluation takes place after the exhibition has opened, at the end of the exhibition production process, but during the running of the exhibition. The findings at this stage might lead to small-scale changes, in the lighting perhaps, but will on the whole become part of the front-end analysis for the next project. This circularity of the evaluation process makes a continuous use and attention to evaluation necessary. There are very few museums employing all of these methods in a planned way. One museum that has used evaluation consistently over a period of years is the Royal Ontario Museum (Lockett, 1991).

Front-end analysis aims to identify and eliminate errors which might occur in exhibitions before the detailed exhibition planning begins. An example from the Natural History Museum demonstrates how the approach to an exhibition altered following the opinions of the target audience. The exhibition British Natural History was designed to appeal to amateur naturalists. This group was defined as those people who answered yes to at least two of five questions concerning their level of involvement in natural history. Visitors to the museum were asked if they belonged to a naturalist club, read two or more books during the year on the subject or owned appropriate equipment (Griggs, 1984: 418). Fourteen of those people who fell into this category were then interviewed for thirty to forty minutes, during which time they were asked about their preferences in relation to the proposed exhibition. One of the questions they were asked was whether they would prefer displays arranged in taxonomic groups, or in habitat groups. The exhibition developers had wanted to make a display based on taxonomic groups, but the visitor preference was for habitat groups. The process of specific hypothesis testing happened at an early enough stage in the process of developing the exhibition to allow major decisions to be taken in an informed manner before resources had been committed.

Front-end analysis can be used in relation to specific exhibitions but can also be used more generally. At the Royal Ontario Museum in Canada 140 visitors were asked how they felt about the way a range of objects (piece of furniture, piece of sculpture, small decorative art object) were displayed. The visitors were carefully selected and variables such as age, level of education, type of interest and so on were taken into account in the analysis. The interviewees were asked to rank four two-dimensional mock-ups representing four typical exhibit techniques in order of preference. The posters showed:

- the object alone with its artefact label;
- a range of similar objects, each with its own artefact label;
- the object in a context of a room setting or vignette with a brief general description;
- the object within a storyline or thematic presentation which included layered text, graphics and artefact labels.

The results showed a distinct split between the last two methods of display, which were preferred in all cases, and the first two, which were ranked third and fourth. This was the case even for those people with fine-art-related hobbies and for the piece of sculpture, which indicates a very consistent preference for informational contexts for objects, including those that are often displayed in aesthetic contests (Lockett, 1991).

Preliminary research can be used to indicate what contexts and which information about objects might be found useful. Rose Kerr, the curator of the T. T. Tsui Gallery of Chinese Art at the Victoria and Albert Museum in London was fortunate in having a sponsor for the gallery that was enthusiastic about the idea of research into an appropriate mode of display. The curator and her colleagues had already spent some time watching visitors and acting as information points in the old Chinese gallery and in the newer Chinese Export Art Gallery. Log-books were kept that documented the questions that visitors asked. One of the things that became clear was that many people had found the labels difficult (Rose Kerr, personal communication). 'Goal-free' evaluation of this kind can be used to discover problems that have perhaps not been identified beforehand.

Work began on the development of the Tsui gallery in 1988, three years before it opened. This allowed sufficient time for a number of consultative measures to be taken. Several seminars were held in the gallery with a range of both museum staff and colleagues from outside the museum including historians, teachers and other museum professionals. These seminars were chaired by a facilitator, and general thoughts were shared. It was decided that the gallery would not be organised chronologically, but by themes. But which themes would be appropriate?

A small in-house questionnaire was carried out by a member of the Museum's Far Eastern Department in the Spring of 1989 to test visitor reaction to initial ideas; this was followed by a visitor survey carried out by National Opinion Polls. The questions visitors asked about the objects were confirmed as: 'What is it made of?'; 'Where, when and by whom was it made?'; 'How did the object enter the collection?'; and 'What does the decoration mean?' These questions were adopted for the introductory cases for the gallery, and also for the chapters in the accompanying catalogue (Kerr, 1991).

Small informal focus group discussions with people representative of specific target groups were held. Focus groups are small groups of people with similar characteristics, who meet for an in-depth discussion with an experienced moderator who uses questions, cues, probes and stimulation material to elucidate attitudes, opinions, reactions, issues and expectations in relation to a specific topic (Rubenstein, 1988). This is a recognised market research technique.

The groups discussing the Tsui gallery included 15- and 16-year-old boys, and girls of the same age, both of whom were studying for the General Certificate of Secondary Education; their teachers; teachers and parents of 8–11-year-olds;

teachers and members of the Chinese community in London. These groups were chosen because they were not frequent current users of the museum, but were groups that the museum wished to encourage. The idea of themes was welcomed, and most people agreed that more information should be provided than had been available in the old gallery. Most people were interested in how the Chinese objects were used and by whom, and this has been adopted as a major theme of the gallery. The idea of objects to touch was greeted as a good idea, and the curator consulted Shape, an organisation working with the arts and people with disabilities. Queries about the use of videos and interactive media in the gallery evoked a mixed response and worries about intrusive noise: in the gallery small-screen silent videos with a number of short sequences have been used.

The old Chinese gallery was organised chronologically, with artefacts spanning the period 3000 BC to the present day. It was presented according to the concerns of the curators and with little attention to the needs of the visitors. Research into visitor perceptions and interests has resulted in the new gallery being organised around six main topics: Burial, Worship, Eating and Drinking, Daily Life, Ruling and Collecting. The use of objects is indicated where possible, partly by discreet contextual arrangements.

There are two wonderful objects to touch, plans explaining the layout of the gallery and seating arranged as an integral part of the display to allow a comfortable pause. Some subject specialists have found the gallery altogether too different to be acceptable. Summative evaluation carried out shortly after the gallery opened tested the reactions of the visitors. The findings of two studies were very encouraging in relation to the general approach of the display, and useful practical suggestions were made about, for example, the siting of gallery plans.

Formative evaluation involves testing sections of the exhibition while in the process of developing the exhibition (Griggs, 1981; Jarrett, 1986; Screven, 1988). In practice this is very difficult, and is time-consuming, although there are some museums that use this approach on a regular basis (McNamara, 1988). In addition, it presupposes enough lead time to try out a number of the design elements of the exhibition, which in many situations is not possible. There are two areas where formative evaluation can be particularly helpful, and these are in the writing of texts and in the development of interactive exhibits.

Texts can be tested in a number of different ways. The vocabulary can be reviewed for unfamiliar and polysyllabic words, and to see if the intended message is being conveyed. Initial checking can assess the structure, complexity and length of the sentences (Coxall, 1992). If texts are read aloud, this often gives a clue as to how the language flows, which is important for communication. Family, friends, teachers, children, security staff and other colleagues can be asked to read the words and to describe what they understand. Many of these methods were adopted in a fairly informal way by the curator of Gallery 33 in the Birmingham Museum and Art Gallery. At the Children's Museum, Boston, trial labels are tested in a special display case, where it is made clear that an evaluation is being undertaken. The labels are hand-written with a large pen on specially prepared sheets, which are blank except for a coloured edge. The curators are able to observe the public interacting with the display and to listen to the way in which they read the labels.

Other aspects of text that need consideration are placing and size. Does positioning affect the meaning of the words and how they are understood? A rough mock-up of part of the exhibit has been used at the Natural History Museum. Visitors were asked to spend a few minutes looking at the mock-up, and were then asked what they understood (Griggs, 1984: 416–17).

Interactive exhibits demand formative evaluation. Those things that are designed for people to use, to handle, to sit on or to manipulate must be tested. If this is not done, breakages and breakdowns are inevitable. Some designers of interactive exhibits would see the whole life of the exhibit as being one long process of formative evaluation. An example from the Franklin Institute in America describes how an exhibit involving ropes and a pulley failed because instead of one child pulling on each of ten ropes to test which made lifting a weight of 500 pounds easy, twenty-five children were all pulling on the ropes at the same time. The number of the ropes was reduced to four, guard rails were erected to narrow the entrance to the exhibit and a sign was erected that read: 'Can you lift 500 pounds by yourself?' (Borun, 1989).

Although this approach to designing exhibits is most often to be found in science museums, some art museums are also working with mock-ups of exhibits and texts. One example is the project at the Musée Picasso at Antibes, France, where formative evaluation is being developed with the help of an American consultant. The long-term aim is to develop enough expertise in audience advocacy in the staff of the museum as a whole so that the museum can act as a training ground for curators and other museum workers. This has grown from the concern of the French Ministry of Culture and Communication to increase the general educational effectiveness of French art museums (Screven and Giraudy, 1991).

Summative evaluation tests the exhibition after it has opened. In most museums where evaluation has been undertaken it is understood that summative evaluation, which judges exhibits after they have been produced, is perhaps less generally useful than formative evaluation that aids in the planning and development of exhibits. However, reviews of the effectiveness of exhibitions on completion can be helpful in the right circumstances.

An example of summative evaluation from the Discovery Room at the Royal Ontario Museum shows one way in which this approach can be used. The Discovery Room consists of modular units designed with handling, exploration and self-guided learning in mind. It has been the subject of fairly consistent assessment in terms of the actual use of specific exhibits and also in relation to the development of theories of discovery learning in the museum (Freeman, 1989: 41; Hooper-Greenhill, 1991a: 183). In 1984 a tracking study revealed that only approximately 7 per cent of visitors came as individuals, and all the others came in informal groups of between two and eight people.

Plate 8 Interactive exhibits, such as this one where electricity is generated at the Museum of Science and Industry, Birmingham, demand formative evaluation. It is vital to test how the different parts of the exhibit relate to each other, to watch how people use the exhibit and to assess what level of wear and tear is likely. Failure to do this will result in an exhibition full of exhibits under repair!

Photo: Birmingham Museums and Art Gallery (Schools Liaison).

79

This observation led to the rearrangement of seating and spacing in the gallery to allow for more than one person per display. The tracking study also identified displays that were rarely if ever used. These displays were subsequently analysed and modified (Lockett, 1991: 41).

The Discovery Room at the National Museums of Scotland was the subject of a summative evaluation in the summer of 1990 (Stevenson and Bryden, 1991). The Discovery Room, which had been piloted in 1987 in the education room of the museum with a budget of £600, had become an enormously popular annual museum event with a capital outlay of £25,000 and an annual budget of £10,000 three years later. The Discovery Room is a space for a 'hands-on' experience, designed to encourage visitors to learn through and about objects and to appeal to people not accustomed to museum visiting. It is based partly on the work carried out at the Royal Ontario Museum and on Merseyside, and partly also on educational theory, but theory of a quite different nature from that used at the Natural History Museum in the 1970s.

The Discovery Room at the National Museums of Scotland derives from the tradition of learning by doing and learning through experience (Bruner,1962, 1966; Cole, 1985; Dewey, 1963). The concept of discovery learning can be traced back to the nineteenth century and beyond (Hooper-Greenhill, 1991c), where finding out about the world through the exploration of real things in real places is seen as one of the best ways of facilitating growth and development. Child-centred learning enables the development of skills and abilities within a structured, but open situation and has been a major element in educational thinking during this century. Currently, school pupils in Britain are being encouraged to find out for themselves through investigations of primary sources, through explorations of sites and environments, using active methods rather than passive book-learning. This approach to education is also to be found at the heart of theories of life-long learning, where people, places, activities and practical experience are all seen as opportunities for self-development throughout the lifetime of an individual.

The Discovery Room at the National Museums of Scotland broke new ground for the museum and it was important for the developers to demonstrate that their expectations concerning the success of the enterprise were in fact correct. A form of summative evaluation was designed using a method adapted from the Open University in Scotland, called Structured Video Recall. A video-tape of the eight themed areas of the Discovery Room was shown to visitors after their visit, and the ensuing conversation recorded. Although several methodological hiccups emerged during the process, the system worked very well and demonstrated that visitors enjoyed the experience so much that they wished for more discovery areas in the rest of the museum. Visitors had become interested in themes that they had not previously considered interesting, and had found answers to questions that had puzzled them for years such as 'How are teapot spouts made?' Some negative factors were identified: 'The doorway was very crowded and I could not see what was in the room.' The meaning that the experience had for individuals began to emerge. In relation to the Masks area: 'Made me smile and use different expressions and voices. The image looked different from "me". I felt naughty!'; 'Not tempted to linger because I felt too self-conscious'.

The Discovery Room has been so successful in the main building of the National Museums of Scotland that it has found sponsorship funding to travel to different parts of Scotland and England. The Discovery Room exhibitions have been dismantled and re-erected in other museums, thus operating as an outreach and marketing arm of the National Museums, and enabling the development of new audiences for the museum outside the capital city of Edinburgh. Evaluation, in demonstrating in a researched and concrete way how the initial museum-based project worked, has been important in securing funding for the outreach developments.

Theoretical approaches to evaluation

Evaluation has begun to be of interest to museum workers, and is of particular concern to museum educators, although very little structured and documented work has been carried out to date. However, the emphasis on accountability and on museum reorganisation has spurred a need to find ways of evaluating the learning outcome of educational activities and events, in addition to the experience of exhibitions. Some curators are also now concerned to investigate the perceptions people have of museums, the attitudes they bring with them when they visit, and the meanings and values visitors attribute to what they see and do. The traditional methods of exhibit evaluation that developed in America do not offer ways of discovering answers to these questions.

Many evaluation studies from North America have been predicated on the idea that exhibitions are an instructional medium, that is, that they are didactic or educational. The view of education on which this attitude is based is very narrow. Education is equated with instruction, rather than with growth, and success is defined as measured against predetermined exhibit-related goals or objectives, as we have seen, rather than in relation to the needs and interests of the learner, which are largely ignored. The evaluation methods which have been developed have focused on analysis, generally of the completed exhibition, through quantitative number-based judgements made against measurable objectives defined by the exhibition developer (or the evaluator!), with the aim of judging the success or failure of the exhibition.

This kind of analysis has its roots in the study of the natural sciences, and in behavioural psychology. The predominant analytical model is laboratory-based testing, with carefully designed experiments carried out in controlled situations in such a way that they can be repeated and verified. In applying these methods in the museum as the test environment, visitors are observed, measured, counted and compared, and the results coded into standardised categories. Responses are converted into numbers so that they can be analysed statistically. Quantitative data is generated from repeatable experiments that test hypotheses.

81

The epistemological model used by these evaluators is 'scientific', stemming from the physical, laboratory-based sciences, and primarily designed to measure observable phenomena. This way of understanding the world studies only that which can be observed, measured and quantified. Within this positivist epistemological model, feelings, attitudes and other intangible elements which are more difficult to measure, cannot be included.

However, other ways of studying the world offer other methods of charting it, and increasingly, these methods are being adopted to try to find ways of understanding how it is that people make sense of museums. These other ways of understanding the world relate, not to the 'hard', physical, laboratory-based sciences, but to the 'soft' disciplines of sociology, ethnography and anthropology. These disciplines are generally field-based, that is, they study people as individuals in their own surroundings rather than as anonymous subjects in laboratories. The methods that have been developed have been designed specifically to study people, rather than, as with behaviourist psychology for example, having their roots in methods designed to study animals or things, such as natural elements.

The field-based methods stress observation rather than analysis, and work towards qualitative rather than quantitive data. Documentation, in-depth interviews and descriptions of case-studies result in narrative accounts, where the responses of interviewees are often quoted, producing 'thick' descriptions of practice. These descriptions look quite different from the reports resulting from the 'scientific' methods, which generally contain figures based on the manipulation of statistics.

'Responsive' or 'naturalistic' evaluation is concerned to describe rather than to analyse, and to understand, rather than to explain. It emphasises the meanings that experiences have for participants, and demonstrates this by using the words of those who were part of an event. Rather than focusing on a narrow set of predetermined objectives, naturalistic evaluation is open to the emergence of spontaneous activities and expressions, and seeks to account for a range of different values and perspectives. Evaluators aim to work jointly as a team with those being evaluated, and to work from the inside towards a mutual understanding, rather than to make judgements from an objective external stance (Korn, 1989; Hein, 1982).

The naturalistic approach to evaluation is beginning to become known in Britain. In the United States it has been familiar for some time and a body of good practice has been built up (Otto, 1979; Wolf, 1980). Interestingly, naturalistic evaluation has been used to study and develop educational programmes as well as to study exhibitions. A long-term evaluation project at the Children's Museum of Indianapolis, for example, enabled the education team to develop its effectiveness by thinking more clearly about its goals as a department, and by considering in depth solutions to issues such as the balance of quality and quantity, the relationship of the museum to schools and the role of the educators in exhibition design. Specific practical information was also produced that related to the design of exhibitions, the structure of the schools programmes and the profile of the audience for one aspect of educational provision (Otto, 1979).

The two paradigms, 'scientific' and 'naturalistic', although stemming originally from different worldviews and different disciplines (Korn, 1989; Fay, 1975), should not be seen as mutually exclusive in practice. There are times when each is useful. For example, we can use an open-ended naturalistic evaluation to explore initial perceptions in relation to a proposed new gallery, as the curator of the T. T. Tsui Gallery of Chinese Art at the Victoria and Albert Museum did, where seminars were held with colleagues, and discussion with members of potential target audiences took place in focus groups. This will yield generalised descriptive data, where patterns, trends and individual comments will be valuable. If, on the other hand, we want to know how many secondary school children used the education department in any one year, a simple counting exercise will tell us.

There are a number of methods text books that can be used to help develop an understanding of the possibilities, although none of them are written explicitly for museums and galleries. *Social Survey Methods: a Fieldguide for Development Workers* (Nichols, 1991), is an excellent easy-to-follow beginners' guide. Written for Oxfam workers operating on a shoe-string budget in under-developed areas, many of the constraints will be familiar to those working in museums and galleries. More formal text books are *Sample Survey: Principles and Methods* (Barnett, 1991), a technical guide to survey data collection and analysis; *A Handbook of Qualitative Methodologies for Mass Communication Research* (Jensen and Jankowski, 1991), which has a good introduction to qualitative and humanistic theory which is then applied to the analysis of the media; and *Research Methods in the Social Sciences* (Frankfort-Nachmias and Nachmias, 1992), which is a comprehensive account of the range of both qualitative and quantitative methods. Methods are also usefully outlined in Korn (1989).

5

Welcoming visitors

Museums and galleries already attract visitors from a broad spectrum and many institutions wish to become more appealing to groups that tend to be under-represented at present. This means that the actual and potential range of visitors to museums is vast. How can museums respond to the needs of all? There are a number of strategies that can be used to begin to unravel the needs of this vast mass of people.

The first thing is to understand that 'the public' can be broken down into constituent groups which tend to have at least some characteristics in common. The concept of 'target groups', borrowed from market research theory, is a useful one. All visitors will have a variety of physical, intellectual and social needs in common, while equally all groups will have their own special needs. Making provision for common needs, and reviewing the museum experience from the point of view of each target group, will go a long way towards enabling most people to enjoy museums. It is important to remember that the concept of target groups is used as an inclusive, not an exclusive, measure (Dickerson, 1991).

Within the total potential audience for museums and galleries we will find a span of learning experiences and aptitudes. Some will be beginners, and some will be capable scholars. Not all beginning or novice learners are children: nearly all adults are novices at something, and it might just be the subject matter of the exhibition that is being visited! Even those who are very capable specialists in one particular area may not be familiar with the subject matter being addressed. Strategies are necessary in exhibitions, presentations and publications to make the basic parameters of the subject matter visible and accessible quickly and easily. This is not 'talking down' to the audience. This is laying out the conceptual framework of the topic for basic intellectual orientation.

People relate to the world in a whole variety of different ways according to the range of their different intelligences, their social and cultural background and their life experience. It is difficult to predict specific communicative techniques for specific types of people, but offering a range of techniques across a broad spectrum will enable people to choose the most appropriate mode for them.

The potential museum audience belongs to a diverse range of ethnic and cultural backgrounds. Have the exhibitions, events, publications been reviewed from the point of view of Eurocentricity? (Shelton, 1992; Fussell, 1991). Are alternative voices and interpretations to be heard anywhere in the museum? What opportunity is there for an Afro-Caribbean teenager to find something of relevance in the museum, or an elderly Asian man or the mother of a Chinese family? Does the café offer a range of snacks that appeal across cultures?

The potential museum audience represents a spread of social backgrounds. Many museum and gallery collections, particularly in art museums, consist of objects that have come from or represent the interests of the higher social groups. The exhibition and events programme should reflect themes that have a general relevance, but equally, the histories and technologies of all social classes have a right to be both collected and displayed (Johnstone, 1991; Fleming, 1991; Frostick, 1991).

The museum audience will include both men and women, although research shows that visitors to science museums are more likely to be men and visitors to art galleries are more likely to be women. The communicative process is at its most efficient when people recognise themselves in the various elements of the process. Most museum and gallery displays have privileged a male view of history, but this is increasingly questioned (Porter, 1988, 1991; Jones, 1991). How are women and men represented in your museum? In an art gallery, for example, are the works of women artists displayed, catalogued and made available?

Research has demonstrated that it is the life-stage which is of particular importance in determining if the museum is visited. The largest groups are people in the 25–44-year-old age range, those people who are likely to have young families. What provision is made for their needs? Are there also opportunities for young couples, older families, the elderly? Single visitors and small groups? School classes of thirty and forty ?

It is helpful if the main user groups are identified through visitor research. Exhibitions and other provision such as special events, publications, items in the shop or types of food in the café can then be reviewed from the point of view of each of the main groups.

Working with target groups

The concept of the target group has been borrowed from market research theory and approaches. It is used to describe particular and distinct groups that are thought to have many of the same characteristics. In market research, this has developed to a very fine art, with groups identified that are likely to buy particular products. With the development of direct marketing through mailing, methods have evolved that link postal districts to house-type to lifestyle to potential markets for specific products. This means that the mailing of promotional material for, say, expensive childrens' clothes, can be targeted at people with young families in affluent areas.

Museums and galleries do not use target groups in quite the same way for quite the same reasons. The imperative of revenue generation is not as acute, and the approach to targeting audiences is less aggressive.

However, it is useful to be able to break down the actual audience into constituent types in order to anticipate their needs. It is also useful to analyse the actual audience to decide how and where to place efforts for audience development.

Target groups can be identified in relation to a number of parameters, which include social class, age, ethnic origin, educational attainment level, geographical location, special needs related to disability and reason for visiting. When researching into the actual or potential audience, most of these characteristics are and should be used.

In relation to the assessment of appropriate provision, the main groups that are used include family groups, school parties, other organised educational groups, leisure learners, tourists, the elderly and people with visual, auditory, mobility or learning disabilities. It is good practice to assess exhibitions and the museum in general in relation to the social, psychological and physical needs of each of these groups. Where research into visitors has been carried out and management is committed to the idea of considering the needs of visitors, a sophisticated and detailed list of types of visitors can be drawn up from which to work (Wilson, 1991: 102–4)

The concept of target groups can be used to define the particular audiences for a particular event, exhibition or publication, or even museum. Once this has been done, the provision for any one group can be assessed over, say, a three-year period, where each audience should be offered something which is particularly relevant to their interests (see Fig.14).

Many museums are now designing exhibitions for specific groups. Educational events have, of course, always been organised for specific audiences with specific needs. Educational curricula have been scanned, teachers' working groups have been convened to help design and assess provision, teaching sessions have been piloted and modified where necessary, and the relationship of sessions to researched needs has been monitored. With a face-to-face teaching or workshop session it is relatively easy (given rigorous research and preparation) to modify the content according to the needs, interest, abilities and experience of whichever group happens to be there at the time. The teaching vocabulary can be altered, the concept level raised or lowered, the pace quickened or slowed, the number of activities lessened or increased, the number and type of objects explored or changed, the time spent in the workshop shortened or lengthened and so on.

This flexibility and range is much more difficult to attain in exhibitions. However, there are measures that can be adopted to increase the flexibility and use of exhibitions. Layered text, the use of images, interactive opportunities, objects to touch, things to listen to, videos, can be used to make the subject matter accessible in a number of ways. We tend to view exhibitions and displays as phenomena which are erected and then remain static. But events can be organised that explore different aspects of the exhibition, sometimes in the exhibition spaces. Sometimes there are opportunities to add material to the displays. For example, at the Ferens Art Gallery in Hull, the austere galleries are enlivened by the sight of children's collages near to the eighteenth-century works that inspired them. At Springburn Museum in Glasgow, 'talk-back boards' are an opportunity for visitors to leave their written comments about the museum. This openness and opportunity for reaction and engagement enables people to become involved and these strategies can be observed and could be explored in all types of museums and galleries.

Some museums have worked with different target groups to develop exhibitions. At Alloa, in Central Scotland, the museum is located next to a centre used by many of the local teenagers, many of whom have not found jobs and are consequently underemployed. The museum put on an exhibition on the subject of Teenagers. This appealed not only to today's teenagers, who helped with the exhibition, but also to those people who had been teenagers in the 1960s and the 1950s. At Warwick Museum, in an effort to develop the elderly audience, and particularly elderly women, an exhibition of war-time women's clothing was mounted called 'We Wore What We'd Got'. The research for the exhibition content meant contacting many elderly women who had been in Warwick during the war, and borrowing clothes and researching information. In many ways, working with target groups means an opportunity to recruit the audience as part of the exhibition process. All the women who had lent material to the exhibition at Warwick came to see it and brought their friends.

Working with specific community groups does not always proceed smoothly. Opening up museum processes to non-museum people, if it is to be more than a token gesture, means the curator abdicating some power and authority. This can be problematic. It is also true that different groups in the community may have differing views on what is appropriate and the museum staff may find it difficult to know how to resolve this (Smith, 1991: 124). Clear forward planning and a policy framework is helpful in resolving priorities.

Working directly with target groups in the development of exhibitions will not be appropriate, or possible, for all museums all the time. It is most appropriate for community museums, for history museums or in relation to the development of new audiences. It is extremely time-consuming and demands communication and negotiation skills that not all museum people will have. However, it is always appropriate to *review* exhibitions and the museum or gallery as a whole from the point of view of target groups.

What language provision is made for tourists; what physical provision is made for people with special needs; what information and help is available for educational groups? Vital questions such as these should be asked early and constantly throughout the development process of any exhibition or display, and should be continually borne in mind as parts of the exhibitions or other museum services change.

	families	schools	further education	special needs	senior citizens	women	men	local art/history natural history societies	local ethnic community	tourists
Science Alive	✳	✳	✳							
Art from Russia							✳			
Discovery Room	✳	✳								
Tactile Sculpture				✳						
Archaeology of the Town										✳
Mexican Festivals									✳	
Remembering the Blitz					✳					
Chinese Customs									✳	
Football in the Fifties			✳		✳					
Music in the Sixties					✳	✳				

Figure 14 Matching a rolling programme of exhibitions to a range of target groups helps to ensure that many sections of the community find something of relevance to them on a regular basis. Each of these groups could be further broken down for more specific targeting, and more groups could be added to the schedule

A welcome in a new place

For visitors to museums and galleries, it is the total experience that will be remembered (Hood, 1989: 168). The total experience includes the exhibitions and activities, and also the shop, whether there is food and drink, the cleanliness of the toilets, the friendliness of the staff and most importantly, the quality of the museum or gallery visit will depend to a large extent on how easy it is to manage, in practical terms, on an intellectual level and socially. Many first-time visitors find it difficult to feel comfortable when first trying out a museum. This is not unique to museums. It is always a little strange to arrive somewhere unfamiliar. Thinking about what we do then might help to empathise with the first-time visitor to a museum or gallery.

On first arriving at an unfamiliar place the immediate feeling is often one of not knowing what to do or where to go. For some people this is an exciting feeling, but for others it leads to a feeling of being out of control and confused. In some, the anxieties caused by feelings like these are such that unfamiliar places are avoided as far as possible. What helps us to cope at times like this?

First, we need some information. If we are in a new town, on holiday perhaps, we need to know what there is to do, where the landmarks are, perhaps where the train or bus station is. We also perhaps want to explore. The information that we need depends on what we want to do, and what our personal needs and abilities are. If we are accompanied by tired and hungry children, rest and food might be the first concern. At a basic level, what we need is a 'menu' that lays out the opportunities for physical comfort (food, drink, rest, cloakrooms) and for the highlights of the town (museum, library, police station, shopping facilities, parks, tourist information). From this information we can build a personal agenda for action, depending on our interests, resources and constraints (time, energy, money, abilities).

In an unfamiliar shopping-centre, the needs are much the same. On arrival we need to know what comfort facilities there are (parking, crèche, café, toilets, seating areas) and where the various shops are (food, clothes, chemist, post office). Many of the new out-of-town shopping centres have become skilled at directing customers to the various facilities in the order in which they are required (parking, toilets, other comfort facilities, then a choice of shops, a cup of coffee half-way through, and back to the car-park). Some of the better motorway service stations deal with things in the same way, and so of course do theme-parks and well-managed leisure venues, such as country houses, countryside parks, castles and so on (Westwood, 1989).

But what of museums? It is still possible to fail to find a museum because of lack of directional signposting. It is not unusual to walk past a museum or gallery building because it has no name on the outside, and it is almost normal to go in to a museum and discover such a dearth of information about what the museum is about that, rather than make the effort to find out, it is easier to walk straight out again.

What do we need to know on entering an unfamiliar museum or art gallery? We need to know what comfort facilities there are and what there is to see or do. We need to have this clearly presented in such a way that it is easily accessible and easily comprehensible. We then need to be able to find our way to whatever we choose to do first. This is so basic that it would seem a waste of time writing it down, except for the fact that there are very few museums that offer information of this nature. Very few museums name the comfort facilities (cloakrooms, café, shop, crèche) and direct visitors to them, and even fewer name the galleries or exhibitions that may be seen, or provide a list of 'top ten' objects that could be seen, or provide suggestions for how to visit the galleries according to particular interests. Sometimes this information can be found in a guidebook or leaflet, which is of course useful, but this basic orientational information must also be made available through panels in the entrance to the museum. Plans of the galleries should be displayed, with key points indicated and rooms named.

Museums are often difficult places to visit. As well as the lack of general information, the expressions used to describe the potential highlights of the visit are not those used in everyday life. The Wolfson Gallery, the Pinto Collection, Decorative Arts, Industrial Art, Ethnography, Recent Acquisitions . . . many of these expressions are in fact technical museological terms and are likely to be unknown to visitors.

In considering the visit as a whole, the demands made on visitors are sometimes very great. Many exhibitions and displays are still set at a concept level that reflects the expertise of the curator rather than the interests of the visitor. In a multi-disciplinary museum each exhibition will have been curated by a different subject specialist, and visitors will be exposed to a vast range of high-level specialist knowledge. Unless some effort has been made to present the exhibition subject matter in such a way that it is accessible without specialist knowledge, visitors will be expected to think like archaeologists in the archaeology galleries, like historians in the history galleries, like art historians in the art galleries, like scientists in the natural history galleries . . . and we are still only half-way through the building!

Each of these areas of exhibition or display is likely to be discrete in itself, part of the domain of the specialist department concerned (art history, archaeology, etc). For the museum staff, each of these physical spaces has its own particular identity, which has evolved through knowing the curators concerned, understanding the level of funding and resourcing for each section, remembering the various displays housed there in the past and so on. Between the different exhibition areas there are huge psychological gulfs. Museum staff understand the spaces according to the way they understand the museum and the experience of working in the museum. They know the beginnings and ends of the various physical territories and recognise the battles lost or won, the team-work achieved that these physical barriers symbolise.

For the visitors to the museum, these psychological barriers do not exist. The divisions between the galleries are invisible. The shift from social history to natural history to archaeology is made at a step. One minute we might be gazing at a display of high-heeled buttoned leather boots; suddenly, with a moment's loss of concentration, the gaze is fixed on a stuffed fox and a dustbin or a panel showing the design on some standing stones. How are visitors to make the jump from an eighteenth-century London salon, to a present-day non-specified city garden, and back to sixth-century Scotland? The level of knowledge and the amount of intellectual energy required to place this experience in any kind of comprehensible framework is enormous.

Very few museums offer any cognitive structure, or framework for making sense, within which to place either the museum, the range of displays within it or the experience of any one individual exhibition. Visitors are often plunged into museums with no information about the institution (date, type, size), no framework relating to the nature of the displays (old, new, subject matter, temporary, permanent) and no guidance about how to make choices as to what to do or see. This lack of information means that the visit begins in a vacuum, and it becomes hard work to make sense of subsequent experiences.

Frameworks for making sense

A recent report from the Getty Centre for Education, which described the results of focus group discussions at eleven art museums in the United States, stated that orientation was a problem at all the eleven museums. Comments from first-time visitors describe how they felt: 'I felt lost when I first entered, like what am I doing here?'; 'I was kind of nervous because I didn't really know where to go'; 'That was a problem I found too. When you first walk in there, which way do you go?'; 'Impossible to find your way around. I felt like I was in a rat maze' (Getty Centre for Education in the Arts, 1991: 18–19).

A museum's buildings and grounds affect the museum experience, and are not merely empty shells to house exhibitions. Perceptions of grand buildings are likely to vary. The Philadelphia Museum of Art was described by a regular visitor as: 'It's really utterly splendid. It's the kind of building that you really don't see anything comparable to in this country or abroad in terms of architecture'; and by someone who didn't visit museums as: 'I think it's just a cold building. It's nothing fun to look at' (Getty Centre for Education in the Arts, 1991: 28).

Many people who are not regular visitors to museums find the atmosphere of some museums intimidating and off-putting (Susie Fisher Group, 1990; Trevelyan, 1991). A disabled person thought of a museum as 'something all fusty, musty and dusty'; a woman with children felt 'frightened to make a noise when you walk through the door'; a young Afro-Caribbean wanted museums to 'really make the atmosphere more warm, more welcome' (Trevelyan, 1991 35–6). One of the main reasons some people never go to museums is because of the image of the museum as a large cold, church-like, unwelcoming building. The fact that many museums are not in the least like this does not impinge on their perception of the museum as unwelcoming.

Regular visitors are likely to enjoy the experience of the museum building, and this is, of course, partly based on the special nature of the building, but this comfort and enjoyment is enabled by the security of familiarity. For those who do not have much or any experience, either of the building itself as a physical space within which to act, or of the ways in which people use the building, or of the contents (collections and people) contained by the building, a first visit can be tricky.

Very specific outreach work, either workshop based (Beevers *et al.*, 1988) or through work with exhibition development (Smith, 1991; Nicholson, 1992) can counteract negative or undeveloped perceptions of museums. However, all this will be wasted if there is not a genuine and helpful welcome at the museum door.

It would be refreshing to see an introduction to the museum on entering:

> This museum and art gallery was opened in 1894. It was then a small museum based on the collection of one of its founders, Lady Smith. Some of her collection of paintings can still be found in the art galleries.

> The museum and gallery is run by Blankshire County Council. The exhibitions include local plants and animals, the history of the town and parts of the county, and paintings and sculpture. There are two display areas for short-term and travelling exhibitions. More information can be found in leaflets or the guidebook.

Having put the institution into a framework, it is next necessary to know what displays can be seen and how they relate to each other. Sometimes this is best done through a plan or a 'bird's-eye view', but it is always helpful to give general simple clues:

> This building contains four art galleries and three social history galleries. The collections relating to science and the history of technology are in the Museum of Science on London Road, where you will also find a science centre.

The Sainsbury Wing of the National Gallery in London offers a useful model:

> The National Gallery was founded in 1824. It houses the National Collection of Western European Painting, comprising more than two thousand paintings dating from the thirteenth century to the early twentieth century. The Collection is divided into four parts located in four different areas of the building.

> | | |
> |---|---|
> | Sainsbury Wing | Painting from 1260–1510 |
> | West Wing | Painting from 1510–1600 |
> | North Wing | Painting from 1600–1700 |
> | East Wing | Painting from 1700–1920 |

Each of the named areas of the building is colour-coded: Sainsbury Wing – blue; West Wing – green; North Wing – yellow; East Wing – red. The colour-coding is used to indicate where the various spaces are on a ground plan. This is accompanied by a list of each room and its contents. From this information, a visitor can see quickly what there is to see, where it is and how to get there.

Visitors need to have an understanding of the building they are in, and will feel more comfortable once this is established. The framework of information, which operates at a very simple but vital level, should be maintained at other points throughout the visit. Thus, on each floor of the museum, there should be indications of what there is to see. This can be compared to visiting a large department store: unless you know what there is you are reduced to wandering around aimlessly, and fatigue and boredom soon set in.

The framework should be maintained within the exhibition galleries. Exhibitions generally have a title; sub-titles can also be useful, and should be used consistently or visitors will become confused. Although it is impossible, and probably undesirable, to have a house-style that is repeated in each exhibition or display area, it is important to maintain a consistency of approach in any one gallery or display area.

Exhibitions, or separate galleries, need titles and introductions as to what they are about.

THE ROMAN WORLD IN BRITAIN

This gallery shows the Romans in Britain.

Here you will find displays on Home Life, The Army, Food ...

In an orientation panel such as the above, where categories are used (Home Life, The Army, Food), these should be the categories used as sub-heads in the display itself. It might be thought that this repetition of categories is boring, but in fact they act as handles on which to hang the experience of viewing. If five categories are given in an introductory panel, once visitors have experienced one sub-section in the display, which relates to one category, it is easy to get a sense of the size of the exhibition as a whole, and to estimate how much attention and effort will be required. Although this happens at an unconscious level, it is a vital part of feeling comfortable and in control of our environment.

The sub-headings Home Life, The Army and Food may also be repeated in leaflets, catalogues, videos and teaching packs. These categories will become the structures that shape the things people think about in the exhibition itself, but might also become the structures that shape the 'educational maximisers', the videos, notes, teaching sessions, events and so on that increase the educational effectiveness of exhibitions. 'Food' as a category, for example, might serve as the basis for a display case with appropriate objects, images and words in the exhibition; 'Roman food' might be a sub-section of a video or teachers' pack; 'Food yesterday and today' might be the topic of a holiday activity for children, or of a lecture for adults; and a cook-book of Roman recipes might be sold in the shop.

It is easy for people to relate to displays if they introduce elements that bear some relationship to everyday experience. For example, the Shropshire Mammoths exhibition devised by Acton Scott Farm Museum used a diary format to introduce the exhibition. The introduction to the exhibition took the form of boards and photographs that documented the find, by a woman walking her dog, of some enormous bones in a large gravel-pit being excavated by mechanical diggers. The boards are arranged by date and take us through the process of halting the excavation, removing the bones, trying to find any others, washing the bones (as a public event) and beginning to decipher the clues as to whose bones they were.

At the end of the introduction, a summary is offered, and new ideas are introduced:

> We now believe that an adult mammoth and three infants were trapped and died in a mud-filled pool or hollow 13,000 years ago, after the last ice-age.
>
> Why did they go in?
>
> Why couldn't they get out?

This set of questions enabled the move from the two-dimensional introductory diary display into the three-dimensional displays. The first thing to be seen after this 'framework' board was quite new in the experience of the exhibition – a reconstruction of an enormous mammoth with a small mammoth in the bog.

At this stage, a further element is being introduced. Secure within the conceptual framework of the exhibition, drama can now be usefully deployed. The plight of the mammoth, graphically demonstrated, enables an emotive response. A different form of reaction is demanded from visitors. Previously, we were thinking and following a logical sequence. This was upheld for a short period, perhaps ten to twenty minutes, in an enclosed area. It was ended in a logical and satisfactory way, with a recap to enable us to recall what we had just read and seen in photographs, and to summarise the main points from quite a mass of data. The response to the reconstruction is much less logical, and much less sequential. The response is immediate, and in many ways physical rather than mental. We feel in our bodies the horror of sinking into the mud, and we feel in our hearts the anguish of the adult mammoth unable to help. The noise of the squealing baby, reproduced as part of the experience, plays a large part in an affective reaction.

This reconstruction is overtly sentimental and a bit crude: however, it works almost because of this. As adults we know we are being appealed to, but we enter into the game of allowing ourselves to feel emotion, partly for fun, and partly because it is, after all a scientific conclusion ... we have just read the evidence. As a child, the scale is vast, and the experience overwhelming. Several very small children have been carried out with their eyes tightly closed. Older children stood in amazement. With families, a wonderful opportunity for parents to be parental, protective, informative, fun, an experience to be shared at a number of levels.

How should exhibitions or displays end? It is sometimes useful to have end-boards. At the Mammoths exhibition the experience is summed up thus: 'This is the most complete adult mammoth in Great Britain and one of the best in Western Europe.' The text goes on to reiterate what has been learnt from the plants and animal remains investigated as part of the project. It reminds us that 95 per cent of the adult skull was discovered along with parts of three infant mammoths, and tells us about further work which is to be carried out in due course.

It is generally not difficult to consider how temporary exhibitions should begin and end, and how people should both enter and leave the spaces concerned. This becomes much more difficult in permanent displays. These are often in place for a very long time, and when renewal or redisplay takes place, it is often carried out in a patchy way. The result can be a patchwork of galleries, with enormous conceptual leaps between them, with little or no framework in place to help visitors cope with the jump from one space to the next.

It is difficult for museum staff to pay attention to the holistic quality of the museum visit. This is partly because of the territorial nature of the display spaces, which means that each display gallery will be seen as the 'property' of a particular colleague, and many different colleagues will be responsible for spaces on, for example, one floor of a large museum. It is also difficult to make links between adjacent display spaces when they are renewed at different times in different circumstances. However, it is important to consider the relationships between spaces, and to think whether a 'framework board' might help.

> This is the end of the social history displays. There are books and catalogues on the themes of the galleries at the main museum shop. More historical displays can be found at Hill House, a few miles out of town. There is a leaflet and guidebook at the shop in this building.

To introduce the new spaces, a title with an introductory sentence would be enough:

DINOSAURS AND OTHER CREATURES

Five galleries that demonstrate the diversity of life.

Clearly, this is an issue which each museum will need to relate to their own circumstances. It may be easier for visitors to construct conceptual frameworks in some buildings than in others. The nature and extent of the frameworks required will vary according to the complexity of the building and the density of the displays. However, what is required is to consider how far the current signing acts to help people make sense of where they are and what they are doing, and how far some rethinking is required. One of the best ways of understanding the need for such help, is to go to a strange town, find and visit the museum, and deliberately look for the signs and the frameworks that should be there to help. This can be an even more useful exercise if a 'worksheet' is used (see Fig.15 for an example).

Welcoming visitors		
	Yes	No
Outside the museum:		
Signs from the railway station/motorway?		
Signs near the museum?		
Leaflet in the Tourist Information Office?		
Museum name on building?		
Disabled access?		
Schools access?		
Welcoming?		
Staff to help?		
Inside the museum:		
Information about the museum itself?		
Information about the collections?		
Information about which exhibitions to see?		
Comfort facilities indicated?		
toilets		
baby-change		
disabled toilet		
café		
shop		
crèche		
Information point with staff?		
Help to plan the visit?		
In the galleries:		
Location information?		
Introduction to temporary exhibitions?		
Introduction to permanent exhibitions?		
Conceptual framework in temporary exhibitions?		
Conceptual framework in permanent galleries?		
Conclusions to exhibitions?		
Conclusions to permanent galleries?		
Opportunities for logical thinking?		
Opportunities for using emotions?		
Social opportunities (in galleries)?		
Seating?		
Refreshments?		

Figure 15 A sample assessment sheet that could be used to test the way in which a museum welcomes its visitors

Using people

People can be the most welcoming device a museum can provide.

Traditionally, museums and galleries have had a limited number of roles for front-of-house staff, and not all of them have been found very encouraging by the visitor. The main role has been security, and the museum security guard with proto-military uniform and in some countries, guns and jack-boots, is a not very helpful stereotype. 'They are quite off-putting actually. It's a bit like going into a shop and a policeman looking over your shoulder', said an Afro-Caribbean in one recent research study in London (Trevelyan, 1991: 51). 'I felt like I was a suspicious person', said a visitor to Toledo Museum of Art in America (Getty Centre for Education in the Arts, 1991: 32).

This forbidding image is well recognised by museum management, and efforts are underway to change it. 'Staff must stop being seen as human rottweilers hired to intimidate visitors, and become exhibitors, showing off a museum's collection with knowledge and pride' (Herbert, 1991: 14). Many security or attendant staff in British museums no longer wear military-style clothing, and an emphasis is now placed on customer care and on helping visitors to find their way around and to feel comfortable. 'Customer care' is the approach taken by other public industries such as British Rail and concentrates on helping staff to give information in an accurate and friendly way. It is likely that this approach will be developed in the future through special training courses, and through the work of the Museums and Galleries Commission. Success may be limited if security staff continue to be recruited from ex-police and ex-military personnel, and if the notion of customer care is not seen to be relevant to all museum staff.

In many museums, and particularly art museums, gallery security remains a priority, and some directors are not happy with the idea of security staff also acting as visitor aides. The demands of security are very real, and the needs of visitors must be balanced against the need to protect the collections from theft or damage. However, there is at present no clear-cut definition of what counts as an appropriate balance (Middleton, 1990: 13). The balance will be resolved in different ways in different institutions according to the prevailing philosophy of management, the value of the collections and the use of other safety measures, such as video cameras, alarms and secure exits and entrances to the building.

Many museums are experimenting with new ways of using security or attendant staff. At Tullie House Museum, in Carlisle, front-of-house staff have been renamed Visitor Assistants, to delineate their main role, which is supported by training in working with visitors. At the Tate Gallery, Liverpool, an elaborate scheme was established to allow front-of-house staff to work on a three-week rota that included some time acting as security staff in the galleries, and some time acting as interpreters, either in the galleries, or working with the education section in workshops both in the museum and in the community. Staff were recruited from the traditional caring professions, such as teaching or social work, rather than from security firms.

A second scheme at the Tate Gallery, Liverpool provides a welcome for new visitors in different way, using existing social and friendship networks. The RSVP (Retired Senior Volunteer Programme) encourages elderly people to get to know the gallery and its staff, before bringing friends, elderly colleagues and day-centre users to show them the gallery.

A different way of doing things is in place at the Museum of the Moving Image in London. Here, costumed interpreters are placed within the displays, which themselves resemble stage sets. Thus, a Russian peasant can be found on the train showing 1930s Russian movies, an usherette shows visitors into the 1950s cinema and cowboys argue on the set of a Western. These interpreters enliven the displays by their actions and performances, and interact with visitors, with a very low-level security role (London-Morris, 1992).

The National Museum of Film Photography and Television in Bradford has maintained its traditional security staff, and employs a resident team of actors to 'act' in the galleries, and also to take workshops out to schools. 'Action Replay Theatre' works closely with curators and museum education staff, using some of the methods of Theatre-in-Education. Members of the group might use mime, discussion or role-play, but each 'performance' relates closely to the galleries and collections within which it is performed. With school groups a more participatory approach is taken, while with leisure audiences less participation is expected. The performances are drawn to the attention of visitors through the loud-speaker system of the museum.

This approach shows a much more clear-cut delineation of function, and for the actors concerned, this is a 'permanent' job, with creative opportunities, and a chance to design small-scale productions, write material and develop a range of skills. The museum has made a conscious decision to use people rather than machines as communicators. Although the museum has been a pioneer in the use of new technologies, the use of people to communicate directly was regarded as a more cost-effective and efficient method.

Demonstrators are used where it is appropriate, and generally enhance the friendly atmosphere of the museum. At Quarry Bank Mill, Styal, for example, the textile machines are demonstrated by older people who are familiar with how they would have worked. In The Ulster American Folk Park in Omagh, Northern Ireland demonstrators bake bread, spin and weave, thatch roofs, make candles and so on.

Many museums and galleries have an information point close to the front door of the institution, where visitors can ask questions and find out what they need to know. In some museums, all museum workers from the Director downwards are expected to take a turn in staffing the information desk, in order to obtain first-hand information about some of the initial needs of visitors, and to observe some of the ways in which the institution is approached.

A welcoming atmosphere is encouraging, particularly to those visitors who are unfamiliar with the museum or gallery. In order to sustain the welcome, and enable a fruitful visit, specific thought should be given to the needs of a range of target groups, such as families, educational groups, people with disabilities and the elderly.

In many museums and galleries, it is the museum Friends group that provides information, offers guided visits, works in the shop or the café and acts as the point of contact between the museum and the public. This can be a very valuable service.

It is difficult for museum or gallery staff to perceive the barriers that some institutions present to some sections of the public. As more market research is carried out and made available it will become clearer how very different are the values of large sections of the public from those of museum professionals, and how little understood are most of the concerns of museums. This knowledge will help museum professionals in finding ways of enabling audiences to understand the values of the museum, to appreciate the benefits of museums, and ultimately, to help create museums and galleries more in their own images.

6

Responding to visitor needs

When thinking about responding to visitor needs, it is important to remember the multi-ethnic nature of modern society. Most cities and towns are made up of a range of different communities with different cultures, first languages and religions. Although many of the needs discussed below, such as those of families or the elderly, are common to all peoples, each community has its own social and cultural patterns. Surveys of museum users in Britain show that unless exhibitions and displays are related to specific areas of interest, such as Caribbean art, or Chinese homes (Hemmings, 1992), visits from minority groups are rare. This is also true of museums in other parts of the world and it is fair to say that all museums and galleries need to improve their provision to include all sections of society (James, 1991).

There is evidence that people from different backgrounds have different perceptions and interests in relation to museum exhibitions. An exhibition opening at the Field Museum in Chicago on the cultures and natural history of Africa has been planned following considerable preliminary research. It was discovered that African-Americans were more interested in the idea of the exhibition than whites or other people of colour. Where people were enthusiastic, there was considerable variation in the degree of interest in specific topics between the three groups. For example, African-Americans were more interested in the people and the culture and less interested in animals and wildlife, while whites and people of colour were interested in animals and wildlife. White people were interested in tribal aspects of culture and lifestyle, but the other two groups were less interested in this topic. The exhibition will build on the common areas of interest and will address the stereotypes uncovered in the research (Simpson, 1992b).

Museums and galleries have a public duty to make provision for all parts of society. This means being aware of the nature of the potential audiences for the museum, and taking care to mount exhibitions and displays that interest as broad a range of groups as possible. Where exhibition topics fall outside the expertise of the curator, if, for example the histories of black groups are being told, or objects related to Arabic languages are displayed, or the story of European migrants is the theme, it is vital to ask for help and advice from members of the groups concerned. When this is not done, much offence may be given. Where it is done consistently and with respect, strong relationships may be built. The exhibition 'The Muslim World' at Leicester New Walk Museum arose from a request from the Leicester Muslim community who wished to use the museum to present positive aspects of their art and culture, following the bad press that Muslim society had received because of the *fatwa*, the command to destroy, against Salman Rushdie, the writer of *The Satanic Verses*.

Museums and galleries can, and should, be seen as neutral ground, where all social and cultural groups have a right to display their histories, their art and their customs, either through the collections of the museum, or using objects from their homes and places of religion. Although all cultural groups have their own specific characteristics, all have general human and social needs. This chapter will consider the requirements of families, school groups and the special needs of the elderly and those with disabilities.

The needs of families

In the past families have rarely been considered when exhibitions have been planned. Designing exhibitions to enable parents to explain the themes to their children, or to allow children to learn in relation to their own physical and mental needs has not been part of the objectives of most displays. Some special events have been organised in order to appeal to families, but these have been unusual and infrequent.

Today, things are changing. Where museums are successful, this success is often based on the fact that parents have judged a visit to be appropriate for the family. Parents have decided that the visit will not be too stressful for them, will be both entertaining and educational for their children and will include enough in the way of food and drink to cope with the demands of growing youngsters. In some cases family visits are an outcome of successful school visits, with the child returning with her own adults in tow.

In Britain, family groups are one of the fastest growing sections of the museum audience. In part this is due to the expansion of the age group 30–44, the group most likely to have young families, which will increase by 1.1 million over the next decade (Middleton, 1991: 140), but it is also because museums are changing to offer something that families find exciting. Half of all the visits made to Leicester Museums, Arts and Records Service, for example, are made by family groups (Prince and Higgins, 1992: 101). Family groups represent the most important and core visiting unit, but choose where to go carefully, and match the museum provision with their own needs, as Table 6 demonstrates.

The New Walk Museum is a traditional type of museum, in a city-centre location, with a range of displays including a Victorian painting gallery and a dinosaur gallery: it does appeal to families, but it is also visited by many people on their own. Families visit the dinosaur gallery and appropriate temporary exhibitions. Donington-le-Heath is a seventeenth-century manor house, only easily accesssible by car, where extremely popular open days are organised. Most visitors are families enjoying an unusual day out, with a chance to explore a fascinating building, watch actors or dancers, take part in demonstrations, buy potions and plants. It is an almost worry-free visit, as children are within a contained (literally, within a walled garden), secure and stimulating environment. On the other hand, the Record Office, where archives and documents are stored with very little on show, is not thought to be a suitable place to take the children.

Table 6 Visits to three Leicestershire Museums, Arts and Record Service venues

Museum	On own	With family	With friends	Other
New Walk Museum	36%	46%	16%	2%
Donington-le-Heath	05%	71%	16%	9%
Record Office	83%	13%	14%	–

Note: The pattern of use shows how different kinds of provision attract different audiences.

Source: Prince and Higgins (1992).

Families are typically no longer the nuclear family, which makes up only 9 per cent of US households (Butler and Sussman, 1989: 1) and approximately 5 per cent of UK households. A 'family' is more likely to be a group of adults and children where a range of relationships may be represented, parents, step-parents, grandparents, step-grandparents, siblings, cousins, friends. A range of relationships may be present in any one group, which may include babies, lively young children, tired parents and elderly grandparents. Teenagers and young people are not likely to be part of family groups. The physical, social and personal needs of a family group include those for all members of the group.

There is a considerable amount of evidence that indicates that for families, the social and educational nature of the museum visit is dominated by practical needs (Falk and Dierking, 1992: 45–7). Routine parenting is going on through-out the visit, with children constantly monitored for physical needs such as trips to the toilet, hunger or tiredness. The needs of children to explore in a new place is likely to take precedence over any chance to indulge a sustained interest on the part of accompanying adults. A recent survey of family experiences at a large national museum in London uncovered a stream of demands for more for the children *to do*, to touch, or interact with displays, and more access for buggies and strollers, some parking for prams, more seats, cleaner toilets and more signs to make the museum easier to use. These practical needs are common across families from all ethnic and cultural groups, and are more extreme the younger the children are. Unless museums and galleries make provision to deal with basic needs such as these, higher levels of use of the museum will not be reached.

Babies need space for both or either parent to change nappies; somewhere to be fed, either breast-fed or in a high chair; room to push the buggy and lifts or ramps rather than stairs. Some museums hire out pushchairs or baby carriers. Some museums have provided a crèche where the target audience for a temporary exhibition included young women likely to be shopping in a city centre.

Young children need some opportunity for physical expression. If this can be supplied as part of the exhibition it is helpful. In the archaeology displays at Tullie House, Carlisle, for example, a display case contains Roman horse trappings. Next to this is a horse similar to the type to be found in gyms, with steps at two levels for mounting. Young children spend happy moments riding, role-playing the Roman horseman they see illustrated nearby. Young children also require feeding and toilets and something to look at and do. Many displays are too high and too complex for young children. This makes the visit very difficult for the parents and where this is the case the visit is not likely to be extended or repeated.

The Insectarium in Montreal, Canada, has arranged its new displays to appeal to all ages and sizes. Most of the displays are in low purpose-built glass cubes, but these are at two levels so that some are virtually at ground level. These very low cases, which involve everyone, except the smallest, in bending, are of great variety. Some of these are very brightly lit; one, for example, has a stunning display of big blue butterflies that 'fly' across the display case. Some involve peering into holes. A case displaying the uses of the cochineal beetle, for example, has underneath it a display called 'Where the beetle goes in winter'. By peering through a tiny hole, a small nest of beetles can be observed. There are many similar interesting things happening at a very low level, which are enjoyed by adults and children alike.

Research indicates that museums have the potential to present ideal opportunities for parents and children to talk about things together, to explore together and to learn by comparing what they know with new things seen: '"Look how big that lion is, Jenny. It looks just like Mrs Wilson's cat, only bigger." "That one over there is just like Bobby's cat"' (Falk and Dierking, 1992: 45–7). Of such apparently trivial exchanges are fruitful family occasions made! The mother and daughter together integrate the new with the known, relate the museum experience to their own family world of experiences, working together actively to construct a world of meaning that includes them both. In so doing they cement their relationship to each other, and together they extend their awareness of unfamiliar things.

Families need a social environment where they can be together with activities that can be shared. In relation to the range of psychographic characteristics described by Hood (1983), families value opportunities for social interaction, and for active participation, and being in comfortable surroundings, more highly than they value the opportunity to learn or do something worthwhile (Hood, 1989). Museums are seen as opportunities to *be together* and to have fun.

Museums with activity areas such as the Natural History Centre at the National Museums on Merseyside, Liverpool, or Launch Pad in the Science Museum, London, offer the kind of experience that families enjoy (Stevenson, 1991). Many museums are now developing ways of using the active and lively responses of youngsters and one or two exhibitions have used children as consultants (Baynes, 1992). Children's museums, such as Eureka! in Halifax, have evolved as a response to children's behaviour (Lewin, 1989; Cleaver, 1988).

Making provision for children entails access to adults. Many adults visit museums in order to take children, and it is likely that adults who are not completely committed museum visitors throughout their lives will become museum visitors while their children are small. We are familiar with the idea of adults teaching children. It is also the case that adults learn through their children (Leichter, Hensel and Larsen, 1989). Some museums have realised this, and provide labels for adults to read aloud to children, or activities that the children can begin, but where adults can also participate. It is important to provide information that adults can access very quickly when asked the inevitable questions that children ask. If the information is not readily available, parents are likely to make it up so as not to lose face (Hood, 1989: 156).

In order to appeal to families, museums and galleries need to provide the family group with problems to solve together, offer ways to promote conversation and discussion (through which relationships will be enhanced and learning will painlessly begin), and to ground potentially unfamiliar objects or ideas in material familiar to the family, so that adults or parents are able to guide younger members of the group from familiar to unfamiliar (Kropf and Wolins, 1989: 79–80).

Educational groups

School groups tend to be the largest of the educational groups that use museums. There are currently about five million school visits to museums and galleries each year in Britain, and suggestions have been made that this has the potential to grow by 50 per cent to 7.5 million by the end of the 1990s (Middleton, 1991). This is an audience that is growing. By the end of the decade in the United Kingdom there will be 17 per cent more school-age children, that is one million more school-aged children. School visits have already increased dramatically in some museums in England with the advent of the national curriculum. At the British Museum, for example, numbers have increased threefold, with teachers using mainly the Egyptian, Greek and Roman galleries in response to specific targets and projects identified by the national curriculum.

Patterns of general educational use are demonstrated by Leicestershire Museums, where primary schools make up 63 per cent of the educational audience, secondary schools 13 per cent, other educational institutions 5 per cent, local authority day centres 3 per cent, and other groups including local societies 16 per cent (Prince and Higgins, 1992: 67).

Plate 9 Many teachers are unfamiliar with the ways in which objects can be used in the learning
process. Here teachers at an in-service training day led by a museum education officer are
studying the evidence for early human settlement in southern England, using artefacts
from Southampton City Museums. Once they have handled objects themselves and seen
how knowledge can be drawn from them and how this can then be matched to archival
information, the teachers will feel much more confident about introducing this method
of learning in the classroom. As most teacher training courses do not introduce people to
this way of working, it is important that museum staff organise courses for teachers
already in schools, for teachers in training and for the teacher trainers themselves. If the
potential for learning from objects is not perceived, museums will not be used.

Photo: Defence of the Realm, Portsmouth.

If a museum or gallery wishes to attract large numbers of school groups, special facilities must be provided. These include sufficient toilets for the numbers expected, spaces in which to eat lunch, cloakrooms and spaces where groups of ten or so can meet in the display areas. Many schools, especially where long distances are travelled, tend to try to maximise their financial outlay by filling a coach, rather than bringing one class group of perhaps thirty. Numbers arriving can sometimes therefore be quite large.

Many of the largest national museums, which attract many hundreds of children per day, either have or are planning large purpose-built educational centres. At the Natural History Museum in London, for example, where 180,000 children visit each year, the basement has been converted into a schools area with space for 1,750 coats and bags, refreshment areas, seminar and meetings rooms. A Teachers' Resource Centre with reference materials, and a small discovery area designed for 7–11-year-olds is also provided (Hooper-Greenhill, 1991a: 90–1).

Teachers require detailed and specific information as to what help is offered, what materials and equipment are provided, what they must bring with them and what facilities are available. Teachers' leaflets advising on the organisation of a visit are useful, as are teachers' notes, slide-packs or videos, to help with visits which are teacher-led. Many museums in England and Wales are producing excellent material at present, spelling out the way in which the displays and collections can be used to satisfy the demands of the National Curriculum. Particularly impressive are the well-researched age-related guidelines produced by Ironbridge Gorge Museum, which take the form of A4 forty-page booklets and which offer suggestions for how to use the museum's many sites. The best teachers' materials are piloted and tested as part of the production process.

Some material is being produced which enables the use of computer-based learning in relation to museums (Stibbons, 1991). As an example, 'Nelson's Navy at Trafalgar', produced in conjunction with the Defence of the Realm, a marketing consortium of museums and sites in Portsmouth, and the Royal Naval Museum, Portsmouth, enables school students looking at 'Ships and seafarers' as part of the National Curriculum to study the muster lists of one of the ships, the Victory, along with contemporary letters and documents, and on a visit to the museum, the artefacts (S. Wright, 1992).

Many teachers value the opportunity to use museum-generated information technology in the classroom. A topic-based compact disc on the subject of the Anglo-Saxons has been produced by the British Museum in association with a computer company. Produced for an exhibition of the same name, 'Anglo-Saxons' is an interactive video structured around artefacts and themes such as Amazing Animals, Marvellous Objects, Making Books and Digging Up London. Interesting techniques are used to explore some of the artefacts, especially where difficulties might be encountered. It is possible, for example, with the manuscripts, to peel away the text, to reveal the modern words underneath. The disc is designed to relate to the National Curriculum, and to cross-curricular approaches.

Many museums and galleries organise special courses for teachers to introduce either the museum or gallery itself, or a particular exhibition (Durbin, 1987). Often these are short, and are held after the school day has ended.

In some of the best practice, teachers' potential use of temporary exhibitions and displays in relation to the national curriculum is carefully considered before final decisions about the nature of the displays are taken. Children aged 9–12 and their teachers made up two of the key target groups for the permanent display, 'Art on Tyneside', at the Laing Gallery in Newcastle in the northeast of England (Millard, 1992). Teachers and educational advisors were invited to comment on the ideas for the exhibition, and their advice was taken as to what to include and what to leave out. Since the opening of the galleries, the use being made of the displays is being evaluated to see if modification is necessary.

Government enthusiasm for relating schooling to work has resulted in an expansion of work-experience placements for both students and teachers. Museums and galleries are often seen as relevant. Teachers on industrial placements have used some large national museums. College students have also found museums and galleries to be useful, being placed in marketing, conservation, curatorial and education departments.

Many educational groups other than schools use museums and galleries. These include university and college students, tourist groups and adult education classes. On the whole, groups of adults or students are generally smaller, and do not always remain as a group. Their leaders need accurate up-to-date information on the availability of assistance, perhaps in the form of a talk, or short introduction to an exhibition or possibly in supplying a space for the group to meet together during the day's studying. These groups are very often self-help groups, but appreciate the specific needs that they have being met.

Special needs for people with disabilities

At a recent conference on 'Museums Without Barriers', organised by the Fondation de France and ICOM, it was suggested that approximately one in ten of the population of Europe has a disability (Weisen, 1991a: 83). Museums and galleries in Britain have increased their awareness of the needs of people with disabilities in recent years, following the work of a number of bodies (Hooper-Greenhill 1991a: 135–42). These include the Committee of Inquiry into the Arts and Disabled People and the Carnegie United Kingdom Trust who published many of the reports connected with the two-year inquiry (Attenborough, 1985; Carnegie Council, 1988; Coles, 1984; Pearson, 1985); the Museums and Galleries Commission, who appointed a Disability Adviser in 1989 on a short-term contract and have since published 'Guidelines on disability for museums and galleries' (Museums Association, 1991b: 450–1) and a disability resource pack; and MAGDA (Museums and Galleries Disability Association), founded in 1986 to provide a focus for work on provision for people with disabilities. A *Checklist* has been produced by the Arts Council (Arts Council, 1989), and some of the Regional Arts Assocations have policies of disabled access. MAGDA has recently produced a set of notes on design for disability (Forrester, Thorpe and Kirby, 1988). The ADAPT fund, organised by the Carnegie United Kingdom Trust, offers grants to those institutions that can raise matching funds for the improvement of buildings to enable greater physical access.

In some museums, the issue of access is taken very seriously indeed, and actions suit words: disabled people were a major key target audience for 'Art on Tyneside', the new permanent gallery at the Laing Gallery in Newcastle (Millard, 1992). Working with Equal Arts, the Northern agency for the arts and disabilities (formerly Northern SHAPE), a list of recommendations was drawn up that related to a number of special needs, including non-reflective glass for visitors with impaired vision, an induction loop in the video area for hearing-impaired visitors, and raised floor-track for blind and partially-sighted visitors. Sponsorship and grants were sought to enable the implementation of the recommendations.

Figures for the number of people with impaired vision in Britain are difficult to determine. Weisen suggests that approximately 2–3 per cent of the population of Britain is visually handicapped (Weisen, 1991a: 83) of which 5–10 per cent are blind (Weisen, 1991b: 112). If we accept Middleton's figure of 57.5 million for the UK population in 1991 (Middleton, 1990: 26) and take the mean of the other figures, then perhaps 1.5 million people are visually handicapped, of whom about 100,000 are blind.

What can museums and galleries do to help people with visual impairment?

Braille texts are useful, although only a very small percentage, perhaps only 3 per cent, of partially sighted people can read braille. Panels with braille labels should be mounted at an convenient angle, on a slight upward slope rather than flat on the top of a surface, which becomes very tiring to work with after a while.

Texts in large type are perhaps more useful, as a large proportion of the audience will also find this helpful, including those with bi-focals, people with reading difficulties and also those who are tired. Sound cassettes are helpful for those with very little or no sight, as these can be used to structure the visit in addition to giving information.

Catalogues or guides in large print and braille could be considered. These are very useful in that they can be taken home and if illustrated, can be studied after the exhibition. A touch exhibition at the British Museum, 'Human Touch', used linear illustrations of the sculpture displayed on the labels in the exhibition and the same illustrations in the catalogue.

Workshops which enable handling, close looking, discussion and personal expression are perhaps the most useful (Kirby, 1991: 118) and if organised sensitively and over a period of time, some workshops can offer new interests and involvement. In many museums and galleries in Britain, this level of provision is rare because of the resource implications.

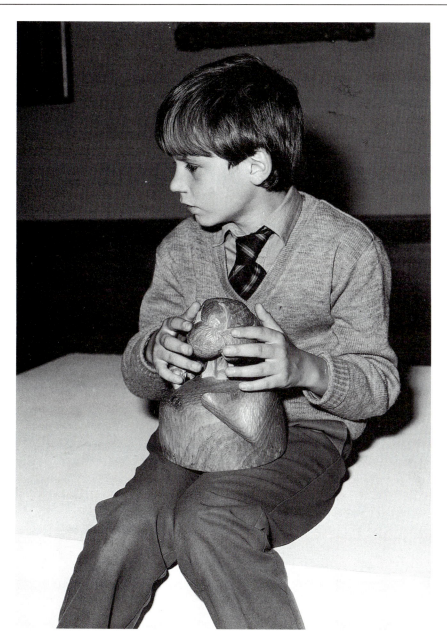

Plate 10 People love to handle objects. This is one of the unique opportunities that museums can offer to all visitors. Here, a boy with impaired vision handles a sculpture from the 'Freedom to Touch' exhibition at the Laing Art Gallery, Newcastle-upon-Tyne. Visitors with visual impairment do not appreciate being singled out for special provision. It is good for everyone to have a chance to handle different kinds of artefacts, and this is most likely to be well used if it is in an easily accessible gallery, preferably near the museum entrance and near refreshments.

Photo: Laing Art Gallery, Tyne and Wear Museums.

109

Opportunities for handling are welcomed, especially when this is integral to the exhibition or permanent display rather than provided as a special event. Although many touch exhibitions have been organised in recent years (Pearson, 1991), most visually impaired people would prefer visits to museums to be facilitated through on-going provision rather than to have to wait for special exhibitions. A touch tour is possible in the Wolfson Galleries at the British Museum (Pearson, 1989).

Tactile thermoform images (raised images of parts of paintings) are one way of enabling people to gain an impression of a painting. The Living Paintings Trust is pioneering developments (Kirby, 1991), and recommendations are made that museums and galleries should have tactile images of paintings and sculpture for sale, loan or reference. Thermoform images in exhibitions need to be accompanied by a taped commentary.

A handrail can be useful, as is a rubber mat to indicate the route through an exhibition like the one used for 'Art on Tyneside'. Where a special mat is not provided, level flooring is recommended. Care should be taken to avoid overhanging or projecting impediments.

Lighting should be bright, without glare, and uniform to help those with residual vision. Sometimes lighting can be used experimentally, as for example at the Tate Gallery, Liverpool, where a sculpture exhibition used light as a way to see, with switches that could be used to change the lighting on a piece of sculpture, using front, back and side-lighting.

The American Foundation for the Blind has published guidelines to help museum guides work with blind and visually impaired people (Groff and Gardner, 1989).

Although it is not always easy to tell, it is possible that a substantial number of museum and gallery visitors may be hearing-impaired. In Britain, for example, approximately one-tenth of the population may have a hearing impairment (Attenborough, 1985). This represents possibly six million people.

In order to help those with hearing impairments, it is important to check that any information that is conveyed audibly is also available in visual form. Sub-titles should be displayed with audio-visual presentations. Where spoken words are used, with for example, talking 'labels', additional graphic panels or supplementary leaflets can be supplied.

Lectures can be signed: where the whole audience is hearing-impaired, the lecture can be signed from the front following the words of someone at the back. Induction loops in lecture theatres can help some of those with deaf aids, and other techniques such as infra-red systems and high frequency communication, both of which use forms of 'walkie-talkie' devices, can be used (Bizaguet, 1991).

Very few museums have deaf staff who use their special skills for the benefit of audiences, but La Villette in Paris has a deaf member of staff who welcomes deaf visitors using sign language (Bouchauveau, 1991).

People who are physically disabled sometimes use wheelchairs or walking-frames. Ramps are easier to manage than steps and should be at a 1:20 gradient. Handrails are useful. To allow wheelchairs to pass, entrances should be level, flat and sufficiently wide. Rotating doors are impossible for the physically disabled and alternatives must be provided which are clearly signed. In the last ten years, several museums in Britain such as the National Portrait Gallery and the Horniman Museum have replaced their old revolving doors with more easily accessible ones.

Many historic buildings have stairs, which can be made accessible through the use of a stairlift. Seating (with seats not too low) and rest areas should be provided.

The main problems for those with physical impairment are those connected with access (it is important to think about ramps, handrails, wide doorways and doors that are not too heavy); freedom of movement within the museum (made easier by wide paths through displays, having a wheelchair available, supplying seating and lifts); sudden changes in floor level; inaccessible toilets and cafés; visibility of signs and labels; and the lack of information and publicity. If there are no suitable toilets, publicity leaflets should state this: if access to upper floors is impossible without climbing stairs, perhaps a sample display or handling table could be made available downstairs.

The Henley Management Centre suggests that the 1990s will see a move away from a culture dominated by youth towards a society dominated by the needs of those over 50 (Middleton 1990: 26–7; Tinker, 1992). If this is the case, we shall see vociferous demands that public services provide for many of the needs considered above. Those becoming older today are people who have been brought up to expect high standards of living, and who have lived through an era of broad access to education, to leisure and to the media. People who have high expectations of life will retain these as they grow older and will be impatient if their needs (no doubt already frustrating enough) are not anticipated.

As people become elderly, hearing, vision and mobility decline. The opportunity to do things at a slow pace, to have access to quiet seating, creature comforts, handling collections and research resources, will all be valued. It may be that separate provision will need to be made to respond to the needs of young families and the needs of the elderly.

Although the same responses will satisfy both groups, the elderly are unlikely to feel completely at ease all the time in a noisy and busy part of the museum.

Many of those over 60 are afraid of going out. Probably the best response to their particular situation is through special workshops organised in association with existing caring groups such as Help the Aged, which is very active in the organisation of events. Workshops for the elderly often perform more of a social function than those for other groups. Cups of tea, refreshments and the chance to talk are very important. Some museums have developed specific outreach programmes for those who cannot make the journey to the museum (Beevers *et al.*, 1988).

In considering how the museum or gallery provides for the needs of specific target groups, the museum building should be evaluated from a number of specific points of view. How does it work for wheelchairs? What about school groups? What information would I get if I were completely deaf? The best way to do this kind of evaluation is to ask a representative of the particular group, or to contact a relevant agency for help, such as SHAPE. The work of one museum, La Villette, in Paris, demonstrates how accessibility for all can be achieved by designing a building without handicaps, where provision for movement was considered in relation to special needs, handling and seeing at the right height was considered for everyone (Grosbois, 1991).

Training of staff is vital and again, relevant agencies such as, in Britain, the Royal National Institute for the Blind, can help. The Museums and Galleries Disability Association can also advise museums on how to begin.

In addition to evaluating the building, exhibitions should be analysed, and where necessary, should be modified. The provision for people with special needs generally means making provision for the use of an alternative sense, where one sense such as sight or hearing, is impaired. If exhibitions and displays incorporate opportunities for the use of a range of senses, then not only are special needs met, but provision is made for those people to access the exhibition content using their preferred learning style, either visually, through looking or reading, through touch or through sound.

A multi-sensory approach to an exhibition

An exhibition at the Boston Museum of Science in America presents a fascinating example. Before modification the gallery consisted of six large dioramas behind glass, with small text panels mounted at adult height. There were few aids to help visitors begin to understand the themes of the gallery, and few people spent very long there. After considerable thought, experimentation and evaluation, the gallery was modified to express the themes of the gallery (animal adaption) more overtly, and in such a way that visitors could respond using many senses rather than just one, as before. The modifications included an orientation panel explaining the aim of the exhibition; a console was added to each diorama (about two feet in front of the glass) which consisted of an audiotape describing the diorama and a smell-box with a relevant smell; two consoles also had something to touch. Other touchables, such as mounted (replaceable) specimens or bronze sculptures, were placed near the other displays. In addition three free-standing hands-on boards illustrating an aspect of animal adaption were added to the gallery (Davidson, Heald and Hein, 1991). The consoles and their constituent parts were consistently placed to make physical access as easy as possible.

The labels were improved by being made easier to read and understand, and some of the material was repeated in the audiotapes. The tone of the wording on the labels was shifted from scientific and academic to conversational and familiar. The first sentence of one of the labels illustrates this: it originally read - 'Whitetail deer, often called 'Virginia Deer', are the most plentiful and best known of American big game animals'; it now reads – 'It is a June afternoon at Squam Lake, in New Hampshire. These whitetail deer, a mother and her two fawns, have come to drink'.

Looking at the animals in their habitats and reading about them can now be supplemented by listening to a description of the habitat, smelling something discussed and handling something relevant. The themes have been drawn out by the improved labels and the introductory board, and can be equally accessed through sight, sound or touch. Summative evaluations indicate that the proportion of family groups visiting this part of the museum increased and the time spent in the gallery has gone up dramatically. Visitors are gaining information from reading, listening, smelling and touching. This information, absorbed through the use of a range of senses, has been synthesised into coherent and articulate understandings. The overall knowledge gain has increased enormously, with a greatly increased number of visitors able to give some information on adaptive features of one of the animals, and the increased range of adaptive features mentioned indicates that information was gained other than through the written label.

The multi-sensory approach to gallery display adopted at the Boston Museum of Science helps everyone. People with one impaired sense are able to use others, and all people have an opportunity to select their preferred sensory learning mode. Tracking studies in the gallery have revealed that although the flow pattern overall seems chaotic, people, and particularly children, move purposefully from, for example, one earphone to the next, or one hands-on activity to another (Davidson, Heald and Hein, 1991: 288). The introductory orientation panel explaining the gallery, the clear exhibition structure with consistently placed physical items and easy to read labels, and the opportunities for interaction make getting to grips with the ideas the display illustrates easier, especially for those with mental handicap, or who find learning difficult or who are very tired.

A whole museum approach

In these sophisticated and competitive days, it is those museums that offer comfortable, welcoming experiences, where many members of varied groups can feel secure but extended, that will flourish and grow. Museums are just beginning to develop the skills of making themselves fun to be in and easy to access, both mentally and physically. There is still a great fear amongst some curators that making it easier for visitors to understand the ideas that collections represent and that exhibitions tackle will begin a slide into commercialism, poor scholarship, facile interpretation and mindless entertainment. This fear must be converted into an understanding and appreciation of the desire of a great many people to like museums and to find them both useful and enjoyable.

113

The task for museums and galleries today is to find appropriate ways to enable the most people to benefit from the resources that we are privileged to hold. Museums today are inescapably part of the leisure industry. This was not the case some twenty years ago, when the leisure industry was itself young and undeveloped. Museums occupy a particular niche in the leisure industry that is open on the one side to leisure, fun and entertainment, but which is firmly joined to the educational world on the other. This link is strong and growing stronger and it is precisely this link to education that constitutes the appeal to leisure audiences. We can enjoy ourselves and try something new and probably good for us at the same time. We can entertain and yet also educate the children.

In addition to this, it must not be forgotten that in recent years, education itself has become closer to leisure. Progressive educational theory has always maintained that we learn while we are involved, committed and enjoying ourselves. The recent stress on learning through doing tasks in the real world, through links with industry, through visits to sites such as shopping centres, museums and galleries and the stress on course-work instead of exams, all have the effect of making the educational process closer to and more open to other social processes. This fundamental change in ways of learning and teaching means that learners no longer think they must suffer to learn, and that learning has to be difficult to be effective.

Fun is only possible in an atmosphere where we feel welcome, comfortable, at home and appropriate. A range of frameworks should support and sustain us in order to allow us the freedom to explore, to experiment, to talk and to make sense of our own reactions to the museum.

7

Language and texts

The power of language

Although museums and galleries are fundamentally concerned with objects, these objects are always contextualised by words. Museums are in fact perhaps as much concerned with words as they are with objects, although in many ways, because of the focus on the material object, the words have become invisible. However, in the classifications used for documentation, in exhibition themes and in the ideas about the museum presented through publicity posters and leaflets, language is necessarily used.

Language is often used without thought, in a natural and common-sense fashion (Belsey, 1980). This apparent obviousness of the use of language hides the power of language to shape thought, to direct perception, to control responses and to present a particular view of the world.

> The world is grasped through language. But in its use by a speaker, language is more than that. It is a version of the world offered to, imposed on, enacted by someone else.
>
> (Kress and Hodge, 1979, quoted in Coxall, 1990: 16)

Spoken language creates a worldview not only through what is said and how it is said, but also by what is *not* said. The gaps and omissions in speech reveal values, opinions, assumptions and attitudes. The same is true of course for written language. Language is both a site of and a stake in struggles for power (Fairclough, 1989), and this is true in museums as elsewhere. The words used in museums create approaches to the past, and attitudes to the present: the choice of a theme for an exhibition, and the nature of the language used to present it, for example, create and display a particular interpretation of experience.

In museums and galleries, messages are carried by a combination of words, images and objects. Both images and objects are capable of carrying many meanings, and are in fact susceptible to the imposition of many meanings (Barthes, 1977; Hooper-Greenhill, 1991b). There are many ways in which artefacts can be explored and presented. However, in museums, a particular approach has evolved over the years to the display of objects, in which they are named and then described in terms of their material, form, design, date and sometimes use or place of origin.

This convention can be observed in art museums, where a dish might be labelled 'STANDING DISH. VENETIAN; early sixteenth century. Wilfred Buckley Collection No. 116. C. 172-1936'; or in science museums, where a piece of machinery might be accompanied by the words 'BEAM ENGINE, eighteenth century'. This terse nomenclature has in the past been so naturalised in museums as to be almost invisible. In some museums, the information given is so embedded in the curatorial code as to be incomprehensible to those who do not understand it. Labels which read, for example: 'Aryballos. Protoattic. 700-650 BC' or 'Fragment of closed vessel, Attic. Late Geometric, *c.* 700 BC', or 'Kantharos. Apulian. *c.* 350 BC' are using specialist names for the objects and archaic place-names drawn from the study of classical Greece. The mode of assembling the words, with the object type and the place of possible origin combined with the curatorial reference is peculiar to museum labels. A viewer without the specialist knowledge and without an understanding of museum conventions is unable to make sense of this information.

Objects are the result of social processes, many of which have been exploitative and conflictual. In museums, this is ignored or diguised by placing the objects in an apparently neutral and factual framework created and sustained through the words which contextualise them. Social objects are treated as though they had spontaneously emerged, through some 'natural' event, and the social relations that are inscribed within the objects are rendered invisible. This is not a neutral process, nor a scientific one. It sometimes has the effect of *neutralising* the power of objects to bear witness to the past. It often creates a past that seems harmonious, productive and comfortable. It frequently produces a present that maintains the existing power relations, where only unquestioning voices are allowed to speak.

Objects are open to manipulation in terms of meaning. This is their strength, but also their weakness. We see things according to what is said about them. The words used to talk about an object fix the way in which this object is to be seen at that particular time. John Berger pointed out in *Ways of Seeing* (1972) that the meaning of Van Gogh's painting of a cornfield was likely to change radically once the words 'This is the last painting Van Gogh painted before he died' are placed underneath it (as they are in the book). The painting doesn't change at all, but what do change are the meanings that we impose on it. The crows become more menacing, more symbolic of impending death, the corn waves more tragically, the movement of the paint appears to herald the onset of madness and oblivion.

In museums, it has traditionally been the curator who has had the task of choosing the way objects should be presented. The linguistic framework, and the resulting intellectual structures within which the objects are placed, have been chosen according to the values and desires of the curator. Thus displays have, until fairly recently, reflected the specialist academic interest of the curator, the subject divisions of the collections of the museum (Decorative Art,

Archaeology or Natural History, for example), and an often minimal approach to giving information in exhibitions with a focus on the names, material properties and places of origin of objects. This process has resulted in very limited and repetitive approaches to objects, with vast areas of potential left untapped and unexplored.

This increasingly outmoded way of working has had the effect of excluding other points of view. It has not, until recently, been very often that other points of view have been able to be expressed. As a result, many sections of the community have felt disenfranchised by museums and galleries. A case-study provides an illustration.

The exhibition 'Palaces of Culture: the Great Museum Exhibition' at Stoke-on-Trent City Museum and Art Gallery, November to December 1987, commissioned six artists to make works that contributed to an investigation into the nature of museums. The 'natural' authority of museums was challenged both by the exhibits and by a specially commissioned essay for the exhibition catalogue (Stoke-on-Trent Museum and Art Gallery, 1987). One of the artists, Jo Stockham, pointed out forcefully in her drawing called *Neutral History* that the messages of the ceramic collection were concerned solely with the aesthetics of the forms and designs of the artefacts, rather than the work of the potters who had made the plates and dishes. Thus the suffering of the women workers through lung diseases caused by the materials used in production, although well documented, was ignored.

Another of the participating artists, Lubaina Himid, used the words 'Success to the Africa Trade', which came from a Liverpool-made eighteenth century punch-bowl in the ceramic galleries at the museum, as the focal point of one of her works for the exhibition. This work *Bone in the China*, was accompanied by the following words:

STATEMENT BY LUBAINA HIMID FOR PALACES OF CULTURE

It would seem to me that museums contrive to do a great disservice to Black people. These palaces of culture are charnel houses full of stolen goods, where the treasures of Black heritage and creativity are hoarded, neglected and ultimately wasted. Those that cannot be accused of these crimes are guilty of others, crimes of denial and bigotry.

Black people have made vast contributions to the culture, wealth and status of Britain for more than four hundred years; try finding the evidence in the local museum. Until the stolen goods are returned and until we take the space to chronicle our own experience as we find it, to honour those who have gone before and encourage our children, there will be nothing great, honourable, honest, or decent about the Museum.

These words accompanying the art-work contextualise it in a very particular way, such that a telling critique is made of museums and their operations as a whole. They demonstrate a great anger at the way museums have ignored a large proportion of the population. These words also enable us to 'see' the works in a different light, to read new meanings out of them.

It is of course perfectly possible to display ceramics and discuss the effects of their production on the producers. The objects remain the same, but the words are different. It is also possible to display ceramics to show 'the blood in the bone', to demonstrate the part played in the history of the object by those people who are normally excluded. The objects remain the same, but the words are different. There is no intrinsic reason not to display or write about ceramics to demonstrate the development of particular styles of decoration, or ways of using materials. But if this is the only way that these objects are displayed or discussed, and if this continues for decades, then the museum is justifiably open to the charges of bias and exclusion from those whose experience is not explored in this approach to the objects. And it becomes clear that the museum is operating within a particular ideological framework that has the social function of supporting, and in fact constructing, the 'natural' authority of those who know about objects in this way, which appears 'academic' and 'specialist', but which ultimately has the function of creating historical myths that sustain the powerful and disenfranchise the others.

Thus we must acknowledge the power of words. Words do more than merely name; words summon up associations, shape perceptions, indicate value and create desire. Words create power relationships, and sustain inclusions or exclusions. The words used in museums are rarely seen in this context, although they are used all the time in exhibitions, in leaflets, in catalogues, in publications and in posters. In all sites of use including museums and their exhibitions, written language works as we have discussed. There is no possibility of producing texts that do not do ideological work.

What, therefore, is a useful way forward? There are two ways of approaching the situation. One is to understand more thoroughly how language works in general and how language works in museums, and the other is to find new ways of producing the words that are used in museums and galleries. The first, a better understanding, will enable us to be more aware of how language is working in the museum environment, and the second, by enlarging the number and nature of writers or producers of museum texts, will break down the curatorial monopoly of the description of experience and will work towards the democratisation of the museum as a social institution. Both of these approaches are necessary. This chapter will concentrate mainly on the first, on exploring how language, in the form of written texts, works in museums. But first we will look at some examples of new ways of generating words for museum use.

Many voices, many contexts

Many museums today have rejected the outdated approach to labelling objects that was discussed above. Instead, other ways of contextualising objects have been found. The reasons for this are many, and they range from the social to the museological. Some reasons are: to enable suppressed histories to emerge; to shift the nature of the information from the academic to the everyday in order to communicate with a broader range of people; to relate the museum experience to experiences in many areas of society; to incorporate real events or actual human feelings; to offer a range of types of response to objects; to incorporate research gathered in a number of ways.

Where exhibition-makers wish to include the experiences and enable the expression of ideas and opinions that are of people other than themselves, consultation becomes necessary. Advisory groups are able to offer points of view on particular ethnic cultures, or information about needs of specific potential audiences, and can be formed to work jointly with exhibition teams. These groups need to be consulted at an early stage in the exhibition development process as texts for both labels and catalogues emerge from concepts and ideas, and it is difficult to write appropriate text if the initial ideas are misconceived.

The Geffrye Museum in London is a small museum which was established as an educational museum in the East End of London by the Greater London Council in the 1930s. Pioneering educational work was carried out by Molly Harrison and others, but by the mid-1980s, the displays appeared tired and irrelevant. The museum had lost its identity and was not sure whether the collection of period furniture should be displayed as social history or as fine art. A more imaginative solution was found, which was to try to develop relationships with the local community. One way of beginning to do this was to commission research into the way in which the collections and existing displays could be used to explore black history (Frazer and Visram 1988; Visram, 1990).

Many practical suggestions were made that resulted in small amendments and additions to the existing period room displays that offered fertile opportunities for discussion; an Indian shawl, for example, was draped over a chair in the Victorian parlour, and a print showing the portrait of a prince from Bantam, Malaysia, who had been the guest of the English court, was hung in the seventeenth-century room. In the William and Mary room, calico curtains with a design originating in Calcutta were hung. The labels for the temporary exhibitions emphasise any appropriate multi-cultural aspects of the topics. The period rooms will all be redisplayed in due course, and so the permanent labels are not being rewritten, but a tape guide has been produced which has incorporated many of the recommendations and suggestions made by Frazer and Visram (1988) (MacDonald, 1990b), and includes references to the histories and work of women, artisans and black people.

In the Early Georgian room opportunities are taken to open up the story:

> The furniture is chiefly of mahogany by this date. At first the principal source for this hard, heavy wood was Jamaica . . .

> Look at the table against the facing wall, on the right. On it are a tea

caddy and cups which attest to the importance of trade with China; and the cookbooks of the eighteenth century are full of recipes calling for any amount of spices from India and the East, and for sugar from the West Indies.

The Victorian parlour is described thus:

This room shows the effects of the Machine Age . . .

A room like this was very labour-intensive. In previous generations the lady of the house had shared the domestic tasks with her maids. . . . Unlike her grandmother, the lady of a house like this was expected to sit in the reception areas of the house and be waited upon. (Note the bell rope by the fire.)

In some museums, policies have been written which state that research and collecting practices should focus on those parts of the community that are currently under-represented by the displays and collections (Hasted, 1990; MacDonald, 1990b) and in others, specific approaches to exhibitions, enshrined in exhibition policies, concentrate on integrating local people (O'Neill, 1990). Through opening up museum processes of collection and display, and finding ways of working in relation to the histories and cultures of the diverse social and cultural groups that make up British society, some museums are developing new languages and new texts. In the process, objects are valued in new ways, and sometimes surprising things happen.

One example must suffice: the 'Women's Pictures' exhibition at Paisley Museum and Art Gallery in Scotland in August 1991 was put together with help from members of local women's groups, using the paintings from the museum's store (Carnegie, 1992). The paintings were all of women and girls, and the labels consisted of the words of the women as they reflected on the works:

'She looks as if she's had a hard life. . . . Aye look at her face . . . but women then did have hard lives. It's real. It shows in her face dinnit, no even her face, look at her hands. It looks as though she's been scrubbing – they'd nae washing machines – scrubbing board and . . . I think she represents every old person that's had a hard time.'

(Comments on the label for an unnamed woman in *The Paisley Shawl* by Fra Newbery
(1855–1946))

There are a number of ways of presenting information other than in the words of the curator. Words can be drawn from the results of oral history, from documents, from poems and from a wide range of sources.

It is now fairly common to see reported speech used to describe particular experiences, where general events or processes are vividly illustrated by the words of an individual. The People's Story in Edinburgh, for example, structures the permanent display around named individuals such as Peggy Livingstone the fishwife, Jimmy Lewis the cooper and Mary Gillon the tram-conductor. The words of each person are used to describe or illuminate the craft or task being displayed. Thus, a progression through the exhibition means moving from the words of the fishwife to those of the cooper and the tram-conductor. In some instances, the words are spoken aloud.

The words have been generated through oral history research with the individuals concerned (although they are spoken by actors), who in addition to being the subject of museum research, also acted as consultants to the displays as they were produced, where the displays show them in earlier times than that of the present. The language used therefore represents the views of both men and women, reflects regional and craft-related dialect, and is drawn from real speech rather than constructed after reading specialist books.

Often, words drawn from the experience of people in real situations has a poignancy and immediacy that could not be achieved in other ways: on an interpretive panel on 'Working Lives' in the same museum:

> I can remember a girl getting badly badly burned in the boiler room up to her waist. She didn't get a penny compensation.

In the exhibition 'The Story of Hull and its People', in The Old Grammar School, the small social history museum in Hull, the storyline of the exhibition is carried through the experiences of two individuals, Ray and Elsie, both of whose families have lived in Hull for five generations and more. In the catalogue, Ray describes how he decided on his career:

> 'I used to see all these kids with five pound notes and packets of 50 Woodbines in their back pocket; all these flash suits, 26-inch bottoms, box backs, hair slicked back with the old brylcream and I thought I wouldn't mind having a go at these trawlers.'

> (Frostick, 1990: 7)

Sometimes archive material can be used effectively. The People's Story in Edinburgh uses a short excerpt from Parliamentary Papers of 1842 to describe the experiences of young women on the panel entitled 'Working Lives':

Women Coal Bearers, 1840s.
The work of Ellison Jack, 11 years.

> 'She first has to travel about 84 feet from wall face to the first ladder, which is 18 feet high; she proceeds along the main road, probably 3'6" high to the second ladder and so on until she reaches the pit bottom, where she casts her load varying from 1cwt - 1½ cwt into the tub.'

This written description is accompanied by a drawing of two young girls climbing a steep ladder with heavy baskets on their backs.

At the Labour History Museum, Merseyside, the issue of unemployment was tackled by using a reconstructed scene of two of the main characters from a television play called *The Boys from the Black Stuff*, by Alan Bleasdale. George in a wheelchair is being pushed by Chrissie along the bridge leading to the dead and derelict docks, which are seen in the background. The men talk about the past, with their dialogue written up on a panel next to the reconstruction. 'Ah, there'd be hundreds of us coming along here, the slip repair men, scalers, dockers, the Mary Ellens who used to swab the big liners, and behind us the great big Shire cart horses.'

In the same museum the story of the nineteenth-century immigrants to America is told in their own words from their diaries, which enables us to empathise with the apprehension with which the journey was undertaken. We are urged to listen through a written panel: 'Please pick up the telephone to listen to extracts from the diary of Dirk van den Bergh who emigrated from Holland, to Canada, via Liverpool, in 1906.'

At Tullie House Museum, in Carlisle, in northwest England, the reconstruction of Hadrian's Wall offers an opportunity to use a quotation from Appian, the Roman historian, to describe the soldiers' rations: 'The soldiers . . . had no wine, salt, sour wine or oil, but fed on wheat and barley, and large quantities of meat and hare boiled without salt, which upsets their digestion.'

In an exhibition, 'Reaching Teaching', which was mounted at Blake's Lock Museum in Reading to demonstrate the effectiveness of using objects from the museum loan service for teaching, the response of one child to a brown glass bottle is illustrated by using her poem about the bottle as the object label.

> There was a murder in the village
> There was a murder in the town
> A policeman came round and asked questions
> But nobody knew
> Nobody knew
>
> One day I was digging in the overgrown garden
> I found a dark brown bottle
> With the writing
> POISONOUS NOT TO BE TAKEN
> On it
> I wonder if . . .

Thus there are many ways of contextualising objects with words. The choice will be made according to the objectives of the exhibition and of the individual piece of text concerned.

How language works

As we have seen, language works to construct and delimit ideas, concepts and mental images. We can often tell by listening to people talk and by hearing the way they use words a great deal about them, including their level of education, social class, geographical origin and profession, their values and attitudes and their personality type. In listening to two people talking, the use of language quickly indicates their relationship. In a work situation, for example, it is generally very easy to see which person has the senior position and which does not. The power to command is indicated by the vocabulary, the register of the language, the way the words are used. How much is said by whom, who interrupts whom and what is not said is also revealing.

Through language, social hierarchies are maintained and reproduced. This has been studied by theorists in the field of critical linguistics, such as Fairclough (1989) and Kress and Hodge (1979). They show how language functions in supporting and also changing power relations and ideology in modern society, and offer methods of analysing language which reveal these processes so that we can become more aware of them, and manipulate them.

Coxall (1990, 1991a, 1991b, 1992) has applied this form of analysis to museum language. By analysing museum texts using an approach drawn from critical linguistics, she demonstrates how values and attitudes are expressed and views of the world are reflected and constructed.

Sometimes these worldviews are exposed as shocking. For example, in analysing an apparently straightforwardly factual text on immigration in London during the nineteenth century, a deeply racist attitude is discovered (Coxall, 1991a). As part of the linguistic analysis of the text, which is not overtly concerned with accommodation, it is found that Jews lived in ghettos, Lascars, Malays and Chinese lived in colonies, and Germans and Russians lived in lodgings. The inference of social worth is clear.

How are such worldviews constructed through museum texts? One of the main points that Coxall makes is not that the text writers are themselves racist, but that in the process of writing the label racist views have been unintentionally expressed. In the writing of museum text, documents relating to the period being studied are frequently used as sources. When ideas and vocabulary from these documents are transferred from the document to the label, which may happen as writers strive for 'historical accuracy', the concepts which were sustained by these words may also be transferred. Here the terms 'Lascars' and 'Malays', which are not in use today, have entered the modern text, and along with them attitudes to the individuals concerned:

> Down in the Docks were colonies of Lascars, Malays and Chinese who had themselves arrived originally as sailors, but who now made a living looking after the domestic needs of the crews of ships and port.
>
> (Coxall, 1991a: 95)

This label did not set out to create a social hierarchy of immigrants, with those from Europe (Germans) presented as more acceptable than those from the Far East. This, however, is the impression given. Nor did the writer set out to present an anti-Semitic view, but the Jews are described as living in a 'clearly defined "ghetto"' in the East End.

Although museum writers do not consciously set out to write biased texts, racist and anti-Semitic attitudes (along with unsupportive attitudes to women, people

123

with disabilities and other disadvantaged groups) are deeply embedded in many sections of our contemporary British society. Where existing social and cultural patterns are felt to be 'normal' or 'natural' rather than socially achieved and historically positioned, it is likely that racist, or biased, attitudes will exist. Many assumptions and values are held just below the level of consciousness, and it is not until the full implications of everyday speech are carefully reviewed that these assumptions are brought to light. One of the ways in which values and attitudes are reproduced is through the kind of unselfconscious text that Coxall discusses.

Coxall asks for more attention to be paid to text, with more awareness of the fact that language communicates values and assumptions. She is critical of the use of readability indexes to analyse text, as these concentrate only on the form and not the content of the texts (Coxall, 1991a: 86–8). She points out that George Klare, an authority on readability formulas, is unable to recommend any of them to writers in general. Coxall recommends that text writers should carefully examine their texts to see that what is intended is in fact expressed.

It is important for museum text writers to be clear that language matters in museums. Language will construct a social worldview whether writers intend this or not, and it is therefore vital to assess text in relation to bias of any sort. What view of women, men, children, different ethnic groups and different parts of the world is being presented?

This construction of a worldview is not of course limited to language. At an exhibition at the Natural History Museum in London entitled 'Man's (sic) Place in Evolution' in the early 1980s, the exhibition's first set-piece presented two three-dimensional life-size white figures – a couple, with the man standing firmly on both legs, and looking directly at the visitor; meekly at his side stood a slightly shorter woman, looking modestly away from the visitor. This 'scientific' pair were flanked on one side by a two-dimensional screen with a range of animals represented, and on the other by a similar screen with a range of non-white races represented. This clearly demonstrated a very particular approach to 'Evolution'! (Anon., 1980).

An awareness of how language works in the construction of values and attitudes should be supplemented with an understanding of the functions of texts in museums, a knowledge of some methods of writing easy-to-read text, a clear idea of the objectives of different kinds of text and a willingness to evaluate written materials. We will look at each of these areas in turn.

Texts in museums

What are the functions of museum texts? Texts can include signposts, interpretive panels, labels, leaflets and catalogues. These can be broadly divided into text that orientates or gives practical information, and text that is knowledge-based, concerned with specific subject matters. We have discussed issues relating to texts for orientation and information in Chapter 6. Knowledge-based text will be discussed here.

Knowledge-based text can be further divided into texts that are experienced as part of the physical environment of the museum, i.e., written on the walls, panels or labels in exhibitions, and texts that *may* form part of this experience, but which have the potential to be read in another place at another time, i.e., leaflets, guides, catalogues, teachers' packs and books.

Exhibition and catalogue text are very often the same, with the same words being used as panels or labels and as parts of the catalogue. There are specific problems with this approach. Exhibition texts and catalogue texts are very different in the way they are experienced: exhibition texts can only be read in the museum, with the special difficulties that this implies; catalogue texts can be read at leisure, in comfort, and more than once. The style of writing that is necessary to cope with the difficulties presented by reading in a museum or gallery environment is quite different from the style that will be successful in something to be read at home.

In the writing of museum texts, there are several basic aspects that should be considered. The first is sentence construction. A good rule of thumb is to keep the structure of the sentence as simple as possible, with only one idea per sentence, and length carefully considered. Vocabulary is important, with active and familiar words being considered the most effective. The presentation of text is all-important, with consideration of line lengths and spacing being vital. Guidelines from Sweden on how to produce easy-to-read texts for adults suggest short sentences, normal word order, line lengths of not more than forty-five characters, the end of the line coinciding with the end of the natural phrase, and no breaking of words into syllables at the end of lines (Ekarv, 1986/7).

Exhibition texts are frequently experienced under very difficult conditions. They are generally read standing up, perhaps while walking, and often in the company of a crowd of strangers. The reader is frequently tired and may be wearing glasses or reading in a foreign language. Very frequently, the subject matter is unfamiliar, and often the vocabulary is a specialist one. It is imperative, therefore, that every effort is made to enable people to read easily, quickly and enjoyably. Text for leaflets and catalogues would also benefit from adopting an easy-to-read style.

One frequent mistake in exhibition texts is to use complex sentences with many parts to them, some of which refer to each other in confusing ways. These two sentences are examples:

> The message of the Buddha, 'the Enlightened One', called Buddhism after him, has, throughout its history, offered salvation from impermanence and rebirth.

> The widespread belief in Buddhas ruling paradises, accessible by grace and faith alone, or in mystical powers, compelling deities to confer material and spiritual advantage, were among the adaptions which, beside monastic disciplines, characterised Buddhism's varied appeal.

> (not original line lengths)

125

Both sentences are complex and are trying to do too much. Too many ideas are carried in one sentence. An over-use of commas, as a device to squeeze in more information, leads to confusion as to which qualifying statement refers to which subject. In the end the overall sense of the sentence is lost as the reader tries to untangle the details.

Sentences are often too long, and use specialised language which is unexplained.

> The rare vagrant species are difficult to fit into any habitat because they often occur around our coast-lines (their first landfall) where they are completely out of context; in the exhibition they are displayed in the habitat which most closely approximates their own.
>
> (not original line length)

In this statement, 'vagrant', 'habitat' and 'landfall' are all used in a specialist way. It is a good idea to use language which is as close to a conversational style as possible, while at the same time, if specialist words need to be used, using them in a context that explains their meaning. The example below shows how this can be done.

THE HIDDEN TRAP OF THE GOLIATH BEETLE

The Goliath Beetle is one of the largest Coleoptera in the world.

When an animal becomes too threatening, the Beetle bends the

front part of its body, allowing the joint in the middle to open

up. By straightening up, the Beetle brutally closes this

sharp-edged trap on the body of its enemy. Ouch!

(original line lengths)

In this passage several technical terms are avoided by expressions such as 'front part of its body', and 'joint in the middle'. This enables readers to understand and empathise (ouch) with the idea of the trap. At the same time, the word 'Coleoptera' is used. This word is used frequently in the displays at the Insectarium in the Botanical Gardens in Montreal, where this text comes from, and it is easy both to understand that this is the specialist word for beetles, and to become familiar with it. The display as a whole uses a limited number of specialist words, each of which occurs more than once. The words used, 'coleoptera' and 'entomologist', for example, have been agreed as being the most important and useful for the target audience (families) to know. Other specialist words are replaced.

The use of abstract nouns referring to ideas (salvation, impermanence, rebirth) leads to language which is highly symbolic and which requires higher-level language skills to decipher. Concrete nouns referring to actual things (body, animal, insect) are to be preferred.

Short sentences using an everyday order of words, rather than long complex sentences should be used.

The message of the Buddha, 'the Enlightened One', called Buddhism after him, has, throughout its history, offered salvation from impermanence and rebirth.

This complex sentence would be better presented as two shorter ones:

Buddhism is the message of Buddha, 'the Enlightened One'. It has always offered salvation from impermanence and rebirth.

The complexity of a sentence can be detected by either reading it aloud, or asking someone else to read it aloud. Any overly complicated structure will become obvious.

It is useful where possible to make the end of the line of text in the panel or label coincide with the end of a natural phrase.

THE HIDDEN TRAP OF THE GOLIATH BEETLE

The Goliath Beetle is one of the largest Coleoptera in the world.

When an animal becomes too threatening,

the Beetle bends the front part of its body,

allowing the joint in the middle to open up.

By straightening up,

the Beetle brutally closes this sharp-edged trap

on the body of its enemy. Ouch!

This arrangement of words enables very fast reading. As museum visitors spend very little time indeed at individual exhibits, it is important to enable fast assimilation of information. Most text writers in museums and galleries write as though they were writing text for a book, with the ends of lines occurring in the middle of a phrase. This makes reading slower, and if combined with specialist words and expressions, reading speed may slow to below 200 words per minute, and comprehension will be severely hampered. Reading will then stop.

As visitors are expected to process an enormous amount of text, visual presentation which encourages reading is vital. Which of the two arrangements of words below is immediately more accessible? The words are the same in each case.

André Derain (1905)

Oc: 394 x 289: signed. Purchased with assistance from the Knapping Fund, the National Art Collections Fund and the Contemporary Art Society and private subscribers 1954.

Matisse and Derain painted portraits of each other while staying at the port of Collioure in the south of France. Using vivid, sometimes arbitrary, colours, Matisse has captured the sensation of sunlight striking the sitter's face and casting a heavy shadow down one side. During his Fauve period Matisse tried to create a dynamic but balanced relationship between complementary colours, such as blue and orange, red and green. Complementary colours literally complement each other: they are at their most intense when placed together. Matisse adjusted his colours to obtain this maximum intensity. This non-naturalistic use of colour can be seen as a radical development of certain aspects of Impressionistic art.

André Derain (1905)

Matisse and Derain painted portraits of each other
while staying at the port of Collioure in the south of France.
Using vivid, sometimes arbitrary, colours,
Matisse has captured the sensation of sunlight striking
the sitter's face
and casting a heavy shadow down one side.
During his Fauve period
Matisse tried to create a dynamic but balanced relationship
between complementary colours,
such as blue and orange, red and green.
Complementary colours literally complement each other:
they are at their most intense when placed together.
Matisse adjusted his colours to obtain this maximum intensity.
This non-naturalistic use of colour
can be seen as a radical development
of certain aspects of Impressionistic art.
Oc: 394 x 289: signed.
Purchased with assistance from the Knapping Fund,
the National Art Collections Fund
and the Contemporary Art Society and private subscribers
1954.

Some labels assume a knowledge that it is most unlikely that viewers/readers will have. The label below refers to three objects that are not present, comparing the object exhibited to others that are similar:

A VIRTUE
Marble
By CHRISTOFORO SOLARI (active 1489–1520)
Lombard: late 15th or early 16th century

This bust may be compared with one of the Virtue Hope (Castello di San Salvatore, Susegana, near Congliano), which also has the head upturned and one breast bare. It is not, however, by Tullio Lombardo, to whom that bust is attributed, and is stylistically closer to Solari's effigy of Beatrice d'Este (Certosa, Pavia) and his Adam (Cathedral, Milan).

(not original line lengths)

This text sounds as though we are eavesdropping on a very erudite art-historical debate. It tells us nothing about what the object is - what *is* a 'Virtue'? Do we care how close it is in looks to other Virtues? This label is written solely for connoisseurs with the same art-historical knowledge as the writer. The public has not been considered at all.

In a recently redisplayed gallery in the same museum more visitor-sensitive texts can be found. A statue of a Buddha is contextualised as follows:

Buddhism originated amongst the followers of an Indian Prince who lived around the year 500 BC, and who renounced his position to lead a holy and monastic life. Thus the first Buddha was a real person, and his teachings were the basis for many later holy texts.

(not original line lengths)

This label starts from the premise that the reader knows nothing about Buddhism, which is likely to be the case for most people. After introducing the theme, as shown above, the label goes on to describe the object and then discuss its significance.

... later holy texts. This gilt bronze figure of about 1750 is an image of the

founder of Buddhism, called Sakamuni Buddha in Sanskrit. It is shown seated in

the lotus position on a lotus throne, with hands in the gesture of 'calling the earth

to witness'. This refers to the climactic event of the Prince's life. Just before he

achieved Enlightenment and became Buddha he was tempted by the goddess of

evil. He resisted her lures, and called the earth goddess to witness his

resistance.

(original line lengths)

The writing here is good and the object well explained. The label would have been easier to read had the line lengths coincided with the natural phrase lengths.

This gilt bronze figure of about 1750

is an image of the founder of Buddhism,

called Sakamuni Buddha in Sanskrit.

It is shown seated in the lotus position on a lotus throne,

with hands in the gesture of 'calling the earth to witness'.

This refers to the climactic event of the Prince's life.

Just before he achieved Enlightenment and became Buddha

he was tempted by the goddess of evil.

He resisted her lures,

and called the earth goddess to witness his resistance.

The presentation of text in this way in museums is new. It looks different, more like a poem than anything else. It has been tried recently at the Herbert Museum and Art Gallery, Coventry, in the exhibition 'Who are the Coventry Kids?' held from April 1992 to April 1993. In this exhibition, the larger text panels use this easy-to-read approach, which enables the very rapid assimilation of the basic ideas of the exhibition. The object labels and other text panels are in a more conventional style.

... AND WHAT

ARE THEY LIKE?

People said they are

Skilled with their hands

Should have worked in a skilled industry

Like weaving or watchmaking

Or auto or aero engineering

Or machine tool production

Ekarv suggests thinking about the rhythm of text. A rhythm appropriate to the theme aids in reading and in comprehension (Ekarv, 1986/7).

Where the rhythmic easy-to-read style can be combined with personal words describing a real experience, the effect can be very powerful. A small 'Lifebox' display organised in 1991 at Coventry focused on the experience of two Polish refugees, Feliks and Stasia Chustecki, who had been separated during the war and after extraordinary journeys half-way across the world had been reunited in Coventry (Pes, 1991). The display was called

FELIKS AND STASIA

Poland . . . Russia . . . Coventry

One part of the text read:

'Stasia . . . On the 10th of February 1940,

At one o'clock in the morning

I heard a commotion.

Two Russian soldiers were pointing their rifles at my father.

I was terrified . . .'

(original line lengths)

Exhibitions are not books on the wall. It is not helpful to construct text without considering how it will be read and by whom. Text in exhibitions should enable easy reading, and should act perhaps more like dialogue in a play, to enhance the emotional effect of the exhibition. Dry, academic and scholarly texts will be read for perhaps fifteen minutes at the beginning of a visit. After this time they will be ignored.

Text should be written considering the needs of readers, which are to assimilate the basics quickly, to be informed and entertained and to be able to find a way of making a personal link with the objects and the themes of the exhibitions. The opportunities for these needs to be satisfied are limited by the physical and mental capacities of the individual reader to stand or walk, to read and to process material inwardly. In all too many museums and galleries, visiting exhibitions still feels like a physical and mental steeple-chase.

One way of planning the content of each piece of exhibition text is to be clear about the objectives for each piece of writing. The next section considers the role each piece of text might play, and discusses the process of text production.

Planning exhibition text

Exhibition text can include titles and sub-titles, introductory panels, group captions, interpretive panels and object captions (see Fig. 16).

The messages or teaching points of the exhibition are carried by the texts, combined with images such as photographs and drawings, and other interpretive media such as maps, charts, posters and so on. Less overt messages are carried by colour, the materials used and other aspects of the design. The planning and production of texts is an integral part of the development of the exhibition. It is not enough to put the objects into the cases and later to 'do the labels'. The messages that are carried in the words of the exhibition must be worked out an a very early stage, as they represent the approach to the subject matter to be taken throughout the display. If these messages are not clearly

Title/heading/sub-heading
    of exhibition or exhibition section
- short
- relevant to exhibition
- familiar words

Introductory Panel
    for exhibition or section
- what the exhibition is about
- how it is organised
- why the objects are worth displaying
- why the exhibition is interesting
- what you can learn

Group caption
    for related objects together
- heading/title
- short descriptive or issue-based text

Interpretive panel
    detailed information
    questions
- use headings and sub-headings
- illustrations/graphs/charts

Object caption
    identify objects
- who, what, where, when
- lender/donor acknowledged
- museum reference number

Figure 16 A hierarchical structure for exhibition texts.

defined at the outset of the exhibition planning process, the exhibition will be very confused.

The production of the text should be a planned and professional process, based on clear objectives for the exhibition and research into audiences. Texts should be piloted and evaluated in order to be useful and accessible to the target audiences. Before beginning, writers should have certain types of information. These include an understanding of easy-to-read writing; a knowledge of the range of ways that text can be generated; information about the overall aims of the exhibition and the objectives of each of its component parts; an understanding of the labelling system to be used; and information on the target audiences and their knowledge about the subject matter of the exhibition.

It is very difficult to write or compile texts unless the objectives of the exhibition overall and the objectives of each section, case, panel and caption are fully understood. There is very often not enough development work carried out in this area, so that writers work in a vacuum and the resulting texts seem like bolt-on extras. Each piece of text should have a specific function and should be part of the system of communication as a whole.

The function of the title of the exhibition is to attract people to the exhibition and to let the audience know when they have arrived. The title should use familiar vocabulary, and should stimulate and motivate. Good examples include 'Shropshire Mammoths', 'Who are the Coventry Kids?', 'The Story of Hull and its People'. These are written in familiar words, they are specific, and they sound as though they might be interesting.

Sub-titles can be used to give more detail to the title, but this can sometimes be distracting and should be used carefully.

Sub-headings indicate the way the exhibition is divided in terms of space and subject matter. They break up the totality of the exhibition into manageable parts, and in order to do this, should be limited to about seven in number. Research has shown that when processing new information, people are only able to apprehend seven pieces of information plus or minus two (Ham, 1983; Miller, 1970) Exhibitions which have many more than seven sub-divisions will confuse the audience. The entire exhibition content should be divided into about seven 'chunks' and these could then be further sub-divided if necessary. It is easier for the audience to assimilate the exhibition content if the structure is simple, straightforward and very clear. The structure can be indicated by a panel that shows the title and the sub-headings and where in space the sub-divisions indicated by the sub-headings are to be found.

Sub-headings need to be short and easy to grasp, using familiar and straightforward language.

Introductory panels set the conceptual agenda for the exhibition and tell the audience what to expect.

GANNIN DOON THE PIT

The story of mining in the south east of Northumberland
(From Woodhorn Colliery Museum, Ashington)

The introductory panel should state what the exhibition is about, and indicate what is interesting and worthwhile about it. It should show clearly how the exhibition is organised, and point out if there are any supporting materials such as catalogues, videos or books.

Group captions can be used to introduce issues that are explored through a group of objects, or through a small coherent section of the display.

Interpretive panels can give detailed information on aspects of the exhibition and may use illustrative material where appropriate. It is useful if interpretive panels can employ a hierarchy of information. In the Colour Museum, Bradford, for example, each display case has an interpretive panel, with the first section using a larger type-size to introduce an issue in brief. The second section in a smaller type-size gives further details. Both sections are supported by suitable images.

The exhibition 'Art on Tyneside' at the Laing Art Gallery in Newcastle uses interpretive panels to introduce each new section. These panels are very lively, and use a mixture of words, drawings, photographs or maps. At the bottom of each panel is a cartoon strip where two children restate the issue in simple and often funny terms. These act to reinforce the more detailed and complex message given by the rest of the panel above. As such they act as a useful and painless reinforcement of the message.

Object captions are used to identify objects and to give essential information, such as the name of the donor, or the museum reference number.

Any exhibition will work with variations on this basic structure. It is by no means prescriptive and not all aspects will be used all the time. The most important thing is to know what the overall objectives of the exhibition are, and what each part of the text structure is intended to achieve and why.

Basic visual layout guidelines suggest using line lengths of not more than approximately forty-five characters (letters), which will make about eight to ten words. The easy-to-read style, with line lengths coinciding with the end of natural phrases, should be considered for the main introduction and interpretive panels. Texts do not need to be justified on both left and right sides. Leaving a line space between paragraphs, rather than using indentation in a continuous block of text, results in texts that are easier to assimilate.

Normal combinations of upper and lower case settings should be used, as text in capitals only slows reading down considerably (Belcher, 1991: 160). Black type on a white background is easier to read than other combinations. It is generally recommended that as a minimum 48–60 point type-size should be used for main headlines, 30–36 point for group labels and 24–30 point for object captions (Belcher, 1991: 161). Opinions vary as to which typefaces are the most legible. The Royal National Institute for the Blind recommends sans serif typefaces, such as Helvetica, or Gill Sans, but Belcher, summarising a range of opinions, suggests that the most legible printed matter is that with which readers are most familiar. For the book and news-paper-reading public, this means an uncomplicated serifed letter (Belcher, 1991: 160).

Ergonomic guidelines, which cover placing of texts, angles of viewing and other practical considerations are given by Belcher (1991), Miles (1982) and Pearson (1985). Detailed practical guidelines on the production of exhibition texts are given in Serrell (1988), Kentley and Neagus (1989) and Punt (1989).

The writing of exhibition texts must be seen as a part of the exhibition process and integral to the planning of the project (Ekarv, 1986/7). Writing should be carried out as the other aspects of the exhibition are being planned, with first drafts being used to clarify the objectives of the exhibition. If at all possible, writing should be done in the room where the exhibition is to be held. Although this is seldom likely, it must not be forgotten that exhibition text is text within an environment, and as such it has a range of environment-related tasks. These include dividing and controlling the space and the way in which people move within it, giving directions as to how to use the space, and shifting the pace or the mood as the exhibition is traversed. When writing the text at a desk, it is all too easy to forget the physical nature of the basic space and display to be installed.

Writing the text should be seen as a process, with several interests represented. The scholarly interest of the curator should seek to maintain the integrity of the subject matter, the concern for clear communication of the educationalist should work towards easy-to-read text and the visual literacy of the designer should enable the production of attractive and accessible words. Many drafts will be necessary, and this should not be seen as a weakness. This *is* the process. As drafts are written and assessed for clarity, bias, style and so on, so the words will change.

One of the most difficult aspects of the production of text is to decide on the hierarchy of information. Exhibition text, panels and labels form part of a continuum of information and knowledge. Generally, too much information is given in words to be read while standing. If this text is seen as just part of a continuum, it is easier to assess what can be said on the walls, what is best in a catalogue or guide, and what might be in a teachers' pack or book (see Fig. 17).

Some museums and galleries are using interactive video to supplement written texts. At the newly redisplayed Imperial War Museum in London, for example, videos with branching hierarchical menus are used to enable visitors to explore a number of topics which relate to either specific objects, or display themes. In the large hall at the entrance to the museum, where many large items such as tanks are exhibited, one interactive video is able to show detailed information and archive film about a number of different types of tank. Several videos are available, together offering a great deal of material for those who wish it, in an unobtrusive way.

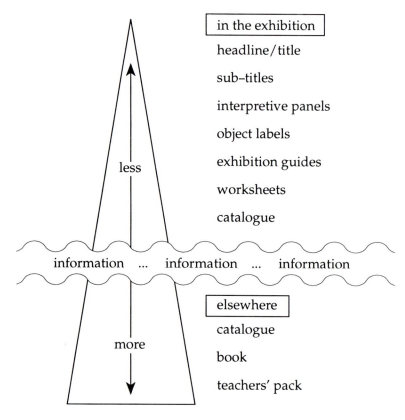

Figure 17 A hierarchy of knowledge-based text, some to be read in the exhibition and some more appropriate for studying at home

Evaluating text

Do museum and gallery visitors read text? For a long time it has been assumed that they do not, and much research based on observations of visitor behaviour in exhibitions has been carried out which 'proves' that texts are not read. Much of this is usefully summarised in Beer (1987). However, as Falk and Dierking assert: 'This is definitely not true. All visitors capable of reading read some labels; no visitors read all labels' (Falk and Dierking, 1992: 70).

McManus has demonstrated through recording the conversations of visitors at exhibits that, even though it is difficult to observe, texts *are* read (McManus, 1989, 1990). Visitors talk back to the text, using what McManus calls 'text-echo', that is – introducing the words of the exhibition text into their own conversations, which are almost always limited to the topics established by the museum writer. Those texts written in a conversational style were (naturally!) the easiest to respond to. In some instances, one member of a group adopted the task of reading the text panel for all the group. It seemed likely that many people processed some of the text as they physically approached the exhibit.

If text is in fact 'read', how is it 'read'? McManus points out that it is unlikely that all of any text will be read no matter how long or short it is (McManus, 1990). This is because visitors are in general more concerned with the social aspects of their visit than the educational aspects, and read just enough to introduce the topic of the exhibit into their conversations. Museum writers are not allowed to dominate the language space and are interrupted as though they were present and talking for too long. Museum readers scan and sample in order to get the gist of the text as fast as possible so that they can integrate this with their own agendas. Fluent readers of well-written text that is placed within a well-structured communication system will appear to be reading very little. 'The surer visitors are of the topic and context of a text and the more familiar with the syntax used, the less they need to read' (McManus, 1989: 184).

Visitors try, sometimes desperately, to relate what they are seeing to their own experiences (Falk and Dierking, 1992: 74). Communication depends on this link being achieved. One of the most basic questions to ask in writing or compiling texts is 'Who is the audience?' It is difficult to write unless it is known whether the audience is a specialist one with a degree of knowledge about the subject or a non-specialist one with very little knowledge and possibly some misconceptions. The Birds Gallery in the Manchester Museum is designed to cater for a general audience, for university students and for school children. An introductory display case poses the question 'What is a bird?', and discusses whether all birds can fly, or have feathers and how flight is enabled by certain characteristics. Central display cases are designed for a non-specialist audience, and contain more birds and less technical information. The side cases are for the specialist and the writing is more technical.

Misunderstandings are common. Bitgood (1989a: 6) describes how the words 'Arctic Tundra' were mistakenly thought to be the name of an animal in an exhibit about arctic foxes. He goes on to say categorically that without evaluation, it is unlikely successful labels will be written (Bitgood, 1989b: 16).

It can seem rather daunting to consider testing labels and texts, but there are a number of ways to do this which are not too difficult. First, knowing what the writing is intended to achieve is vital. What does this piece of text need to tell people? Second, it is essential to realise that it is impossible to get all the text right first time. With any piece of text, the one you are now reading included, writing is a process. It consists of the production of a series of notes and ideas, a structuring of those ideas into a sequence or outline, the writing of a rough but complete draft, and the gradual completion of the draft through numerous trials. It is helpful to discuss each part of this process with a colleague. It is extremely unhelpful to delay this consultation process until the final complete version, when any suggested changes may be felt as attacks on personal competence. Early consultation allows the writer to expand and review ideas at all stages, and to accept or reject suggestions as appropriate. Sometimes suggestions are made that cannot be acted upon for a variety of reasons, and the text writer should have the confidence, based on the knowledge of the objectives of the writing and of the constraints that bear upon it, to put those suggestions to one side.

Both the content and the style need to be considered. Content will relate to the subject matter, the approach of the exhibition and the target audience. Do these words relate to the exhibition's message and will the audience find them both useful and interesting? Am I saying the right thing? The evaluation of this means checking with the curator for content accuracy and with the audience advocate or educationalist for audience relevance.

If there is no audience advocate, the text writer must first make sure that target audiences have been identified, and must then endeavour to discover what they know or think about the exhibition subject matter. This 'front-end evaluation' might mean a small-scale questionnaire carried out in the museum or, if the audience is not represented by the existing museum audience, it will mean finding a representative group and talking to them. Hopefully, some of this work will have already been carried out as part of the initial development of the idea of the exhibition. If not, some findings may suggest that the basic concept of the exhibition is flawed, and this finding could prove very difficult.

Content should be examined for bias, looking carefully at the underlying assumptions that might have crept into the text.

Style relates to comprehensibility and accessibility. Do these words mean what I want them to say, and can they be understood easily? This can be tested as part of 'formative evaluation' by showing the words to people and asking them what they understand by them. This can be done with colleagues, preferably those not involved in the exhibition, or with friends or family. It will soon become clear where assumptions have been made and where one section of text relies upon another. Most of the text reproduced below stands very well on its own, but it is assumed that we know what a neotropical zone is. If this text is not part of a larger section sub-titled NEOTROPICAL ZONE (with this expression explained either here or in a nearby panel), then it should have been explained in the text itself.

WHAT IS THE BIGGEST COLEOPTERA IN THE WORLD?

Among insects the notion of size poses a problem.

Entomologists do not agree on the subject. Is the biggest insect

the longest, the widest, the thickest or the heaviest one? Since

the neotropical zone is home to several enormous Coleoptera, we

will let you decide which one is the record-holder!

(original line lengths)

Avoid an impersonal, formal tone, and limit the number of abstract concepts; where technical words are used they should be defined; use familiar words where possible; limit the amount of information to a few key points (Coxall, 1992).

Formative evaluation should also be carried out with museum visitors if there is any doubt about audience reactions. Content can be tested with low-cost mock-ups, and design features such as placement or lighting can be tested by trial and error before the final decisions are made (Griggs, 1981; Jarrett, 1986). 'Summative evaluation' will point out where mistakes have occurred which may provide useful information for the future.

Although 'museum labels' have had a bad press for a number of years, it is clear that the simple label is in fact of much greater importance than might be supposed. All labels are part of a museum language system.

Language in museums works in the same way as elsewhere to create worldviews and to express values and attitudes. In understanding how language works, and how ideologies are constructed, museum language users can be more specific and more in control of what they wish to say.

Visitors use museum texts to help them negotiate the museum experience. Although visitors come with their own personal and social objectives, they use text to elaborate and achieve these aims. Text must therefore be accessible, easy to read, and meaningful both within the context of the exhibition and in relation to the personal context of the visitor.

The language used in museums and galleries is as important as the objects. It structures the visitor's experience, it welcomes or discourages, it informs or mystifies. We need to understand it, and use it well.

8

Museums: ideal learning environments

Some basic philosophical issues

In recent philosophical discussions about the role of museums and galleries as we approach the twenty-first century, the following three functions have been proposed: to preserve, to study and to communicate (Weil, 1990). 'Preservation' includes the collection and care of artefacts and specimens; 'study' refers to research carried out on these objects and 'communication' includes all those activities and professional practices that enable people to have access to both the objects and the results of their study.

'Communication' is then a large area, and one that gives rise to confusion. What do we mean by 'communication' in the museum and how is it different from 'education'? In many ways these questions are a waste of time as each expression is capable of carrying such a large range of meanings and it is unlikely that any finite agreement will be reached over their use. Communication as a major museum function includes those activities that attract visitors to the museum (publicity and marketing), investigate their needs (research and evaluation) and provide for their intellectual needs (education and entertainment). Educational and entertainment-related needs are provided for through exhibitions, workshops and demonstrations. This penultimate chapter discusses the provision for educational and entertainment-related needs.

Education and entertainment will be discussed together, as related and complementary aspects of the museum experience. Museums and galleries are fundamentally educational in character, that is, they offer opportunities to people for increasing reservoirs of knowledge and experience. They are not fundamentally about entertainment; entertainment in museums always has the ulterior motive of offering something new, exciting and potentially valuable. Entertainment in museums, however it might be presented, is used as a method of education, in the full knowledge that learning is best achieved in circumstances of enjoyment.

Plate 11 Learning is most effective if it is provoked through active enjoyment followed up by reflection and analysis. Museums are places without many of the restraints that characterise other places of learning. Dynamic and imaginative projects can be developed that explore familiar subjects in new ways, using methods that are more difficult to achieve in the classroom. Here children dressed in replica Victorian costume explore the old walled town of Stirling with the museum education officer. The Town Trail and the costumes (which were later loaned to the school for close study) were only two of a number of activities developed by the education officer from an exhibition of Victorian paintings. Exploring history through walking through its remains, wearing its clothes and looking at the creative expressions of its inhabitants is much more fun than just reading about it. Later, information acquired through reading and discussion is put into this concrete framework, thereby becoming more meaningful and interesting. The quality of learning is enhanced.

Photo: Central Regional Council, Scotland.

Education is beginning to be explored by museum professionals in new ways. In the past, education has been equated with schooling (Leichter, Hensel and Larsen, 1989: 25). This has been true for educational theorists and for museums. As education has been redefined in society, and the concept broadened to include more than merely formal provision in formal institutions such as schools and colleges, so education in museums has come to have a very broad brief. Instead of meaning the organisation of workshops or guided tours for school or other formal groups, education in museums is now understood to include a range of types of provision, including exhibitions, workshops and publications, for a greatly increased range of types of visitor, including schools, families and adult learners. Museum education may take place both in the museum and in the community.

Education has sometimes been understood as focused on outcomes (exam results, grades) rather than process. However, this form of focus tends to limit and narrow educational possibilities, and although some politicians have tried to promote this form of approach to education, most teachers know that this helps very few learners. Attention to educational processes, such as the skills and activities necessary to reach an outcome, enables a more in-depth exploration of experience, the potential for creative side-tracking and opportunities for redefining the outcome as part of the process. Thinking of education in terms of processes facilitates the idea of education as a way of life, as being desirable in order to negotiate life-events and as being a problem-solving way of approaching the world. In museums and galleries, there is a natural emphasis on processes; outcomes are far less important. There is no 'syllabus' to be followed; educational activities can be exploratory, broad and experiential.

Education is not mono-dimensional: it is complex and multi-layered. An educational achievement may be as small as the observation of a blade of grass, or as large as the understanding of the Roman Empire. Education may happen in a haphazard and unplanned way, as well as within specifically designed structures. Equally, social and leisure-based activities may give rise to educational moments. Many people will be experts in one field of knowledge, but beginning learners in others. Museums and galleries are perhaps the only institutions in society that have the potential to satisfy the needs of learners at all levels, who are looking for experiences ranging from those with a great deal of overt educational content to those with very little.

The educational role of the museum or gallery is fulfilled through two main types of communicative method, mass communication and interpersonal communication. We may characterise these methods as distance-learning and face-to-face teaching. Distance-learning has many of the characteristics of mass communication: it is one-way (indirect), impossible to modify at the moment of communication (unresponsive) and takes place in the absence of one of the partners (unequal). In spite of these characteristics which can be seen as potential drawbacks, the distance-learning methods of the museum, which include exhibitions, displays, publications, loan services and mobile museums, can be strikingly successful.

Face-to-face teaching is direct, 'natural', or interpersonal communication. It can enable interpretation through shared experience, modification or development of the message in the light of on-the-spot responses, and involves many supporting methods of communication (body movements, repetitions, restatements, etc.). In the museum it includes many different forms of teaching and many different types of activity, such as working with handling collections, drawing, or role-play (see Fig. 18).

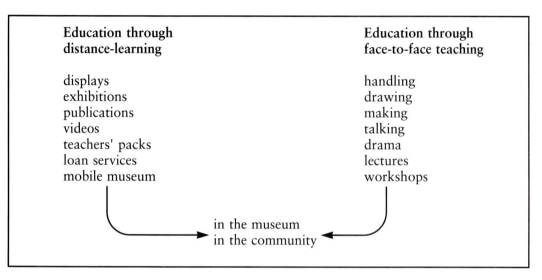

Education through distance-learning	**Education through face-to-face teaching**
displays	handling
exhibitions	drawing
publications	making
videos	talking
teachers' packs	drama
loan services	lectures
mobile museum	workshops

in the museum
in the community

Figure 18 The educational task of the museum is achieved through a number of distance-learning and face-to-face teaching methods

Both these forms of communication can operate in the museum and in the community. Most museums today are very conscious that they need to expand their audiences and to be of relevance to more parts of their supporting constituencies. Museums and galleries are opening their doors, and are taking their staff and collections outside, into community centres, hospitals, prisons, schools and day centres. Working in some of the more informal community venues means considering education, not from the point of view of 'high levels of educational achievement. Rather it is concerned with negotiating, confidence building and providing opportunities. It is about empowering community groups' (Dodd, 1992: 31). Focused on processes rather than outcomes, and informal and needs-driven rather than formal and curriculum-driven, community-based museum and gallery education represents some of the most innovative aspects of the museum today (O'Neill, 1991; Plant, 1992; Hemmings, 1992).

What is learning ?

Learning involves acquiring and absorbing new information, skills or experiences and making sense of these in relation to that which is already known (Bruner, 1960: 48). True learning has not occurred until the new matter is integrated with the old. For most people, this relationship must be made by starting with the familiar, with what is known, and then proceeding to the unfamiliar, extending the known into the unknown through comparison, contrast, analogy or analysis (Schouten, 1983). Any visit to a museum is almost bound to introduce some new material of some kind, and on many occasions will involve a great deal of new knowledge or experience.

Learning is the satisfaction of a higher-level human need and cannot take place until lower-level needs have been satisfied. Before we feel free to accept and relate to new information, we must feel physically safe and secure, immediate physical needs such as hunger and tiredness must be under control and we need to feel comfortable and loved, or at least welcome. If all these needs are met we are able to look to satisfying higher-level needs, such as looking for new information, enjoying aesthetic sensations or extending our range of knowledge.

When we do become exposed to new information, the form of exposure is instrumental as to whether the new information will mean anything to us. Memory is related to our level of involvement with information. Unless we are working very hard at it, we remember approximately 10 per cent of what we read, 20 per cent of what we do, 30 per cent of what we see, 70 per cent of what we say and 90 per cent of what we say and do (see Table 7).

Real learning and long-lasting changes in perception take place through activity and involvement. Reading a recipe book has a very low chance of effecting much change in attitude to a sixteenth-century meal compared with preparing the meal and eating it in a reconstructed sixteenth-century kitchen.

We can relate these ideas to a more broadly-based approach to teaching, which suggests three main ways of making contact with material to be learnt. Each of these enables people to learn using different modalities, which tend to operate at different levels (Suina, 1992). The first, the *symbolic* mode, is the most abstract and tends to take a verbal form. It requires sophisticated skills and understanding and generally operates at a high level of language use. The second, the *iconic* mode, consists of learning through imagery or other representations of reality, such as paintings, drawings, films or dioramas. This is a more concrete way of learning. The third, the *enactive* mode, consists of learning through using real things such as objects, or learning through people and events or through activities.

It is easier to become involved in the enactive mode. This demands involvement, and people at all levels of ability and experience often find this way of learning, or handling new experiences, inviting and enjoyable. It demands fewer of the skills associated with formal education. However, those people who are used to learning in a formal way may find it difficult to loosen up enough to become involved, and may feel themselves to be exposed if asked to participate. Museums which use interactive exhibits, organise practical work-shops and encourage handling are employing the enactive mode of learning.

Table 7 Modes of learning and involvement relate to how much we are able to recall

We tend to remember . . .	Type of activity	Mode of learning and level of involvement
Read 10%	reading	symbolic mode
Hear 20%	hearing words	abstract passive
See 30%	looking at pictures looking at objects watching a film looking at a diorama watching a demonstration watching a play	iconic mode concrete passive
Say 70%	participating in a discussion giving a talk	enactive mode
Say and do 90%	giving a demonstration handling and talking about objects using interactive exhibits giving a demonstration doing a dramatic presentation	experimental active

The iconic mode enables learning through a variety of representations, both two- and three-dimensional. This is perhaps the most familiar in museums. In many ways exhibitions are iconic experiences, with visual means being deployed to convey ideas. At its best the iconic mode should enable a great many people to learn. It is concrete and therefore does not demand higher-level reasoning skills or experience. It is immediate, as it appeals to the senses. However, images are complex things and their use is not always as straightforward as it might appear. In addition, many exhibitions do not maximise this learning potential, and rely less than they might on iconic devices to carry messages. A greater variety of channels of communication using the iconic mode would enable the communication process to develop more easily, especially where the images make references to everyday experience.

Museums perhaps rely too much on the symbolic mode. Text is often used too much in exhibitions, and the potential for other means of learning not explored. Lectures that do not offer slides or objects for handling or close scrutiny offer only the symbolic mode of learning. The symbolic mode enables learning for those who can read and understand at a high level, work with abstractions, can sustain one form of attention for a long period of time and have the self-confidence to know that it is worth beginning this demanding process.

The symbolic mode means understanding how words and experience relate, how words represent experience. This is inevitably a culture-bound process, and very often it is class-bound too. The way people represent the world to themselves will be an expression of their social, cultural, educational and ethnic identity. It is not a universal representation. The language and structures of thinking that are used, the choice of issues to address and ways of relating them one to another, the relationship of the text to the object or the image, all these reveal the unique subjective position of the text writer in the world. For those who do not share this position, the text will be difficult in varying degrees, according to how close to the writer's world-position the reader is.

Where the possibilities of iconic and enactive learning are not offered, reliance on the symbolic mode alone will produce an exhibition, or a presentation, with only one major communicative channel. This will inevitably restrict the range of audiences with which the exhibition will sucessfully communicate. The more opportunities for different modes of contact with ideas that are offered in any exhibition or presentation, the more possibilities will open up for the communication process. The more possibilities that are offered, the more they are likely to be exploited.

Museums and galleries are immensely rich in possibilities of enactive and iconic involvement. New approaches to displays such as discovery rooms, hands-on exhibits, film, interactive video and drama exploit these modes of learning and by doing so, enable new approaches to learning to take place. New ideas about how people learn, and new theories about the nature of intelligence also offer fruitful opportunities for museums and galleries.

A range of intelligences

Until recently intelligence was understood to be related to verbal and logical-mathematical ability. Intelligence tests and other standardised tests were devised to measure this ability along an axis that could be applied to everyone. Widespread dissatisfaction with this approach emerged during the 1960s and 1970s when it became clear that this way of measuring intelligence led to the exclusion and failure of large proportions of the (school) population. In addition, intelligence tests were unable to measure skills and abilities that might be highly developed, but which did not come within the narrow accepted definition of 'intelligence'. Musical talent, craft skills or expertise in dance, for example, were some of these abilities. 'Intelligence' became a difficult and often discredited concept.

Plate 12 Enactive learning is particularly effective with younger children, who find it easy to enter into role-play. In Britain, the Victorian schoolroom is a popular way of linking the past with the experiences of children in the present. Dressing up in typical boys' and girls' outfits and trying to carry out handwriting exercises with chalk on slates was one event in a busy day spent at Ironbridge Gorge Museum in Shropshire for a local primary school.

Photo: News Team International.

The Squatter's Cottage at Blists Hill, by Emma, aged 6

A dark, dark, night
In the mist
Is the little squatter's cottage
Low and cosy.
Looking through the windows I see
A vase
A bottle
And a lumpy bed.
A fire burns in the cast iron
grate. The lumpy grey big big bed.
Wooden shutters like eye lids
to keep out the wind

Figure 19 Linguistic ability is one of the multiple forms of intelligence proposed by Howard Gardner. From *Primary Schools and Museums – Key Stage One – Guidelines for Teachers* (Ironbridge Gorge Museum, 1991)

Recently, however, a new approach to the study of mind and intelligence has been developed, which presents a more complex way of considering abilities and skills. Gardner (1983; 1990) has produced a pluralist view of the mind and a theory of multiple or multi-faceted intelligence, which offers a spectrum of seven types of ability: linguistic, logical-mathematical, spatial, musical, bodily-kinesthetic, interpersonal and intra-personal intelligences. This theory has much to recommend it while considering how to increase the communicative potential of the museum. If we can ensure that museums and galleries offer menus of opportunities that relate to all of these opportunities, we should be broadening the possibility of relating to people with many different skills and abilities.

Linguistic intelligence is the ability to use words precisely and evocatively, to discriminate between the varied meanings of words and to use rhythm and tone to good effect. This is displayed at its most developed by poets, but many children have this form of intelligence, which may often go unrecognised. *This Fitz Me Fine* is a book of poetry produced by children visiting the Fitzwilliam Museum in Cambridge which demonstrates the way in which an experience stimulated by artefacts can enable children to write with great skill. Very young children visiting Ironbridge Gorge Museum were also moved by what they experienced, and Emma, aged 6, wrote about it (see Fig. 19). It would be interesting to see what response there would be if museum visitors were asked to write a poem about, say, a specific object. Clever marketing and a public prize-giving would arouse interest. Inviting an adult literacy class, or a class studying literature or language to the museum to use the collections and experiences for stimulus would also open up the museum to the use of linguistic intelligence.

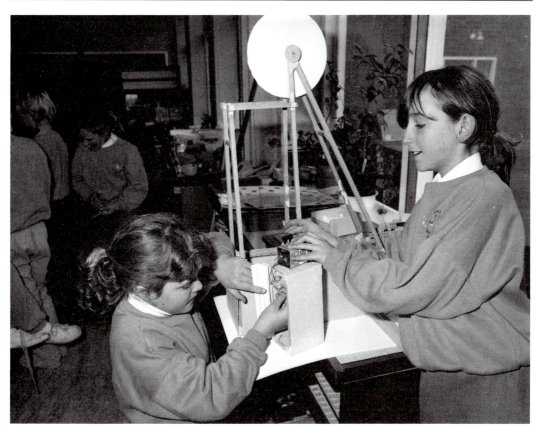

Plate 13 Logical-mathematical abilities can be stimulated by many activities in museums. Here, two 11-year-old girls are making a working model of the winding gear at the top of a coal-mine. In addition to increasing their skills, these girls are learning that it is appropriate for them to be interested and knowledgeable about coal-mines and winding gear. One of the most exciting potentials for museums is the possibility of counteracting social stereotypes.

Photo: Ironbridge Gorge Museum Trust.

Logical-mathematical intelligence is the ability to work in a logical and mathematical way. This is very close to what was formerly understood to be 'intelligence', and what was formerly studied by theorists such as Piaget under this guise (Gardner, 1990: 14). Some interactive exhibits, including computer programs, offer the chance to exercise logical-mathematical intelligence. Since the introduction of the National Curriculum, some museums have been developing ways of using the displays to support the development of mathematical skills. The Geffrye Museum in London, for example, produced two booklets in 1991 entitled *Maths at the Geffrye* and *Science at the Geffrye* which show teachers how to use the English domestic interiors in the development of numeracy and problem-solving. In *Maths at the Geffrye*, for example, children using the Early Georgian room are encouraged to estimate how many cups of tea the teapot would hold; to work out the ratio of black notes to white notes on the spinet and to speculate on what would happen if this were changed; and to identify patterns and shapes in the room. One of the science projects is developed from the question 'How did they light their rooms?'

Spatial intelligence is the ability to form a mental model of a spatial world and to be able to operate and manoeuvre using that model. Sailors, surgeons, sculptors and painters all have highly developed spatial intelligence. Mapping a historic site, making a reconstruction of a historic house and working from collections to evolve a personal statement through sculpture are opportunities to increase spatial ability. Producing a map of a site, with features marked on it, and specific information given about the features, would be one way of enabling people to use spatial ability to access knowledge.

Musical intelligence is the fourth category of intelligence, and is, of course, the ability to play music and to make musical compositions. Some museums are able to offer the opportunity to use unusual contemporary musical instruments. The Horniman Museum in South London, for example, has a Ugandan lyre collected as part of a handling collection that can be played. Musical intelligence also includes the ability to listen and to discriminate between different types of sounds. Many teenagers have this as a very highly developed intelligence within a narrow range of sounds. This intelligence could be used in museums and galleries through playing music in the galleries, or through organising musical events.

Bodily-kinesthetic intelligence is the ability to solve problems or make products using one's whole body or parts of the body. This might sound a bit unlikely for a museum, but in fact many museums offer opportunities to employ this kind of ability. Bodily-kinesthetic intelligence is demonstrated by craftspeople, dancers, athletes and surgeons. Craft demonstrations of all sorts including rural crafts (spinning, weaving, thatching), domestic crafts (cooking, cleaning), industrial crafts (knife-making, using a forge), artistic crafts (pottery, painting) and many more are offered in museums, either as organised workshops, or as demonstrations. Clearly the more people can do rather than observe, the greater the possibility of exploiting this form of intelligence. The potential is there.

Dancing is also something to be found in museums, although not as often. Children visiting the Indian galleries at the Victoria and Albert Museum in London, for example, were asked to adopt the postures of some of the sculptured gods and goddesses. This led into a dance workshop. There are potentials for development here, particularly using modern dance techniques, where anything from a combine harvester to a painting by Turner could provide a stimulus. Some forms of modern drama would also enable the development of bodily-kinesthetic intelligence.

The last two forms of intelligence Gardner proposes are not well understood and are difficult for psychologists to study. These are interpersonal intelligence, the ability to understand other people and to work co-operatively with them; and intra-personal intelligence, which is the ability to form an accurate model of oneself and to be able to use that model to operate effectively in life.

Interpersonal intelligence is likely to be highly developed in successful teachers, doctors, sales-people and politicians. It can be developed by carrying out activities in small groups, exploring how other people think, work and feel. Many of the activities offered by museum education departments offer exactly this experience. In cooking a meal in a reconstructed sixteenth-century kitchen, for example, there are ample opportunities both to work collaboratively, and to discuss how people solved problems in a different way when different resources were available. Part of interpersonal intelligence is the ability to understand that other people are not like oneself, but that their way of being is just as valid, but different. One aspect of this is experience of these differences in thinking, carrying out tasks, in prioritising and in according value. Museums, with their collections from throughout the world and from different times, are full of potential for the exploration of similarity and difference.

Intra-personal intelligence is more difficult. How can museums help people to develop realistic views of themselves, and to act in the real world? This intelligence is, of course, linked to the former kind. Knowing about how other people operate, in order to work with and understand them, requires the development of a self-view. Cooking in the reconstructed kitchen offers the chance to try out a way of acting, of operating, of being, within a world which has many of the characteristics of reality, but which is not in fact real.

Museums offer numerous opportunities of enabling children or adults to enter real (but protected) or reconstructed worlds where they may play out skills that are vital to acting in the real world. In addition to enabling people to use multiple intelligences, the building of confidence through speaking out in a group, the opportunity to test an idea in a sympathetic environment, the ability to become a useful member of a group with a common task, all these activities go towards forming a self-view. Perhaps one of the most useful things a museum can offer at the end of a visit is for someone to leave thinking: 'Well, I didn't know I could do that.'

One of the things which is noticeable in working with school groups in museums and galleries is the displacement of the existing hierarchies of relationships in the class. Children who find learning in school difficult suddenly discover they can shine in the museum. Some other form of intelligence than the linguistic/logico-mathematical model still used in classrooms has been called for, and children discover that their abilities are, at last, both useful and able to command respect. This release of often unrecognised intelligences suggests that museums are already demanding the use of a greater range of intelligences than is required in some other environments. This is an enormous strength for museums and galleries, and could be maximised by the serious consideration of how the ideas of Howard Gardner can be applied in the museum context.

Working with objects

It is their collections that distinguish museums and galleries from other social institutions. In recent years the study of objects and their social functions has become more familiar (Schlereth, 1982; Pearce, 1992; Csikszentmihalyi and Rochberg-Halton, 1981; Csikszentmihalyi and Robinson, 1990). Anthropologists, psychologists and museum professionals, among others, have begun to explore the complex ways in which objects sustain our worlds, structure our thoughts and are used for prestige, power, comfort and a sense of identity.

In a study of the meaning of things in the home, Csikszentmihalyi and Rochberg-Halton discovered two broad types of homes. One type of home was where objects were signs of warm symbolic ties between people, and where the objects themselves were understood to have symbolic meaning. In homes where there were no positive shared emotional meanings, the objects were barren of symbolic meaning, and had no other value than to be used and consumed as material items. The researchers suggest that where people are incapable of calling upon symbolic meaning they are unable to break out of the proscribed environment in which they live, and 'are consigned to live on the one dimension of agreed-upon reality, without the skills to break out of its constraints' (Csikszentmihalyi and Rochberg-Halton, 1981: 246). Material consumption becomes the main goal and objects represent nothing more than their financial cost and their role in the market-place.

It is important to be able to become free of already determined meanings in order to be able to redefine the meanings of objects, and in doing so, the meanings of experience and existence. The act of perception is the first key to being able to release the symbolic power of things. The ability to be able to see things both objectively and subjectively at the same time enables the viewer to make new relationships with the objective stimuli of the environment. These new relationships extend beyond immediate personal needs and beyond the hierarchies of material goods that our modern consumer society demands. Seeing more than immediate material values in objects enables the individual to transcend the lower-level goals of immediate material existence and to move towards higher levels of understanding the world and the place of the self within the broad context of the community, the human species, the ecology as a whole.

If it is important to be able to understand objects both objectively and subjectively in order to be able to relate to them both in terms of their material existence and also in terms of their possible symbolic existence, then museums and galleries have a role to play. Many museum objects are collected precisely because of symbolic meanings. At the National Portrait Gallery in London, for example, a portrait of the Brontë sisters, painted by their brother Branwell, is on display in the nineteenth-century galleries, and is in fact one of the most popular paintings. This painting is cracked and damaged, badly painted and very dark. Why is is popular? And why is it there at all?

The painting, dated about 1834, shows Anne, Emily and Charlotte Brontë. In the background is a large column, under which can clearly be seen the outline of a man, Branwell, who at some stage painted himself out. The painting was well known to friends of the family, but disappeared after the death of the sisters. It was discovered in 1914 by the second wife of Mr Nicholls, Charlotte's husband, folded up on top of a cupboard in Ireland.

This painting hangs in London because of its symbolic meaning within the family it depicts, but also because of the importance of this family to the history of literature. This symbolic meaning can be unpicked and discussed, compared with other forms of symbolic meaning and contrasted with other possible symbolic objects people might have in their homes. One of the strengths of using objects is the potential to explore a plurality of meaning for any one object, and in the exploration of the range of possible meanings, to show how objects can carry meanings to do with love, memory, a particular event, a special person, in addition to meanings connected to their material nature, individual history and so on.

Csikszentmihalyi and Robinson have also researched the nature of the aesthetic experience. In a number of interviews with curators and museum educators, they studied responses to works of art and discovered four types of challenge represented by the objects: the formal structure of a work; its emotional impact; the intellectual references it carries (its art-historical, cultural, historical and biographical implications); and the communicative possibilities it presents (opportunities for dialogue with the artist, his/her times, and within the viewers themselves) (Csikszentmihalyi and Robinson, 1990: 178–9). The researchers discovered that although the *nature* or *structure* of the aesthetic experience was very similar for most people regardless of age, training or professional role, the stimuli that triggered the experience was very different for different people.

The structure of the aesthetic experience is similar to the structure of all 'flow' experiences. The researchers have examined the way experts in intrinsically rewarding activities such as rock-climbing and chess describe their experiences. They found that it was the experience of 'flow' that motivated people to spend time doing things where there was no reward other than the act itself. 'Flow' was a term frequently used by these experts to describe what it was that they found enjoyable. It refers to a feeling of deep involvement and effortless progression.

Three conditions have been identified as critical to 'flow' experiences: the tasks must be equal to the present ability of the individual to perform; attention must be focused on a field of limited stimulus; and the experience must contain coherent, non-contradictory demands for action and provide clear and unambiguous feedback. In other words, during a 'flow' experience we feel challenged, but competent; we concentrate on the activity to the exclusion of other matters; we know what is expected of us and know that we are getting it right.

Among the rewards of the 'flow' experience are a sense of being freed from normal cares, a sense of being competent and in control of the situation, a sense of discovery and a sense of personal enrichment (Csikszentmihalyi and Robinson, 1975; Chambers, 1990). The aesthetic experiences of professionals in museums and galleries are 'flow' experiences, and similar pleasures are felt as in any other 'flow' experience.

The triggers for the aesthetic experience, however, varied with different people, with for example, art historians perceiving the challenges of the aesthetic encounter mainly in terms of knowing more about the objects, while art educators found the challenges in communicating about the object to a wide range of people. These triggers related to the competences and abilities possessed by the individuals. It was found that corresponding to the different fields for action posed by the perception of challenges were the skills that the viewers possessed, which then allowed interpretation of and response to the challenges perceived. In other words, curators felt challenged to discover more about an object and knew how to go about doing this, while educators felt stimulated by the possibilities of using the objects with audiences and felt confident in designing appropriate programmes.

Perceptual skills to compare, contrast and evaluate visual stimuli were always necessary to some degree, with the study suggesting that someone without these skills would be unable to derive an aesthetic experience from any but the most familiar paintings. The depth of the aesthetic experience is directly related to the number of dimensions for interpretation included in the response to the work. These dimensions include emotional responsiveness, knowledge of the period, of the culture and of the artist, a familiarity with techniques and schools of art and an ability to communicate with the work and its contents (Csikszentmihalyi and Robinson, 1990: 179–80).

The researchers insist that these perceptual skills which are necessary to the aesthetic experience are acquired, not inherited. One of the most valuable aspects of their extremely important study is the demonstration that connoisseurship, taste and powers of discrimination are not innate, but are learnt, through exposure to objects, opinions and experience.

A second very valuable lesson from the research is that 'flow' experiences, seen at their most developed in experts, are also possible at a lower level of skill. One of the key characteristics of the 'flow' experience is the feeling that skill levels are adequate to the challenge perceived. This combines with an opportunity to find personally meaningful insights and to feel competent and in control of the situation. 'Flow' experiences are optimal experiences, and lead to a more intense interaction with the environment, to a development of potentialities; they change and expand the being of the viewer. However, we are all capable of experiencing 'flow', if the criteria outlined above can be met.

How, the researchers ask, can we enable the 'flow' experience to develop in museums and galleries? This is the challenge for the art museum educator. How can we teach people to see, to develop discrimination and judgement in relation to works of art? How can we identify the skills required to study paintings and sculptures?

But this is what art museum educators have been doing for some years; this is precisely the work of the museum and gallery educator and good practice is in place and has been documented (Hooper-Greenhill, 1991a). Csikszentmihalyi, in describing 'flow', describes the experience that characterises the learning process that progressive educationalists work towards: an experience where the learner is stretched, but feels competent, is focused and is able to find personal relevance. The emphasis on enabling individuals to discover meaning for themselves in experiences is well known in theories of both successful teaching and communication (Tilden, 1957; Ham, 1983).

What is new in the 'flow' theory is the distinction between the structure of the experience and the stimulus, and the fully researched description of the structure of the experience which enables us to make connections with aspects of existing practices in art galleries and museums. From the work of Csikszentmihalyi we can see exactly why many people feel so uncomfortable and incompetent in those museums or galleries that do not enable them to use their own interests and levels of skill. Although it is desirable to enable people to increase their levels of skills to allow them to experience 'flow' at a higher level, this can only begin by enabling the practice of the talents people already have. Museums and galleries, then, if they wish to encourage 'flow' experiences in more of their visitors, must organise the museum to meet the needs of those with a range of skills, from very limited to extremely sophisticated, and must offer opportunities for people to increase those skills through using them.

If the characteristics of the structure of the 'flow' experience are in fact transferable across a range of environments, then it is justifiable to consider how we can facilitate this type of experience in all types of museum, working with all types of object. Some American museum educators have begun to explore this (Chambers, 1990; Roberts, 1990). From the results of the research discussed above, it is likely that although the characteristics of the 'flow' experiences will remain remarkably similar in any type of museum, triggers are likely to be radically different. Triggers in museums or galleries will, however, be related to the skills for responding to the challenges posed by the artefacts. A concentration on developing the skills to respond to objects is therefore of very general use.

Plates 14 & 15 Knowledge and skills are required to reach a 'flow' experience. In museums, in order to feel comfortable and in control when looking at artefacts, it is necessary to possess knowledge of the subject area and general skills of intellectual analysis. Museum educators work to enable everyone to be able to do this at their own level, to reach their own experience of 'flow'. One of the ways in which this is achieved is through demonstration and explanation followed by exploration. Here, for example, the children are first shown how the washing was done using nineteenth-century artefacts. Then they try the process for themselves. When looking at these objects again, this practical experience combined with the knowledge gained through looking and listening will hopefully enable spontaneous and confident response, a feeling of recognition and a sense of personal ownership of the process the objects represent. This, perhaps rudimentary, 'flow' experience, will give the student the confidence to go on to develop more sophisticated and elaborated responses.

Photo: Warwickshire Museum and Archive Education Service.

Working with objects has been discussed at length elsewhere (Hooper-Greenhill, 1991a: 126–8, 1991c, 1992d; Durbin, Morris and Wilkinson, 1990; Morris, 1989) and some problems and benefits have been outlined (Husbands, 1992; Morris and Wilkinson, 1992).

The most basic method of working with objects is the use of questions. This will be discussed here, with examples which demonstrate first, how asking questions of objects may be organised; second, how the use of questions opens up many of the areas of expertise in relation to objects identified above (Csikszentmihalyi and Robinson, 1990: 179–80); and last, how the perceptual skills required for the 'flow' experience in museums may be fostered.

Learners can be introduced to objects through a number of types of question that demand a range of types of response (Durbin, 1989). The mental processes involved move from simple recall, through convergent, divergent and judgmental thinking to a synthesis of the intellectual process as a whole.

Memory questions demand the recall of facts, a recognition of things and a description. They tend to begin with: 'How many . . .?'; 'What is the . . .?'; 'Name the . . .'.

Convergent questions focus on specifics, that which is already known or understood. They require answers giving explanations, making comparisons or discussing relationships. 'What does this lever do?'; 'How is this bag like that bag?'; 'How do these two pieces of fabric differ?'

Divergent questions open things out, and more than one answer may be appropriate. Imagination, hypothesising, the use of knowledge to solve problems, prediction, inference and reconstruction are all required. Questions typically begin with: 'What if . . .?'; 'How many ways . . .?'; and 'Imagine that . . .'.

Judgemental questions demand personal unique answers based on choice and evaluation. The formulation of opinion is required, and views will have to be presented, justified and supported by evidence. These questions ask: 'What do you think about . . .?'; 'Do you agree that . . .?'; 'What is your reaction to . . . ?'; 'Which do you think . . . and why?'

Questions which demand a synthesis are very useful at the end of a discovery or thinking process. 'What have we learnt about . . .?' and 'What did . . . tell us?' demand the recall of recent experience, enable a review and evaluation of what has happened, and enable the contextualisation and assimilation of new knowledge or material. This incorporation of new information, skills and experience into existing knowledge, combined with practical work that has been discussed from a range of personal points of view makes an ideal learning environment.

These questions, with their various demands, enable moves through thought processes which will encourage the development of thinking skills in relation to objects. They enable an accumulation of intellectual expertise, and call on existing knowledge to be applied to new artefacts.

'Flow' experiences are possible for all ages and all abilities when taking part in this kind of work. The 'flow' might not be that of an aesthetic experience, but this is not important. What is important is to enable people to feel that the museum objects being investigated are of interest and relevance to them, that they know how to respond to them and that they feel enriched and invigorated by the experience of working with them. For some individuals at a later stage, 'flow' experiences might be possible in relation to the aesthetics, or the scientific (or other) aspects of the objects. Facilitating the 'flow' for pure intellectual enjoyment is more than enough to begin with!

Structuring learning materials: exhibitions, for example

All learning materials, whether exhibitions, lectures, workshops or teachers' packs, need to pay attention to some very basic rules in order to achieve successful communication. This is particularly important for 'distance-learning' materials such as exhibitions and teachers' packs, where instant modification in relation to manifest needs is impossible.

It is perhaps useful to summarise these basic considerations before discussing them in more detail. Preliminary research on the needs and knowledge of target audiences will make a positive response more likely; the content to be 'learnt' should be limited, and material structured into seven (plus or minus two) main chunks (although these can be sub-divided); subject matter should move from the known to the unknown, with links made with everyday life; analogy, comparison and example aid understanding; ideas should be expressed in as concrete a way as possible, but links between concrete and abstract ideas should not be ignored; frameworks for processing the subject matter should be incorporated. The material should be evaluated.

These basic guidelines will be discussed in relation to exhibitions. Two of these issues have already been discussed at length and will only be touched on here. These are research (Chapter 4) and frameworks for making sense of new material (Chapter 5).

We have already seen that preliminary research in relation to visitors to any proposed exhibition or display is helpful. Once target audiences have been defined, their use of an exhibition and their level of interest and knowledge can be examined. If visitor figures matter, perhaps in relation to revenue-generation, some fairly simple questions may save later embarrassment. For example, if teachers are expected to visit the exhibition, it makes sense to see if the topic relates well or badly to the curriculum. If the latter, teachers are unlikely to come. Timing and cost are other important factors. Education staff, or local education authority representatives can be consulted, as can curriculum documents, or visiting teachers. A small impressionistic survey will quickly reveal the situation.

Some exhibition producers, on considering how visitors are responding to the subject matter of an exhibition, have discovered after the exhibition has been

159

mounted that visitors did not understand the general concepts on which it was based. For example, visitor knowledge of characteristics of the eighteenth century were found to be hazy in a review of how visitors were responding to an exhibition on an eighteenth-century scientist. This was the case even where visitors said they were interested in and knowledgeable about history. It would have been simple, if this had been discovered beforehand, to erect an introductory panel that reminded people through text and images of what they had perhaps forgotten about the eighteenth century, with some scientists named and some broad aspects indicated.

One basic mistake that is often made in exhibitions is to have too much material. Visitors sometimes drown in information, facts and objects. Sometimes this is the result of the exhibition team not being clear about the objectives of the exhibition and including a great many irrelevant aspects. A recent exhibition in the North of England had twenty-eight categories of information, many of which overlapped. The planning had been muddled, and as the main aims of the exhibition were not clear, they changed whenever external circumstances (the offer of some additional objects, the requests of a member of the museum's governing body) changed. A clear set of aims for the exhibition, carefully thought out and then followed will facilitate planning and enable priorities to be determined.

Once the content of the exhibition has been agreed, then the question of structuring the material arises. Cognitive psychologists tell us that it is difficult to relate to more than about seven pieces of new information at once. This represents the span of immediate memory and is about the limit that most people can cope with (Miller, 1970: 21–50). If a large amount of information is organised and grouped into recognisable 'chunks', then we can begin to process it. Figure 20 demonstrates how perception and therefore both assimilation and recall is eased by the process of grouping. Using familiar reference points helps the process.

LEAGEMNCIQICOMAAMMA

LEA GEM NC IQ ICOM AAM MA

Figure 20 Material presented with no structure is very difficult to process and to remember. Structuring the material using familiar and recognisable 'chunks' makes it much easier. Try testing this using acronyms that are familiar to your audience. These acronyms are familiar to British museum education staff

These 'chunks' can be further sub-divided, which expands the amount of information that we can assimilate. If the ideas are themed as part of the structure and if the structure is hierarchical, the possibility of communication is enhanced (Ham, 1983). Each part of the overall message should be related to a larger part and then to the overall theme. In this way, even small points can be integrated into the structure and have therefore a greater possibility of being absorbed and remembered (see Figs 21 and 22).

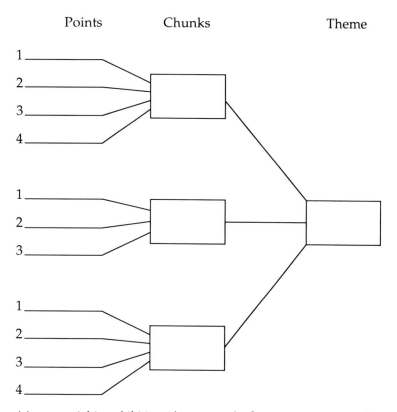

Figure 21 Organising material in exhibitions, lectures or leaflets. Discrete points should be organised into 'chunks' or topics which relate to the overall theme

Visitors find it easier to pay attention to exhibitions where the structure used can be related to their personal experiences. Relating new information to long-term memory is essential for understanding and to enable the making of meaningful links. In the example in Figure 22 the 'chunks' 'men', 'women' and 'children' are easy to relate to and come within the sphere of everyone's experience.

Visitors should be encouraged through the display to make comparisons with today, for example their own childhood, or their parents' childhood, in order fully to grasp and understand the similarities and differences between the experiences of the Tudors and Stuarts and their own. New knowledge is

161

only fully assimilated once the link has been made with existing knowledge. The development of knowledge of the Tudors and Stuarts comes more easily if integrated with comparisons with today.

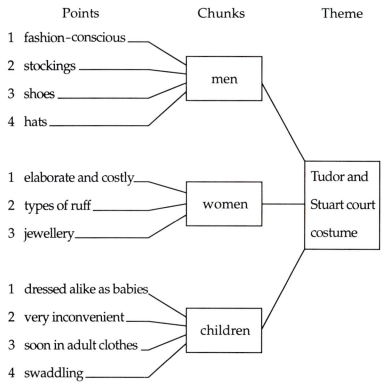

| | Points | Chunks | Theme |

Figure 22 The various points to be made in this exhibition are grouped into easily understood categories which relate to the experience of the visitors rather than the categories of the collections

Continuous information is difficult to process if it is presented in a self-contained vacuum. It has been shown that people will continue to process information, to learn, as long as they can continue to make meaningful and relevant links with the material that is being presented. If these links cannot be sustained the learning process will stop (Ham, 1983). If an exhibition offers, therefore, first a structure to frame the ideas, and second, some ways of making links with the existing experience of the visitor, the communication process will remain alive. If not, the process will die.

Concrete ideas that can be easily understood make the best jumping-off point for the introduction of abstract ideas. Looking at a young sixteenth-century girl's dress soon leads to the idea that Tudor children were dressed like adults at a very early age, which easily progresses to the more abstract notion of the differences in the concept of 'childhood'. These more abstract notions should not be avoided, but do benefit from growing out of the familiar and the concrete. This is something that museums and galleries, full of real things, should be able to do with the greatest of ease. Unfortunately, it is rarely done. It is more likely that the dress will be presented with a label saying what it is, how old it is and where it came from, rather than pointing out the interesting thing, which is what can be learnt from it.

Most teaching material is automatically trialled and piloted before it is finally released. This is, of course, much easier with a worksheet than a teachers' pack, and infinitely much easier than with an exhibition. However, if the exhibition is to work genuinely as a medium of communication, then some effort at both naturalistic and scientific evaluation must be built into the development process.

Preliminary research (front-end evaluation) will reveal audience characteristics and knowledge. Trialling texts and individual exhibits, even in a fairly crude way, will give some idea of whether messages are being received and understood. It will be suggested that this is all too time-consuming, but if formative evaluation shows up basic design problems, the time is well spent (Griggs, 1981; Jarrett, 1986; Lockett, 1991).

Summative evaluation will offer information on who did in fact come to the exhibition, what they felt about it, how the exhibition was used, how much revenue was generated, how sales in the shop were increased and so on. Summative evaluation has often been discussed in relation to improving the exhibition itself: this, of course, it cannot do. What it can do is provide concrete evidence of performance, and hopefully, if the other research and evaluation has been effective, of success. In these days of accountability, it is very valuable to be able to spell out goals and objectives and then detail how these have been met. Only an ongoing commitment to evaluation and research can help you do this.

These basic structural matters, drawn from the principles of both successful communication and successful teaching, should, of course, be considered in relation to the facilitation of 'flow' experiences. If these guidelines are followed, then the preconditions should be in place for visitors to feel competent, in control and able to discover personally meaningful insights.

Face-to-face teaching

The potential for face-to-face teaching in museums and galleries is enormous. The vast range of educational possibilities, the varieties of communicative method and the great spread of potential audiences mean that many opportunities open up.

Teaching in museums and galleries is based on the collections held in each institution. Methods focus on ways of exploring these collections and of finding relevant and immediate links with a range of audiences. These links are carefully researched through discussions with group leaders, through examining curriculum documents and through building up banks of experience. General connections between the resources of the museum can be identified and made available to groups of all sorts, and, with the potential of direct and 'natural' communication, specific and detailed modifications can be made after discussion of the objectives for individual visits, or, if necessary, during the teaching process itself.

Face-to-face teaching in museums is enormously flexible. The collections, the exhibitions, the buildings, the site, the staff and the shop, including the publications and videos, all present a huge resource for learning. There are, of course, restraints to do with other institutional and individual priorities, which mean that not everything can be used in all ways at all times, but nevertheless the potential is virtually limitless. Given this great resource, and given the power of interpersonal communication to be tailored to specific needs, an explosion of possibilities can ensue (see Fig. 23).

Museum name
Address
Date of review
Name of reviewer

Services	Slide lectures	Gallery talk	Art/ science work- shops	Films	Teachers' packs	Teachers' courses	Work- sheets	Loans	Talks in schools	Talks in commu- nity
Audiences										
KS1										
KS2										
KS3										
KS4										
Sixth form										
Teachers										
Student										
Adult education group										
Family										
Elderly										
Disabled										
Tourist										
Cultural group										
Group leaders										
Other audiences										

Figure 23 A profile grid to plot the range of audiences and activities of a museum education service. The scatter pattern of the completed cells would show where the balance of provision fell.

The collections and displays of museums and galleries can provide opportunities that relate to a range of age and interest-related requirements. In the reconstructed kitchens of a grand historic palace in Britain, for example, Key Stage One children (5–7 years) can study the five-foot-long soup ladle and the stuffed peacock as indicators of the passage of time; at Key Stage Two (7–11 years), where Tudors and Stuarts are a prescribed study unit, children can investigate the court appetite that required a fifty-room kitchen to feed it, using 1,240 oxen per year, 8,200 sheep and 300 barrels of ale. They can handle pewter plates, and find out that holly was used to clean the butcher's block and goose wings to baste the roast. It will be revealed that tooth decay was a serious problem at court and that social status dictated the kind of bread that was eaten (different grades of white for different grades of courtier – only the peasants ate brown). Key Stage Three students (11–14 years) can be introduced to court administration, the kitchen policing system managed by the clerks of the green (baize) cloth that was necessary to ensure that the right ingredients were delivered, paid for and reached the dining table. Numerous other topics connected to the royal cult, with its hierarchies, liveries, artifice and extravagance can be introduced according to the needs of the various groups.

It is important that museum educators consult the curricula that schools and colleges are using. These groups are unlikely to make much use of museums unless their provision relates fairly closely to the areas which are being studied.

The National Curriculum in England and Wales, for example, has laid down teaching objectives for the classroom. Coincidentally, these have proved enormously productive in the museum. Museum educators are now able to review their collections to see how, for example, they could be used to indicate types and uses of materials. Although this is officially part of the science curriculum, collections of social history material have been usefully used to explore this theme. Types and uses of materials to be discovered at the seventeenth-century manor house Clarke Hall, for example, include varieties of wood, stone, clay, cloth, glass, pewter and many others. Problem-solving activities in relation to one of the materials, 'Fabrics', include working out what could have been used to dye fabric, experiments with red cabbage, beetroot, blackberries and lily of the valley roots, testing to see whether temperature affected the results and so on. (Hooper-Greenhill, 1991: 174–81). Art museums could equally be used to respond to the science curriculum in this way.

This rereading of artefacts and specimens has demonstrated how objects can be interpreted and reinterpreted from an enormous number of points of view. These approaches have resulted in exciting new ways of thinking about objects which have the potential of being adapted to suit broader audiences.

Health and hygiene, for example, can be studied as part of the National Curriculum at Hampton Court in London, using the disposal of waste from the kitchen (into the Thames), recipes, and diets (75 per cent meat and a 5,000 calories per day intake). However, this approach to historical evidence which uses current interests and concerns such as diet as an analytical tool, is an approach of very general potential. It could be made of specific interest to people at various life-stages by comparing the diet of the early sixteenth-century with an early twentieth-century diet (for the elderly), a 1950s post-war diet (for the young retired), and a 1990s health-conscious diet (for the young adult). Comparisons with diets elsewhere in the world (Japan, India, Africa, America) would make links with the experience of many different cultural groups. Such a project would relate well to the characteristics of a cross-generational multicultural group such as a London school group accompanied by parents and grandparents, or working jointly with a day centre for the elderly.

Face-to-face teaching in museums or galleries employs a number of methods. These are adapted to suit the specific audience. At the National Gallery in London, for example, many talks and lectures are given for adult and student audiences. These are sometimes linked to Art History courses at the University of London. These lectures may be presented in a lecture theatre where the use of slides enables comparison of objects in the collections with paintings from elsewhere. A high academic standard is offered combined with well-developed lecturing techniques. This formal method of teaching suits this audience well and is very successful.

For the frail elderly, other techniques must be used. In Warwickshire and Oxfordshire, boxes of objects that may be handled have been put together on a thematic basis and taken into nursing homes and day centres. These objects have been used to stimulate memory and discussion through handling, close examination and comparison. Other museums, such as the People's Story in Edinburgh, have, as we saw in the last chapter, used the memories and experiences of older people, recalled through talking stimulated through contact with artefacts, to research and build displays (Beevers *et al.*, 1988). On the completion of the displays, the people involved in the original research became part of the museum communication team, available in the museum to share their experiences with visitors.

Workshops and active learning of all sorts are preferred in museums. There is a concern to offer a form of experience that is not possible elsewhere. In general, this means enabling close contact with the collections through handling, careful looking, drawing and discussion. Sometimes the need to examine the objects is motivated by a role-playing situation, or by the need to solve a problem.

Plate 16 Examining a small group of specimens in the Science Centre in São Paulo, Brazil,
enables the use of the skills of observation, classification, comparison, hypothesising,
imagining and summarising. In addition, social skills are required to work in a group.
The live displays of snakes and spiders are supplemented by snake skins for handling,
models of how snakes' jaws work and jars of dead specimens for close looking.
Enablers or demonstrators are on hand to chat informally to school or family groups.
The handling material is easily available in a self-help chest or pull-out drawers.

Photo: Eilean Hooper-Greenhill.

167

For young audiences, museums, galleries and sites offer opportunities of learning through doing. In part this is because it is impossible to avoid. The journey to arrive at the museum, being in what is generally an unfamiliar place, with often huge buildings or outdoor spaces, means the generation of a level of excitement and expectation that can be used. The channelling and conversion of expectant energy into productive learning is best achieved by using practical methods of, for example, making masks, playing contemporary but unusual musical instruments, doing a small-scale scientific experiment, watching a demonstration of skill and then trying it out.

In addition to physical and practical experiences, museums can enable the development of thinking skills. Examining a small group of objects will demand the use of the skills of observation, comparison, summarising, classification, criticising, looking for assumptions, collecting and organising information, hypothesising and imagining.

Face-to-face teaching in museums soon opens up a multitude of questions as to what museums are for and how they operate. Working with objects in a direct teaching situation produces discussion about why and how objects are collected, looked after, conserved and used. The various processes that museum workers are engaged in become open and easy to understand. The élitist mystique of the museum evaporates as museums become accessible places with their own special characteristics, like libraries or zoos or garden centres.

Much of the experience of visiting the museum can best be used by group leaders using analysis, discussion and workshop techniques after the visit. It is important for museum educators to ascertain how a museum visit is to be used, and sometimes to give advice on the development of either initial objectives or possible follow-up work.

Many of the best practical workshops are led by specialists such as artists, scientists or poets, who use their particular skills to interpret, with their group participants, some aspects of the collections. Tania Kovaks, for example, worked with the Serpentine, the British Museum and the Museum of Mankind, looking at artefacts as ways of making, inventing and preserving history, and went on to relate this to art history, anthropology and colonialism (Clarke, 1991).

Successful and innovative museum and gallery education is often based on the establishment of strong, mutually supportive networks. Thus the Tate Gallery, London, the Living Paintings Trust and Edmonton School worked together to enable older school students to produce tactile paintings for visually-impaired people (Wolf, 1991), and the British Museum and the Royal Opera House worked together with 200 children from Suffolk to produce an Anglo-Saxon opera, partly inspired by the exhibition 'The Making of England' at the British Museum (Davidson, 1992).

Most museums and galleries balance the amount of time spent on face-to-face teaching with time spent in preparing teachers' materials (Fraser, 1991), and working with curators on displays. The balance of time will vary with the philosophies and objectives of the institution concerned (Hooper-Greenhill (ed.), 1992).

Museums and galleries: ideal environments for learning

Museums and galleries have the potential to be ideal learning environments across the age-range. They are perfectly placed to play an important role in life-long learning. Life-long learning insists that people learn throughout their lives and not until they reach a certain rather young age. Life-long learning is seen to occur in many different situations, and not just institutions of formal learning. Laying a patio, decorating a room, making a dress and visiting a new place are all opportunities for learning new things. People are understood as resources for learning, as are places and activities. Learning throughout life occurs according to personal desire and opportunity and is paced according to the needs of the learner. In many ways, learning is seen as a way of living, of continually expanding horizons and of tackling personal challenges, however small.

Museums and galleries can offer a range of opportunities for formal and informal learning, active participation or observation, structured long-term courses or single memorable occasions. Museum staff are full of expertise in an impressive array of areas. Museum buildings and sites as environments offer new places to learn in and topics to learn about.

Museums teach about themselves as part of their communicative role. This happens imperceptibly as people engage with the experience of the museum, its staff and its people. Lessons will be learnt about how the museum views visitors, how people are valued and cared for, and how the collections are valued and cared for.

Increasingly, educators in other fields are looking to museums and galleries as places to help them attain their educational objectives. This can be observed across all age ranges. Howard Gardner (1991: 200–3, 208, 215) has identified Children's Museums as the perfect environment for stimulating the natural curiosity of the young child and has designed specific projects, working jointly with the Children's Museums in Boston and Indianapolis. Given that many museums are now developing display methods that adapt the interactive, problem-solving approach taken by Children's Museums, this development deserves close investigation.

In response to demands from new educational approaches and the new curriculum in Scotland, older children are using museums to develop their critical faculties in art and design (Campbell, 1992) in historical study and in cross-curricular projects where investigative work spans maths, English, craft and design (Capernos and Patterson, 1992).

Strong links are being made in America with university-based adult learning provision. Both formal and informal educational programmes have been developed which are offered broadly across the community (Solinger, 1989). These include masters programmes in the decorative arts, black oral history projects and many others.

In Britain, families are recognised as one of the largest and fastest growing sections of the museum audience. Provision for families to learn and enjoy themselves together are rapidly being developed.

Museums and galleries are institutions with an almost unimaginable potential for enabling learning and enjoyment. Some museums have exploited some aspects of this, others have concentrated their efforts on other approaches. Many museums have achieved very little. In most institutions at the present time, money is short, and hard decisions have to be made over priorities. What structures need to be in place to manage effective museum communication and to identify useful actions?

9

Managing museums for visitors

A SWOT analysis for the future of museums

A number of forces demanding the development of the museum as a communicator were discussed earlier. Increased competition from within the museum industry and from other parts of the leisure industry, greater demands from audiences, especially the school audience, and increased accountability to government and museum governing bodies, all emphasise the need to develop new ways of demonstrating relevance and value for money, and new ways of attracting and satisfying audiences. What are the Strengths, Weaknesses, Opportunities and Threats that will influence the ways in which museums will repond to these demands?

Museums have many strengths. They represent ideal learning environments, and they have enormous resources in their collections, buildings and staff. New methods in museum communication are being developed and within a close and collaborative profession are quickly shared. The public perception of museums is, on the whole, good: they are seen as places of worth, value and integrity.

There are also some weakness. Fear of getting too close to people is one of them; some museum workers find it difficult to contemplate incorporating either other museum professionals or representatives of the audience into work patterns. Lack of training is another; many museum workers are undertrained and this can lead to narrow horizons, lack of vision, lack of knowledge of alternative ways of doing things and fear of change. The training that is required must enable museum professionals to expand their horizons, to explore new and sometimes controversial ideas, and to act in problem-solving and creative ways.

Lack of strategies and forward plans, and lack of policies, particularly in the area of communication, is another area of weakness. This leads to a paucity of management information in relation to visitors and audiences in general. Without information, planning for exhibitions, education and marketing represents no more than a stab in the dark and a waste of resources.

The opportunities for museums are sometimes not perceived. In general, the early 1990s is felt to be a period of desperate survival in the face of decreasing resources, and it is true that some museums are facing severe cutbacks, and lack of support. But what opportunities are there? Radical change must by its very nature stir things up, which offers possibilities for new practices and new partnerships. As structures change, so new potentials present themselves. Changes in the education curriculum offer enormous opportunities. The responses that most people have to handling objects is extremely encouraging. The uses families make of museums can be exploited. A greater 'green' consciousness in society in general emphasises the kind of values that underpin museums. An emphasis on quality and customer choice means that planning high-quality services for specific groups is likely to be successful.

What are the threats? These are easier to define. Inertia in museums and galleries at a time of vast structural and value changes in society will mean almost certain failure. Positive response to change, a proactive attitude, and seizing the initiative will give the museum the best chance of being part of processes of change, rather than being ignored and marginalised, later to be eradicated. Severe funding restrictions, lack of forward consensus in local authorities and reorganisation of many social structures means uncertainty, and can lead to short-term responses in local authorities, central government and elsewhere. Museums without clear visions of what they are and might become will be blown by the wind.

Writing in the depths of a very severe recession, when many social institutions are examining their financial and philosophical viability, it is clear that opportunities must be discovered, grasped hold of and exploited. They will not arrive unsolicited, and they may arrive in strange guises. One of the uses of a SWOT analysis is the demonstration that, through creative and lateral thinking, some threats can be turned into opportunities. In museums, as everywhere else, the fixed parameters are in flux, and new approaches are emerging all the time. In many ways, the nature of museums and galleries as we have known it for many decades is now changing radically, and it is important to be clear about what museums may be and when museums are no longer museums (Hooper-Greenhill, 1992a).

The management of communication: forward planning

The potential power of the museum as a communicator lies ultimately in the hands of the managers of the museum. It is the managers who must have the vision to see where this potential lies and how it may be achieved. It is managers who must have the courage and strength to experiment with new methods and to remain committed to the ideal of communication if or when failures occur. It is managers who must set up the internal structures to enable the best use of resources and the achievement of objectives, and it is managers that must empower their staff and audiences to initiate and sustain the variety of two-way communication processes that are required.

Museums are now required to be more customer-oriented. Local authorities in Britain are encouraged to review their museums and galleries through a process of market research which will identify what the objectives of the museum are, and who it is trying to serve (Audit Commission, 1991: 29). Managerial arrangements of museums should identify responsibility for market research, attracting customers, delivering services and customer care (Audit Commission, 1991: 6–7).

In the United States the major report from the American Association of Museums, *Excellence and Equity: Education and the Public Dimension of Museums* (American Association of Museums, 1992) presents the findings of the Task Force on Museum Education that was established in 1989 following the American Association of Museums report *Museums for a New Century*. This report states unequivocally that there is an educational dimension in every museum activity, and insists on the range and depth of the public service role of the museum.

All museums and galleries in Britain are being encouraged to develop forward plans, and these will shortly be required in some areas as a precondition of grant-aid. It is in this context that museum communication should be developed. Forward plans take a variety of forms; they may be business plans, corporate plans or development plans (Ambrose and Runyard, 1991). Forward plans should cover collections management, interpretation and education, research, marketing, financial planning, staff training and future developments (Museums and Galleries Commission, 1991: 70). Issues relating to buildings, retail and catering and other areas may also be included. All aspects are discussed in relation to the history and current position of the museum. Objectives and methods are set out, targets and performance indicators identified and stated. The process of planning which underpins the forward plan should be carefully managed, call on experts where necessary and be realistic (Lord and Lord, 1991: 1–16).

The communication policies, strategies and action plans will form one tranche of the policies and plans contained within the forward plan and should consist of marketing, exhibition, education and customer care policies. Policies for the management of volunteers may be relevant in some museums or galleries. These policies will be informed by several sets of guidelines recently published by the Museums and Galleries Commission. These are *Quality of Service in Museums and Galleries: Customer Care in Museums – Guidelines on Implementation,* 1992; *Guidelines on Disability for Museums and Galleries in the United Kingdom,* 1992; and *Guidelines for the Use of Non-Sexist Language* (available from the Museums Association).

The communication policies are intimately related to the other museum policies and are informed by the overall objectives or mission of the museum (see Fig. 24). In some instances, especially where the museum or gallery is part of local authority provision, the museum policies will be linked into a larger Service Plan.

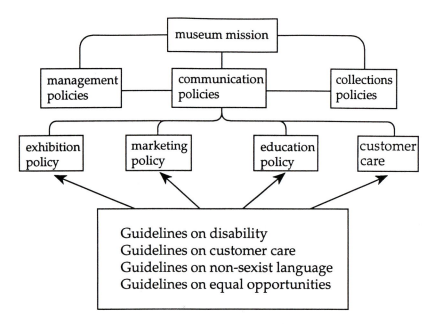

Figure 24 Communication policies are intimately related to other museum policies and are
informed by a range of guidelines that should underpin all the museum's activities

The Museum of Contemporary Art, Sydney, Australia, a public university
museum that has recently been reorganised as a 'not-for-profit' company (The
Museum of Contemporary Art Limited) provides an excellent example of one
way of presenting integrated policies. The collection/exhibition/education policy
is contained in one document (Museum of Contemporary Art, 1992), and is
managed by a committee of representatives from each of these programme areas,
the CEE Committee. The three policies for the three programme areas are
preceded in the written statement by a General Policy, where the objectives,
functions and obligations of the gallery are stated, key words (contemporary,
artist) are defined, visions and philosophies are set down. The document is
available to the public. Some short excerpts follow from the General Policy:

1   The MCA affirms the power of art and creative activity, and will
    seek, in all its activities, to communicate this to a wide and varied
    audience.

5   The MCA, in accordance with its commitment to embrace the 'most
    recent' ideas, theories and works of art, will critically assess its own
    values, concepts and practices in relation to changes occurring within
    the institutional and cultural formation of art.

6   The MCA will address a wide range of educational objectives in the
    field of contemporary art. ... The MCA will foster criticism and

scholarship, while seeking to make contemporary art challenging and engaging to a broad spectrum of public audiences.

15 The MCA will seek to prevent, in all its activities, any exercise of discrimination on the basis of race, culture, creed, gender or sexual preference.

21 The MCA will support the spirit and intention of the following statement, from paragraph 18 of the Mexico City Declaration, UNESCO world conference on cultural politics, Mexico, 1982.

> Culture springs from the community as a whole and should return to it; neither the production of culture nor the enjoyment of its benefits should be the privilege of *elites*. Cultural democracy is based on the broadest possible participation by the individual and society in the creation of cultural goods, in decision-making concerning cultural life and in the dissemination and enjoyment of culture.
>
> (Museum of Contemporary Art, 1922: 2–4)

Marketing policies and plans

Marketing in museums is still in its first decade, and in some museums is conceptually limited to publicity. Marketing, however, involves more than mere advertising. This statement from the Marketing Plan 1991–1994 from the Museum of Science and Industry in Manchester, England, indicates the scope of marketing departments:

> This Marketing Plan outlines the aims and objectives of the marketing function within the museum. It presents information on the current visitor profile, the marketplace within which the museum operates, the potential for development in the main segments of that market and the strategies which will be developed to increase the existing customer base and attract new audiences.
>
> (Sharkey, 1992: 3)

Marketing policies evolve through careful assessments of the marketing needs of the museum and the resources available to meet them. The Museums and Galleries Commission in Britain will shortly be publishing *The Museum Marketing Handbook*, which will give guidance on how to produce a policy.

Market research into the perceptions of users and non-users of the museum is rapidly becoming a requirement for museums (Audit Commission, 1991: 37; Museums and Galleries Commission, 1993; American Association of Museums, 1992: 16), and, as we saw in Chapter 5, important results are being produced and are being acted upon. Marketing policies and plans are informed by the results of research, and these results in turn are fed into exhibition and education policies (Museums and Galleries Commission, 1991: 106).

175

A marketing plan describes the key objectives of the marketing department of the museum, which might relate to increasing visitor numbers, increasing a particular target audience, carrying out specific research in the museum or the community or raising the museum's profile. The potential audience, within a given geographical area, and the current visitor profile are described, in the context of demographic trends and local or national population information. The results of any evaluation or research into visitor response are incorporated. Commercial and retail activities, and sponsorship, if part of the remit of the department, are discussed. The current promotion of the museum through leaflets, television advertising or free listings is outlined. Joint marketing initiatives with other museums, or tourism organisations, or other bodies are noted. The charging policy is laid out. Specific relevant factors (such as, for example, particular grants, events or other influencing matters) are specified.

Following these statements which outline the present position, proposals for future action are outlined, perhaps over a three-year period. Broad aims are stated and specific objectives or targets to be achieved are set out. These are related to particular sites if relevant. Strategic projects, such as the development of a new house-style, or work with focus groups in relation to a proposed exhibition are described. Links with other museum departments, perhaps on evaluation, for example, are indicated. Campaigns in relation to specific audience sections are discussed. The role and functions of the Friends group might be included here.

An action plan set out as a simple chart over at least the next year is useful. Budgets and allocation of funds should be specified over the period covered in the plan. The staffing levels of the department, with any planned increases, should be described. Other resources, such as space, for example, might also be mentioned to give a clear operational picture.

Measures of performance need to be identified in relation to key objectives: for example, if the objective is to achieve greater use of a particular site through increased publicity and the removal of charges, performance might be measured by counting visitor numbers at the site before and after the proposed action, and by carrying out structured interviews with some visitors to research perceptions and attitudes.

Graphs with information on demographics relating to visitor figures, spend per head, for example, may be included. Quotes from qualitative audience research may be added.

The marketing policy should be reviewed annually as the marketing plans roll through. Changes may be necessary when circumstances change.

The exhibition policy

The exhibition policy describes the underlying principles on which exhibitions will be based, and sets out the intentions of a rolling programme of exhibitions.

The exhibition policy informs the exhibition action plan, which describes the actual exhibitions that are planned over a certain period. The policy may cover permanent and temporary exhibitions, and where relevant, travelling exhibitions and mobile museums.

The exhibition policy needs to address the following areas: target audience, resources, types of provision, roles and functions of temporary exhibitions and permanent displays within the museum, and in the community, research and evaluation. At one level these are practical questions, but at another they are deeply philosophical and relate to the very core of the identity of the museum.

In many museums, exhibitions occur for a variety of pragmatic reasons, rather than for a planned and carefully thought out purpose. Some museums do little except buy in temporary exhibitions from elsewhere. In some museums, the relationship between temporary exhibitions and permanent displays is tenuous, to say the least. The relationship between the two, the objectives of the one and the other and the resources allocated to each, should be part of the programmed and managed development of the museum.

The exhibition policy from the Museum of Contemporary Art, Sydney, provides an interesting example. The policy is prefaced by the following philosophical statement:

> The MCA exhibition programme constitutes its most immediate, varied and energetic interface with the community. All other MCA activities will be drawn together and pivot around the function of exhibiting works of art for direct engagement with a public audience.
>
> It is through the exhibition programme that both 'the latest ideas and theories' and 'the most recent contemporary art of the world' (as conceptualised by the founding benefactor, J. W. Power) will be brought into prominent focus within the life of the MCA. It is through the exhibition programme that works of art will be experienced not only as discrete objects, but also as vehicles of more comprehensive and complex meanings, within the wider context of the production, interpretation and experience of culture within the community.
>
> (Museum of Contemporary Art, 1992:11)

This statement provides a challenging intellectual context for the mounting of exhibitions. It goes beyond the functional organisation of objects in spaces, and acknowledges the social and cultural issues that arise when objects are placed within museums or galleries.

The policy goes on to discuss the scope and balance of temporary exhibitions (the responsibilities for the permanent collections are fully acknowledged in the General Policy), ethics, related events and support activities, audiences, sponsorship and funding and implementation of the policy.

Exhibition policies in Britain must acknowledge the guidelines on customer care, disability and the use of non-sexist guidelines produced by the Museums and Galleries Commission and the Museums Association. Approaches to

177

display bearing in mind the needs of audiences should be considered. Phased renewal of permanent displays should be set out, with costings and target dates. Potential themes for displays and exhibitions, issues in relation to local circumstances, current gaps and omissions should be identified.

The exhibition action plan specifies what developments are taking place within which time-frame and at what cost. This is generally planned over a three- or five-year period, with staff time, resources, use of space, employment of outside contractors or designers and educational use carefully considered.

In Britain, at the present time, exhibition *plans* are frequently to be found within forward plans, where actions to be taken are described. It is much rarer to find an exhibition *policy* that takes a philosophical stance in relation to the functions of exhibitions, and makes statements about the issues that should underpin any exhibition, such as a commitment to disabled access, avoidance of sexist, racist or other bias, approaches to the writing of accessible text. It might seem that these can be taken as given, but where things are taken for granted this often means they have not been fully considered and therefore they will not be fully implemented.

In considering the role of the audience advocate, the staff member responsible for promoting the needs of visitors, in developing, reviewing and revising exhibitions, D. D. Hilke proposes that all exhibitions should be:

> accessible to the widest possible audience (including those with visual, physical, auditory, and learning disabilities);
>
> informative and relevant to the widest possible audience (e.g. beginners and scholars; browsers and studiers; first-time visitors and returning visitors; foreigners, non-native speakers and native speakers; visitors from diverse ethnic and other social backgrounds; children, teenagers and adults, etc.);
>
> effective in communicating their messages;
>
> structured to complement the natural learning strategies that visitors use;
>
> supportive of a variety of learning styles;
>
> supportive of the visitors' agendas as well as the museum's agendas;
>
> supportive of individual and group experiences;
>
> empowering, stimulating and fun;
>
> comfortable, uncrowded, and not overly structured or sequential.
>
> (Hilke, n.d.)

These are excellent guidelines, and museums and galleries should be working towards ensuring that all exhibitions and displays conform to them. To achieve these objectives it is necessary first to have general information about, for example, the nature of the museum's audience, the needs of people with a range of impairments, or an understanding of the range of learning strategies and intelligences people bring with them to any exhibition; second to have information on specific matters relating to each exhibition, such as attitudes and possible misconceptions in relation to particular topics, likely reactions to specific exhibition vehicles and particular factors that will influence the use of the exhibition by any particular audience segment.

An exhibition policy should be written to include these audience-related matters, rather than simply as a matter of resource allocation.

Education policies

Many museums and galleries in Britain have produced education policies in the last two years and many more are currently being written. Education policies have been recommended by successive reports (Audit Commission, 1991; Museums and Galleries Commission, 1991; Museums Association, 1991a) and guidelines with representative case-studies have been produced (Hooper-Greenhill (ed.), 1991). These guidelines and case-studies are available free of charge from the Department of Museum Studies, University of Leicester. In the current situation, where opportunities are great, but funding structures are insecure and uncertain, educational policies have played their part in demonstrating the educational potential of museums.

An educational policy discusses the role of education in the museum, and outlines the current and planned future provision. The document should include the education mission statement, the education policy, the education strategy and the education action plan.

The mission statement relates closely to the museum mission statement, and explains how 'education' is to be understood in the context of the policy document. Although education is a museum-wide function, the document might in some instances be concerned only with organised provision for groups. The education policy sets out the intentions of the educational service and identifies priorities, and the action plan shows how the objectives will be met by carrying out certain activities over a specified time period.

The education policy discusses audience, budget and resources, types of educational provision, roles and functions within the museum, networks outside the museum, training, marketing and evaluation (Hooper-Greenhill (ed.), 1991).

Policies are likely to vary according to the resources of the institution, the expertise represented by the staff and the approach taken to the educational responsibility of the museum. Policies may state that the educational function

179

will be achieved through carefully planned and targeted displays supported by written materials for group leaders; or may set out the role of an education department in face-to-face teaching.

The *Policy on Education* from the Ulster Museum, Belfast, asserts first, quoting from the *Policy on Collections*, that collections and their acquisition, curation, conservation and interpretation constitute the central activity of the museum. The document continues with the 'Aim and strategic objectives', with a general statement on interpretation, a quotation from the museum mission statement, and then eight strategic objectives:

1   to enlist the active co-operation of all Museum staff in the educational process;

2   to establish the Education Service as the recognised centre for educational co-ordination in the Museum with primary responsibility for educational organisation and development;

3   to involve Museum education staff in the various approaches to interpretation and presentation since they serve as advocates for museum audiences;

4   to emphasise in interpretation and presentation, the unique characteristic of the museum experience which is the encounter with objects. It is about 'learning from things';

5   to maintain and expand the museum visitor base by all appropriate means;

6   to respond to the following challenges (followed by ten challenges covering developments in all educational sectors, demographic and social matters);

7   to ensure an appropriate commitment of financial and human resources so that the Museum realises its full education potential;

8   to keep educational needs in view in all future planning and development of the museum.

These broad strategic objectives are followed by a discussion of the role and function of the museum education service and then a detailed outline of the strategic plan. This covers issues related to the curriculum in Northern Ireland, and plans for gallery development, on-site museum education services, outreach museum education services and staffing and resourcing the education service. The document concludes with a reiteration that museum education is a responsibility shared by all museum staff, with the Education Service acting as the centre of educational co-ordination and taking the lead in educational development.

The Education Service acts as audience advocates within the museum, and also as museum advocates in the community (Ulster Museum, 1992: 2–3).

Customer care policies

All museums and galleries need to consider their customer care policies. Guidelines published by the Museums and Galleries Commission are based on the 'National Code of Practice for visitor attractions' developed by the English Tourist Board, which is mandatory for membership of a tourist board (Museums and Galleries Commission, 1993). The guidelines are not mandatory, but indicate the quality of service that all museums should strive to achieve. They amplify the English Tourist Board Code of Practice and place it in a museum and gallery context.

The Museums and Galleries Commission Guidelines acknowledge the Audit Commission's 1991 report *The Road to Wigan Pier?* and quote from it:

> Scholarship and conservation are essential to a museum. Without them displays, though lively, may be superficial and uninformed and may even be misleading or incorrect. But scholarship and conservation have little point if people do not visit a museum or use its services.
>
> (Museums and Galleries Commission, 1993: 1)

The Museums and Galleries Commission Guidelines also acknowledge and quote from the 1991 Office of Arts and Libraries *Report on the Development of Performance Indicators for the National Museums and Galleries*:

> Spending money on service provision is of little value if the level, mix and quality of service is at odds with the requirements and preferences of those for whom the service has been provided and whose needs it has been agreed should be met.
>
> (Museums and Galleries Commission, 1993: 1)

The Guidelines cover all those areas that impinge on visitors, including collections management, access, marketing, display and education, training, on-site care, safety, evaluation and the development of a customer care policy.

Volunteer policies

Many museums and galleries use volunteer staff to deliver their educational or interpretive services. On the whole these are very professionally managed in North America, and much less well managed in Britain. The North American pattern is to deploy volunteers as a matter of policy, to designate a member of the museum's staff as a volunteer co-ordinator and to develop extensive training and management arrangements. In many instances, large numbers of 'docents', volunteer teachers, deliver programmes that have been designed and piloted by paid staff; usually this is very successful, and is certainly built on a long and well-known tradition (Newsom and Silver, 1978: 242–55). There is no shortage of guidance on how to develop and manage volunteers to work usefully and successfully with visitors (Wilson, 1976; Grinder and McCoy, 1985; Groff and Gardner, 1989).

181

In Britain, volunteers are not always used as part of a policy decision. In many cases, individual staff members adopt volunteers to work with them, and little training or management ensues. In some museums or galleries, the use of volunteers is closer to the North American model, but this is rare. Policies are essential for the successful integration of volunteers into the museum culture. There are suggestions, particularly in the Independent sector, that many museums will depend more heavily on volunteers in the future, although at the same time, the enhanced status of volunteering may mean that museums will be competing with other sites (Millar, 1991a). The development of better volunteer management should be a priority (Millar, 1991b).

Conclusions

Museums and galleries are vital to the educational and cultural health of society. This, however, is not always either seen or understood, and as long as this is the case, the continued existence of museums will be tenuous.

The future for museums and galleries lies in the hands and the hearts of their users; those social institutions that cannot demonstrate a real and perceived need for their continued viability will not last for long in the climate of radical change that are we are currently experiencing.

In this chapter we have considered the type of policy that is necessary to enable museums and galleries to maximise their use in society, and to develop new approaches that will broaden their appeal. However, policies alone can achieve nothing. Without a genuine and heartfelt conviction, a passion, on the part of museum staff to reach out to the people who will pay for their futures, those futures will not come into being. Without visitors who are contented, fulfilled, and eager to return, museums and galleries will perish.

Glossary

Area Museum Services/Councils regional advisory bodies for non-national museums and galleries in the United Kingdom.

audience advocate the museum staff member that speaks on behalf of actual and potential museum visitors. He/she should sit on gallery planning teams, and carry out visitor research and evaluation. This role is sometimes played by an education specialist.

customer care comprehensive attention to the needs of visitors, which includes a welcome on arrival, intellectually and physically accessible displays and events, adequate facilities and a safe environment.

discovery room a space within the museum or gallery where artefacts and specimens may be handled and investigated.

easy-to-read text initially devised for adults with reading difficulties, this has now been adapted for museum use.

evaluation assessment of exhibitions, projects or almost anything.

Formative evaluation takes place as the project or exhibit is being developed and aims to test it before major resources are invested.

Front-end evaluation takes place before a project begins, is sometimes goal-free or open-ended, and acts as preliminary research before the project is finally agreed.

Summative evaluation takes place at the end of a project and assesses its success. Lessons are learnt for future projects.

face-to-face communication communication between two people in the same place at the same time; also known as interpersonal communication.

focus groups groups of between six and twelve people of similar characteristics. Often used in market research, or in the collection of qualitative data.

goal-free evaluation open-ended assessment which uses questions which are not devised in relation to previously defined criteria or standards. Allows for unforeseen outcomes and the generation of new ideas.

goal-referenced evaluation assessment where criteria and standards have been devised, and where outcomes will be measured against these goals. Tests hypotheses.

holistic considers the complete phenomenon rather than parts of the whole.

mass communication communication with a mass audience, generally used of advertising, newspapers, television and cinema.

Museums and Galleries Commission central government body in the United Kingdom with responsibility for overseeing the welfare of museums, administering grants, and developing guidelines for good practice.

naturalistic evaluation assessment and research using methods adapted from human and social sciences, such as ethnography and sociology.

Office of Public Censuses and Surveys central government department in the United Kingdom responsible for collecting and publishing general social data. A few museum visitor surveys have been produced for national museums.

outreach taking the museum or gallery out into the community, through workshops or exhibitions in community centres such as hospitals or libraries, mobile museums or exhibitions, loan services.

performance indicators measures developed to assess how specific areas of an institution have performed in relation to established criteria, which may be qualitative or quantitative.

piloting trying out a small sample before deciding to go ahead.

qualitative research research based on qualitative data, i.e., small-scale but very detailed investigations, where small amounts of in-depth information are more important than a broad picture. Data often includes descriptions of practice and reported speech.

quantitative research research based on quantitative data, i.e., large-scale impressionistic research, where a general picture is required. Data is generally converted to statistics and presented in the form of tables and graphs.

research research in museums traditionally meant collection research. It now includes audience research. This may sometimes overlap with some forms of evaluation; it is generally more open-ended and more concerned to discover new knowledge.

science centres consist of exhibits specifically designed to be used and to demonstrate scientific or technological principles as they are used. Science centres may or may not be part of a science museum, but fall within most definitions of museums and are generally accepted as part of the museum community.

scientific evaluation research and assessment based on the laboratory-based methods of the natural or behaviourist sciences, such as botany or psychology.

teaching points the main concepts or themes to be communicated.

Bibliography

Adams, G. and Boatright, J. (1986) 'The selling of the museum 1986', *Museum News*, 64(4), 16–21.

Addison, E. (1986) 'Is marketing a threat . . . or is it the greatest challenge that museums have ever faced?' *Muse*, Summer, 28–31.

Allwood, R. (1992) 'All change at Oxford County Museum service', *Museums Journal*, 92(6), 8.

Alt, M. B. (1977) 'Evaluating didactic exhibits: a critical look at Shettel's work', *Curator*, 20(3), 241–58.

—— (1980) 'Four years of visitor surveys at the British Museum (Natural History) 1976–79', *Museums Journal*, 80(1),10–19.

—— (1983) 'Visitors' attitudes to two old and two new exhibitions at the British Museum (Natural History), *Museums Journal*, 83, 145–8.

Alvarado, M., Gutch, R. and Wollen, T. (1987) *Learning the Media: an Introduction to Media Teaching*, Macmillan Education, Basingstoke and London.

Ambrose, T. and Runyard, S. (eds) (1991) *Forward Planning: a Handbook of Business, Corporate and Development Planning for Museums and Galleries*, Routledge, London and New York.

American Association of Museums (1984) *Museums for a New Century*, American Association of Museums, Washington, DC.

—— (1992) *Excellence and Equity: Education and the Public Dimension of Museums*, A Report from the American Association of Museums, Washington, DC.

Ames, P. (1989) 'Marketing in museums: means or master of the mission?' *Curator*, 32(1), 5–15.

—— (1991) 'Measuring museums' merits', in Kavanagh, G. (ed.) *The Museums Profession: Internal and External Relations*, Leicester University Press, Leicester, London and New York, 57–68.

Anon. (1980) 'Adam's ancestors; Eve's in-laws', *Schooling and Culture*, 8, 57–62.

Arnell, U., Hammer, I. and Nylof, G. (1980) *Going to Exhibitions*, Riksutstallningar, Stockholm.

Arts Council (1989) *Arts and Disability Checklist: a Quick Reference Guide for Arts Officers on Arts and Disability Issues*, Arts Council, London.

—— (1991a) *Target Group Index 1990/1*, British Market Research Bureau/Arts Council, London.

—— (1991b) *RSGB Omnibus Arts Survey, Report on a Survey of Arts and Cultural Activities in GB*, Research Surveys of Great Britain/Arts Council, London.

Attenborough, R. (1985) *Arts and Disabled People*, Carnegie United Kingdom Trust and the Centre for Environment for the Handicapped, Dunfermline and London.

Audit Commission (1991) *The Road to Wigan Pier? Managing Local Authority Museums and Art Galleries*, The Audit Commission for Local Authorities and the National Health Service in England and Wales, HMSO, London.

Baker, N. (1990) 'Worlds apart?', *Museums Journal*, 90(2), 27.

Barnett, V. (1991) *Sample Survey: Principles and Methods*, Edward Arnold, London.

Barthes, R. (1973) 'The great family of man', *Mythologies*, Paladin, St Albans, England, 100–2.

—— (1977) 'The rhetoric of the image', *Image – Music – Text*, Fontana/Collins, Glasgow, 32–51.

Baynes, K. (1992) 'Lessons from the Art Machine', *Museum Development*, February, 29–39.

Beer, V. (1987) 'Great expectations: do museums know what visitors are doing?' *Curator*, 30(3), 206–15.

Beevers, L., Moffat, S., Clark, H. and Griffiths, S. (1988) *Memories and Things: Linking Museums and Libraries with Older People*, WEA South East Scottish District, Edinburgh.

Belcher, M. (1991) *Exhibitions in Museums*, Leicester University Press, Leicester, London and New York.

Belsey, C. (1980) *Critical Practice*, Methuen, London and New York.

Berger, A. A. (1982) *Media Analysis Techniques*, Sage Publications, London.

Berger, J. (1972) *Ways of Seeing*, British Broadcasting Corporation and Penguin Books, Harmondsworth.

Berry, N. and Mayer, S. (eds) (1989) *Museum Education, History, Theory and Practice*, The National Art Education Association, Reston, Virginia.

Bitgood, S. (1988) 'Problems in visitor circulation', in Bitgood, S., Roper J. T. Jr and Benefield, A. *Visitor Studies – 1988: Theory, Research and Practice. Proceedings of the First Annual Visitor Studies Conference*, Centre for Social Design, Jacksonville State University, Jacksonville, Alabama.

—— (1989a) 'Deadly sins revisited: a review of the exhibit label literature', *Visitor Behaviour*, 4(3), 4–13.

—— (1989b) 'The role of evaluation in the development of exhibit labels', *Visitor Behaviour*, 4(3), 16.

Bizaguet, E. (1991) 'Sufferers from defective hearing and the new techniques for communication', in Fondation de France and ICOM, *Museums Without Barriers*, Routledge, London, 156–9.

Board of Education (1931) *Museums and the Schools: Memorandum on the Possibility of Increased Co-operation between Public Museums and Public Educational Institutions*, Educational pamphlets, 87, HMSO, London.

Borun, M. (1989) 'Assessing the impact', *Museum News*, 68(3), 36–40.

Bott, V. (1990) 'Passmore Edwards Museum – a change of name?', *AMSSEE News*, 5, November, Area Museum Service for South Eastern England, London.

Bouchauveau, G. (1991) 'Reception services for the deaf at the Cité des Sciences et de l'Industrie at La Villette in Paris' in Fondation de France and ICOM, *Museums Without Barriers*, Routledge, London, 160–2.

Bradford, H. (1991) 'A new framework for museum marketing', in Kavanagh, G. (ed.) *The Museums Profession: Internal and External Relations*, Leicester University Press, Leicester, London and New York, 83–97.

British Tourist Authority (1991) *Sightseeing in the UK, 1990: a Survey of the Usage and Capacity of the United Kingdom's Attractions for Visitors*, BTA/ETB Research Services, London.

Bruner, J. (1960) *The Process of Knowing*, Vintage Books, New York.

—— (1962) *On Knowing: Essays for the Left Hand*, Belknap, Cambridge, MA.

—— (1966) *Towards a Theory of Instruction*, Norton and Co., New York.

Burrett, F. G. (1982) *Rayner Scrutiny of the Departmental Museums: Science Museum and Victoria and Albert Museum*, Office of Arts and Libraries, London.

Butler, B. H. and Sussman, M. B. (eds) (1989) 'Museum visits and activities for family life enrichment', *Marriage and Family Review*, 13(3/4).

Cameron, D. (1968) 'A viewpoint: the museum as a communication system and implications for museum education', *Curator*, 11(1), 33–40.

Campbell, G. (1992) 'Beyond the classroom wall', in Greeves, M. and Martin, B. (eds) *Chalk, Talk and Dinosaurs: Museums and Education in Scotland*, Scottish Museums Council and Moray House Institute, Edinburgh, 26–8.

Capernos, Z. and Patterson, D. (1992) 'Chalk and cheese', in Greeves, M. and Martin, B. (eds) *Chalk, Talk and Dinosaurs: Museums and Education in Scotland*, Scottish Museums Council and Moray House Institute, Edinburgh, 35–7.

Carnegie Council (1988) *After Attenborough: Arts and Disabled People – Carnegie Council*

Review, Carnegie United Kingdom Trust, Dunfermline and London.

Carnegie, E. (1992) 'Women's pictures', *Scottish Museum News*, 8(1), Spring, 8–9.

Chambers, M. (1990) 'Beyond "Aha!": motivating museum visitors', in Serrell, B. (ed.) *What Research Says about Learning in Science Museums*, Association of Science-Technology Centres, Washington, DC, 10–12.

Clarke, M. (1991) 'Serpentine connections', *Times Educational Supplement*, 25, 10 May.

Clarke, P. (1992) 'Peter Clarke', in Hooper-Greenhill, E. (ed.) *Working in Museum and Gallery Education – 10 Career Experiences*, Department of Museum Studies, University of Leicester, 14–15.

Cleaver, J. (1988) *Doing Children's Museums: a Guide to 225 Hands-on Museums*, Williamson Publishing, Charlotte, Vermont.

Cole, P. R. (1985) 'Dewey and the galleries: educational theorists talk to museum educators', *The Museologist*, 48, 12–14.

Coles, P. (1984) *Please Touch: an Evaluation of the 'Please Touch' Exhibition at the British Museum 31st March to 8th May 1983*, Committee of Inquiry into the Arts and Disabled People and Carnegie UK Trust, London.

Commission on Museums for a New Century (1984) *Museums for a New Century*, American Association of Museums, Washington, DC.

Coneybeare, C. (1991) *Museum Visitor Surveys: a Practical Guide*, Area Museum Council for the South West, Taunton.

Copeland, T. (1991) *A Teachers' Guide to Maths and the Historic Environment*, English Heritage, London.

Coxall, H. (1990) 'Museum text as mediated message', *WHAM*, Women Heritage and Museums, Newsletter, 14, 15–21.

—— (1991a) 'How language means: an alternative view of museums text', in Kavanagh, G.(ed.) *Museum Languages: Objects and Texts*, Leicester University Press, Leicester, London and New York, 83–99.

—— (1991b) 'The Spertus Museum of Judaica: Chicago', *New Research in Museum Studies*, 1, 211–14.

—— (1992) 'Museum text: accessibility and relevance', *Journal of Education in Museums*, 12, 9–10.

Csikszentmihalyi, M. (1991) 'Notes on art museum experiences', in Getty Centre for Education in the Arts, *Insights: Museums, Visitors, Attitudes, Expectations*, J. Paul Getty Museum, Malibu, California.

—— and Robinson R. E. (1975) *Beyond Boredom and Anxiety*, Jossey-Bass, San Francisco.

—— and Robinson, R. E. (1990) *The Art of Seeing: an Interpretation of the Aesthetic Encounter*, J. Paul Getty Museum and the Getty Centre for Education in the Arts, Malibu, California.

—— and Rochberg-Halton, E. (1981) *The Meaning of Things: Domestic Symbols and the Self*, Cambridge University Press, Cambridge.

Dabydeen, D. (1987) 'High culture based on black slavery', *The Listener*, 24 September, 14–15.

Danilov, V. (1986) 'Promoting museums through advertising', *Museum News*, 64(6), 33–8.

Davidson, B., Heald, C. D. and Hein, G. E. (1991) 'Increased exhibit accessibility through multisensory interaction', *Curator*, 34(4), 273–90.

Davidson, P. (1992) 'Buried treasures', *Times Educational Supplement*, 20 March, 47.

Department of Education and Science (1989a) *National Curriculum – from Policy to Practice*, HMSO, London.

—— (1989b) *The Curriculum from 5–16* (2nd edn), Curriculum Matters, 2, HMSO, London.

Dewey, J. (1963) *Experience and Education*, Coolier Books, New York.

Dickerson, A. (1991) 'Redressing the balance', *Museums Journal*, 91(2), 21–3.

Divall, P. (1989) 'Museum education – a new ERA?', *Museums Journal*, 89(2), 23–4.

Dixon, B., Courtney, A. and Bailey, R. (1974) *The Museum and the Canadian Public*, Arts and Culture Branch, Department of the Secretary of State, Government of Canada, Toronto.

Dodd, J. (1992) 'Whose museum is it anyway?' *Journal of Education in Museums*, 13, 31–3.

Duffy, C. (1989) 'Museum visitors: a suitable case for treatment', paper for the 1989 Museum Education Association of Australia conference.

Duncan, C. (1991) 'Art museums and the ritual of citizenship', in Karp, I. and Levine, D. (eds) *Exhibiting Cultures: the Poetics and Politics of Museum Display*, Smithsonian Institution Press, Washington, DC, 88–103.

—— and Wallach, A. (1980) 'The universal survey museum', *Art History*, 3(4), 448–69.

Durbin, G. (1987) 'Practical courses for teachers', *Journal of Education in Museums*, 8, 4–5.

—— (1989) 'Improving worksheets', *Journal of Education in Museums*, 10, 25–30.

—— Morris, S. and Wilkinson, S. (1990) *A Teachers' Guide to Learning from Objects*, English Heritage, London.

Eckstein, J. and Feist, A. (1992) *Cultural Trends*, 12, 1991, Policy Studies Institute, London.

Edeiken, L. R. 'Children's museums: the serious business of wonder, play and learning', *Curator*, 35(1), 21–7.

Ekarv, M. (1986/7) 'Combating redundancy – writing texts for exhibitions', *Exhibitions in Sweden*, 27/8, 1–7.

English Tourist Board (1982) *Visitors to Museums Survey 1982*, Report by the English Tourist Board Market Research Department and NOP Market Research Limited, English Tourist Board, London.

Esteve-Coll, E. (1991) 'The people's choice', *The Guardian*, 12 June, 37.

Fairclough, N. (1989) *Language and Power*, Longman, London and New York.

Falk J. H. (1988) 'Museum recollections', *Visitor Studies – 1988*, 61–5.

—— (1991) 'Analysis of the behavior of family visitors in natural history museums: the National Museum of Natural History', *Curator*, 34(1), 44–50.

—— and Dierking, L. D. (1992) *The Museum Experience*, Whalesback Books, Washington, DC.

Farmelo, G. (1992) 'Drama on the galleries', in Durant, J. (ed.) *Museums and the Public Understanding of Science*, Science Museum in association with the Committee on the Public Understanding of Science, London.

Fay, B. (1975) *Social Theory and Political Practice*, George Allen & Unwin Ltd., London.

Fleming, D. (1991) 'Second class citizens', *Museums Journal*, 91(2), 31–3.

Fondation de France and ICOM (1991) *Museums Without Barriers*, Routledge, London.

Forrester, W., Thorpe, S. and Kirby, W. (1988) *Disability Design Museums*, Museums and Galleries Disability Association and GDIM, London.

Foster, R. (1988) 'Reconciling museums and marketing', *Museums Journal*, 88(3), 127–30.

Frankfort-Nachmias, C. and Nachmias, D. (1992) *Research Methods in the Social Sciences*, Edward Arnold, London.

Fraser, J. (1991) 'Do you have any Teacher's Packs?', *Scottish Museum News*, Winter, 3–4.

Frazer, P. and Visram, R. (1988) *Black Contribution to History*, Geffrye Museum, London.

Freeman, R. (1989) *The Discovery Gallery: Discovery Learning in the Museum*, Royal Ontario Museum, Toronto.

Fronville, C. (1985) 'Marketing museums: for-profit techniques in the non-profit world', *Curator*, 28(3), 169–82.

Frostick, E. (1990) *The Story of Hull and its People*, Hull City Museums and Art Galleries, Hull.

—— (1991) 'Worth a Hull lot more', *Museums Journal*, 91(2), 33–5.

Fussell, A. (1991) 'Adding to the collection', *Museums Journal*, 91(2), 28–9.

Gardner, H. (1983) *Frames of Mind*, Paladin Books, London.

—— (1990) 'Developing the spectrum of human intelligences', in Hedley, C., Houtz, J. and Barratta, A. (eds) *Cognition, Curriculum and Literacy*, Ablex Publishing Corporation, Norwood, New Jersey.

—— (1991) *The Unschooled Mind: How Children Think and How Schools should Teach*, Basic Books, New York.

Getty Centre for Education in the Arts (1991) *Insights: Museums, Visitors, Attitudes, Expectations*, J. Paul Getty Museum, Los Angeles, California.

Goodhew, E. (ed.) (1989) *Museums and Primary Science*, Area Museum Service for South Eastern England, London.

Greater London Arts (1990a) *Arts in London: a Survey of Attitudes of Users and Non-users*, Greater London Arts, London.

—— (1990b) *Arts in London: a Qualitative Research Study*, Greater London Arts, London.

Greene, M. (1991) 'More jobs lost at the Museum of London', *Museums Journal*, 91(8), 8.

Greenwood, E. F., Phillips, P. W. and Wallace, I. D. (1989) 'The Natural History Centre at the Liverpool Museum', *The International Journal of Museum Management and Curatorship*, 8, 215–25.

Greeves, M. and Martin, B. (1992) *Chalk, Talk and Dinosaurs: Museums and Education in Scotland*, Scottish Museums Council and Moray House Institute, Edinburgh.

Griggs, S. A. (1981) 'Formative evaluation of exhibits at the British Museum (Natural History), *Curator*, 24(3), 189–201.

—— (1984) 'Evaluating exhibitions', in Thompson, J. M. A. (ed.) *Manual of Curatorship*, Butterworths, London, 412–22.

—— (1990) 'Perceptions of traditional versus new style exhibitions at The Natural History Museum, London', *ILVS Review: a Journal of Visitor Behavior*, 1(2), 78–90.

—— (1992) *Evaluating Museum Displays*, Committee of Area Museum Councils Museum Factsheet, Committee of Area Museum Councils, Cirencester.

Grinder, A. L. and McCoy, S. (1985) *The Good Guide: a Source Book for Interpreters, Docents and Tour Guides*, Ironwood Press, Scottsdale, Arizona.

Groff, G. and Gardner, L. (1989) *What Museum Guides Need to Know: Access for Blind and Visually Impaired Visitors*, American Foundation for the Blind, New York.

Grosbois, L. P. (1991) 'Ergonomics and museology', in Fondation de France and ICOM, *Museums Without Barriers*, Routledge, London, 60–9.

Gurian, E. (1992) 'The importance of "and"', in Museum Education Roundtable, *Patterns in Practice: Selections from the Journal of Museum Education*, Museum Education Roundtable, Washington, DC, 88–9.

Hall, J. (1992) 'Museum education: adapting to a changing South Africa', *Journal of Education in Museums*, 12, 10–14.

Ham, S. (1983) 'Cognitive psychology and interpretation: synthesis and application', *Journal of Interpretation*, 8(1), 11–28.

Handy, C. (1990) *The Age of Unreason*, Arrow Books Ltd, London.

Harlen, W., Van der Waal, A. and Russell, T. (1986) *Evaluation of the Pilot Phase of the Liverpool Interactive Technology Centre*, Centre for Research and Development in Primary School Science and Technology, Department of Education, Liverpool University, Liverpool.

Harris, N. (1990) 'Polling for opinions', *Museum News*, 69(5), September/October, 46–53.

Harvey, B. (1987) *Visiting the National Portrait Gallery*, OPCS/HMSO, London.

Hasted, R. (1990) 'Museums, racism and censorship', in Baker, F. and Thomas, J. (eds) *Writing the Past in the Present*, St David's College, Lampeter, 152–62.

Heady, P. (1984) *Visiting Museums: a Report of a Survey of Visitors to the Victoria and Albert, Science, and National Railway Museums for the Office of Arts and Libraries*, Office of Population and Census Surveys, HMSO, London.

Hein, G. (1982) 'Evaluation of museum programs and exhibits', in Hansen, T. H. (ed.) *Museums and Education*, Danish ICOM/CECA, Copenhagen.

Hemmings, S. (1992) 'Chinese Homes', *Journal of Education in Museums*, 13, 33–4.

Hennigar-Shuh, J. (1982) 'Teach yourself to teach with objects', *Journal of Education*, 7(9), 8–15, Department of Education, Nova Scotia.

Herbert, S. (1991) 'Inmates of a beautiful prison?', *Daily Telegraph*, 25 January, 14.

Hiemstra, R. (1981) 'The state of the art', in Collins, Z. (ed.) *Museums, Adults and the Humanities*, American Association of Museums, Washington, DC, 61–72.

Hill, T. and Nicks, T. (1992) *Turning the Page: Forging New Partnerships Between Museums and First Peoples*, Assembly of First Nations and Canadian Museums Association, Ottawa.

189

Hilke, D. D. (n. d.) 'What is an audience advocate? A position paper', unpublished paper.

Hodge, R. and D'Souza, W. (1979) 'The museum as a communicator: a semiotic analysis of the Western Australian Museum Aboriginal Gallery, Perth', *Museum*, 31(4), 251–67.

Hong Kong Museum of History (1990) *Law Uk Folk Museum*, Urban Council of Hong Kong, Hong Kong.

Hood, M. G. (1983) 'Staying away – why people choose not to visit museums', *Museum News*, 61(4), 50–7.

—— (1989) 'Leisure criteria of family participation and nonparticipation in museums', in Butler, B. H. and Sussman, M. B. (eds) *Museum Visits and Activities for Family Life Enrichment, Marriage and Family Review*, 13(3/4), 151–70.

Hooper-Greenhill, E. (1983) 'Some basic principles and issues relating to museum education', *Museums Journal*, 83(2/3), 69–70.

—— (1988) 'Counting visitors or visitors who count', in Lumley, R. (ed.) *The Museum Time Machine*, Comedia/Routledge, London, 213–32.

—— (1990) 'The space of the museum', *Continuum*, 3(1), 56–69.

—— (1991a) *Museum and Gallery Education*, Leicester University Press, Leicester, London and New York.

—— (1991b) 'A new communications model for museums', in Kavanagh, G. (ed.) *Museum Languages: Objects and Texts*, Leicester University Press, Leicester, London and New York, 47–61.

—— (1991c) 'Learning and teaching with objects', in *Actes du colloque 'A propos des recherches didactiques au musée'*, La Société des Musées Quebecois, Montreal, 48–52.

—— (1992a) *Museums and the Shaping of Knowledge*, Routledge, London.

—— (1992b) 'The past, the present and the future: museum education from the 1790s to the 1990s', *Journal of Education in Museums*, 12, 1–3.

—— (1992c) 'Museum education', in Thompson, J. M. A. (ed.) *Manual of Curatorship* (2nd edn), Butterworths, Cambridge, 670–89.

—— (1992d) 'Object lessons for schools', in

Greeves, M. and Martin, B. (eds) *Chalk, Talk and Dinosaurs: Museums and Education in Scotland*, Scottish Museums Council and Moray House Institute, Edinburgh, 9–15.

—— (forthcoming) 'Museum education: past, present and future', in Miles, R. (ed.) *Towards the Museum of the Future: European Perspectives*, Routledge, London.

—— (ed.) (1989) *Initiatives in Museum Education*, Department of Museum Studies, University of Leicester, Leicester.

—— (ed.) (1991) *Writing a Museum Education Policy*, Department of Museum Studies, University of Leicester, Leicester.

—— (ed.) (1992) *Working in Museum and Gallery Education: 10 Career Experiences*, Department of Museum Studies, University of Leicester, Leicester.

Hull, K. (1990) 'A new leaflet for the service or the beginnings of a marketing strategy?', *AMSSEE News*, 7, November, Area Museum Service for South Eastern England, London.

Husbands, C. (1992) 'Objects, evidence and learning: some thoughts on meaning and interpretation in museum education', *Journal of Museum Education*, 13, 1–3.

Ironbridge Gorge Museum (1991) *Primary Schools and Museums – Key Stage One – Guidelines for Teachers*, Ironbridge Gorge Museum Trust, Ironbridge.

James, R. (1991) '"Could do better . . ." Marketing museums in a multicultural society', West Midlands Area Museum Service, Bromsgrove.

Janes, R. R. (1987) 'Museum ideology and practice in Canada's Third World', *Muse*, Winter, 33–9.

Jarrett, J. E. (1986) 'Learning from developmental testing of exhibits', *Curator*, 29(4), 295–306.

Jensen, K. B. and Jankowski, N. W. (1991) *A Handbook of Qualitative Methodologies for Mass Communication Research*, Routledge, London.

Johnstone, C. (1991) 'Documenting diversity', *Museums Journal*, 91(2), 29–30.

Jones, S. (1991) 'The female perspective', *Museums Journal*, 91(2), 24–7.

Kavanagh, G. (1988) 'The first world war and its implications for education in British museums',

History of Education, 17(2), 163–76.

Kelly, J. (1991) 'Bodelwyddan close to sale', *Museums Journal*, 91(10), 11.

Kentley, E. and Neagus, D. (1989) *Writing on the Wall: a Guide for Presenting Exhibition Text*, National Maritime Museum, London.

Kerr, R. (1991) *Chinese Art and Design: the T. T. Tsui Gallery of Chinese Art*, Victoria and Albert Museum, London.

Kirby, W. (1991) 'Paintings and visually impaired people', in Fondation de France and ICOM, *Museums Without Barriers*, Routledge, London, 118–21.

Knez, E. I. and Wright, G. (1970) 'The museum as a communication system: an assessment of Cameron's viewpoint', *Curator*, 13(3), 204–12.

Knott, C. and Feber, S. (1991) 'Infantile behaviour', *Museums Journal*, 91(8), 16.

Koe, F. (1991) 'Small museum, big plans', *Museum News*, 70(1), 61–4.

Korn, R. (1989) 'Introduction to evaluation: theory and methodology', in Berry, S. and Mayer, S. (eds) *Museum Education: Theory and Practice*, The National Art Association, Reston, Virginia, 219–38.

Kress, G. and Hodge, R. (1979) *Language as Ideology*, Routledge and Kegan Paul, London.

Kropf, M. B. and Wolins, I. S. (1989) 'How families learn: considerations for program development', in Butler, B. H. and Sussman, M. B. (eds) (1989) *Museum Visits and Activities for Family Life Enrichment, Marriage and Family Review*, 13(3/4), 75–86.

Leichter, H. J., Hensel, K. and Larsen, E. (1989) 'Families and museums: issues and perspectives', in Butler, B. H. and Sussman, M. B. (eds) *Museum Visits and Activities for Family Life Enrichment, Marriage and Family Review*, 13(3/4), 15–50.

Lewin, A. W. (1989) 'Children's museums: a structure for family learning', in Butler, B. H. and Sussman, M. B. (eds) *Museum Visits and Activities for Family Life Enrichment, Marriage and Family Review*, 13(3/4), 51–73.

Lockett, C. (1991) 'Ten years of exhibit evaluation at the Royal Ontario Museum (1980–1990)', *ILVS Review: a Journal of Visitor Behavior*, 2(1), 19–47.

London-Morris, H. (1992) 'What's the catch?', Report on the first UK conference on the use of drama in museums, insert in *Museums Journal*, 92(8).

Loomis, R. J. (1987) *Museum Visitor Evaluation: New Tool for Management*, American Association for State and Local History, Nashville, Tennessee.

Lord, G. D. and Lord, B. (1991) *The Manual of Museum Planning*, Museum of Science and Industry, Manchester and HMSO, London.

Lucas, A.M., McManus P. and Thomas, G. (1986) 'Investigating learning from informal sources: listening to conversations and observing play in science museums', *European Journal of Science Education*, 8(4), 341–52.

Lumley, R. (1988) *The Museum Time Machine*, Comedia/Routledge, London.

MacDonald, S. (1990a) 'Discovering what Croydon people want from a museum', *AMSSEE News*, 6, November, Area Museum Service for South Eastern England, London.

—— (1990b) 'Telling white lies', *Museums Journal*, 90(9), 32–3.

—— (n.d.) 'Your place or mine?' unpublished paper, Croydon Museum Service, London.

McManus, G. (1991) 'The crisis of representation in museums: the exhibition "The Spirit Sings"', *New Research in Museum Studies*, 2, 202–6.

McManus, P. M. (1987) 'It's the company you keep … the social determinants of learning-related behaviour in a science museum', *International Journal of Museum Management and Curatorship*, 6, 263–70.

—— (1988) 'Good companions … more on the social determination of learning-related behaviour in a science museum', *International Journal of Museum Management and Curatorship*, 7, 37–44.

—— (1989) 'Oh, yes, they do: how museum visitors read labels and interact with exhibit texts', *Curator*, 32(3), 174–89.

—— (1990) 'Watch your language! People do read labels', in *What Research Says about Learning in Science Museums*, Association of Science-Technology Centres, Washington, DC, 4–6.

—— (1991) 'Making sense of exhibits', in Kavanagh, G. (ed.) *Museum Languages: Objects and Texts*, Leicester University Press, Leicester, London and New York, 33–45.

McNamara, P. A. (1988) 'Visitor-tested exhibits', in Bitgood, S., Roper, J. T. Jr and Benefield, A. *Visitor Studies – 1988: Theory, Research and Practice. Proceedings of the First Annual Visitor Studies Conference*, Centre for Social Design, Jacksonville State University, Alabama,150–4.

McQuail, D. (1975) *Communication*, Longman, London and New York.

—— (1987) *Mass Communication Theory, an Introduction*, Sage Publications, London.

—— and Windahl, S. (1993) *Communication Models*, Longman, London and New York.

MAGDA (1988) *Disability Design Museums*, Museums and Galleries Disability Association and Group of Designers and Interpreters in Museums, London.

Malcolm-Davies, J. (1991) 'Lincolnshire faces likely change in direction', *Museums Journal*, 91(10), 11.

Markham, S. F. (1938) *A Report on the Museums and Art Galleries of the British Isles*, Carnegie United Kingdom Trust, Dunfermline and London.

Merriman, N. (1989) 'The social basis of museum and heritage visiting', in Pearce, S. (ed.) *Museum Studies in Material Culture*, Leicester University Press, Leicester, London and New York.

—— (1991) *Beyond the Glass Case: the Past, the Heritage and the Public in Britain*, Leicester University Press, Leicester, London and New York.

Middleton, V. (1990) *New Visions for Independent Museums in the UK*, Association of Independent Museums, West Sussex.

—— (1991) 'The future demand for museums 1990–2001', in Kavanagh, G. (ed.) *The Museums Profession: Internal and External Relations*, Leicester University Press, Leicester, London and New York, 137–59.

Miers, Sir H. A. (1928) *A Report on the Public Museums of the British Isles*, Carnegie United Kingdom Trust, Dunfermline and London.

Miles, R. S. (1982) *The Design of Educational Exhibitions*, Unwin Hyman, London.

—— (1985) 'Exhibitions: management, for a change', in Cossons, N. (ed.) *The Management of Change in Museums*, National Maritime Museum, London, 31–3.

—— (1986a) 'Museum audiences', *The International Journal of Museum Management and Curatorship*, 5, 73–80.

—— (1986b) 'Lessons in "Human Biology": testing a theory of exhibition design', *The International Journal of Museum Management and Curatorship*, 5, 227–40.

—— (1988) 'Museums and public culture, a context for communicating science', in Heltne, P. G. and Marquardt, L. A. (eds) *Science Learning in the Informal Setting*, Chicago Academy of Sciences, Chicago, 157–69.

—— (1989) *Evaluation in its Communications Context*, Technical Report no. 89–10, Centre for Social Design, Jacksonville, Alabama.

—— and Tout, A. F. (1979) 'Outline of a technology for effective science exhibits', *Special Papers in Paleontology*, 22, 209–24.

—— and Tout, A. F. (1991) 'Impact of research on the approach to the visiting public at the Natural History Museum, London', *International Journal of Science Education*, 13(5), 534–49.

Millar, S. (1991a) 'Policy planning for volunteers', in Ambrose, T. and Runyard, S. (eds) *Forward Planning: a Handbook of Business, Corporate and Development Planning for Museums and Galleries*, Routledge, London and New York, 112–16.

—— (1991b) *The Management of Volunteers in Museums*, HMSO, London.

Millard, J. (1992) 'Art history for all the family', *Museums Journal*, 92(2), 32–3.

Miller, G. A. (1970) *The Psychology of Communication*, Penguin, Harmondsworth.

Millward Brown (1991) *Galleries and Museums Research Digest*, British Market Research Bureau, London.

Minihan, J. (1977) *The Nationalisation of Culture*, Hamish Hamilton, London.

Moore, K. (1991) '"Feasts of reason?" Exhibitions at the Liverpool Mechanics Institution in the 1840s', in Kavanagh, G. (ed.) *Museum Languages: Objects and Texts*, Leicester University Press, Leicester, London and New York, 155–77.

Morgan, J. and Welton, P. (1986) *See What I Mean*, Edward Arnold, London and New York.

Morley, D. (1980) *The 'Nationwide' Audience: Structure and Decoding*, British Film Institute, London.

Morris, S. (1989) *A Teachers' Guide to Using Portraits*, English Heritage, London.

—— and Wilkinson, S. (1992) 'What are the differences between "objects" and "documents" as historical sources and what is the value of using objects?', *Journal of Education in Museums*, 13, 24–8.

Mounin, G. (1985) *Semiotic Praxis: Studies in Pertinence and in the Means and Expression of Communication*, Plenum Press, New York and London.

Munley, M. E. (1986) 'Asking the right questions: evaluation and the museum mission', *Museum News*, 64(3), 18–23.

—— (1992) 'Back to the future: a call for co-ordinated research programs in museums', in Museum Education Roundtable, *Patterns in Practice: Selections from the Journal of Museum Education*, Museum Education Roundtable, Washington, DC, 196–203.

Murdin, L. (1991) 'Newcastle upon tenterhooks – possible job cuts', *Museums Journal*, 91(9), 9.

Museum Education Roundtable (1984) *Museum Education Anthology, Perspectives on Informal Learning: a Decade of Roundtable Reports, 1973–1983*, Museum Education Roundtable, Washington, DC.

—— (1992) *Patterns in Practice: Selections from the Journal of Museum Education*, Museum Education Roundtable, Washington, DC.

Museum of Contemporary Art (1992) *Collection/Exhibition/Education Policy*, Museum of Contemporary Art Limited, Sydney.

Museums and Galleries Commission (1991) *Local Authorities and Museums: Report by a Working Party (the Last Report)*, Museums and Galleries Commission, London.

—— (1992) *Guidelines on Disability for Museums and Galleries in the United Kingdom*, Museums and Galleries Commission, London.

—— (1993) *Quality of Service in Museums and Galleries: Customer Care in Museums – Guidelines on Implementation*, Museums and Galleries Commission, London.

Museums Association (1991a) *A National Strategy for Museums: The Museums Association Annual Report 1990–1991*, Museums Association, London.

—— (1991b) *Museums Yearbook 1992*, Museums Association, London.

Myerscough, J. (1988) *The Economic Importance of the Arts in Britain*, Policy Studies Institute, London.

—— (1991) 'Your museum in context: knowing the museum industry; the background statistics', in Ambrose, T. and Runyard, S. (eds) *Forward Planning: a Handbook of Business, Corporate and Development Planning for Museums and Galleries*, Routledge, London and New York.

National Audit Office (1988) *Management of the Collections of the English National Museums and Galleries*, HMSO, London.

National Curriculum Council (1990) *The National Curriculum: a Guide for Staff of Museums, Galleries, Historic Houses and Sites*, National Curriculum Council, York.

—— (1991) *History in the National Curriculum*, DES/HMSO, London.

Newsom, B. Y. and Silver, A. Z. (1978) *The Art Museum as Educator*, University of California Press, Berkeley, Los Angeles and London.

Nichols, P. (1991) *Social Survey Methods: a Fieldguide for Development Workers*, Oxfam, Oxford.

Nicholson, H. (1992) 'Cultural centres or trading posts', *Museums Journal*, 92(8), 31–4.

Office of Arts and Libraries (1991) *Report on the Development of Performance Indicators for the National Museums and Galleries*, Office of Arts and Libraries, London.

Olds, A. R. (1992) 'Sending them home alive', in Museum Education Roundtable, *Patterns in Practice: Selections from the Journal of Museum Education*, Museum Education Roundtable, Washington, DC, 174–8.

O'Neill, M. (1990) 'Springburn: a community and its museums', in Baker, F. and Thomas, J. (eds) *Writing the Past in the Present*, St David's College, Lampeter, 114–26.

—— (1991) 'The Open Museum', *Scottish Museum News*, Winter, 6–7.

Ontario Ministry of Citizenship and Culture (1985) *Developing an Interpretation and Education Policy for the Museum*, Museum Notes – Practical Information on Operating a Community Museum, 11, Ministry of Citizenship and Culture, Toronto.

193

—— (n.d.) *Developing an Exhibition Policy*, Museum Notes for Community Museums in Ontario, 9, Ministry of Citizenship and Culture, Toronto.

Ontario Ministry of Culture and Communications (1985) *The Community Museum and the Disabled Visitor*, Ontario Museum Notes, 12, Heritage Branch, Ministry of Citizenship and Culture, Toronto.

Otto, J. (1979) 'Learning about "neat stuff": one approach to evaluation', *Museum News*, 58(2), 38–45.

Owen, D. (1991) *A New South African Challenge: Teaching History in Multi-Cultural Schools*, Albany Museum New History Series, 1, Albany Museum, Grahamstown, South Africa.

Parsons, L. A. (1965) 'Systematic testing of display techniques for an anthropological exhibit', *Curator*, 8(2), 167–89.

Pearce, S. (1992) *Museums, Objects and Collections: a Cultural Study*, Leicester University Press, Leicester.

Pearson, A. (1985) *Arts for Everyone*, Carnegie United Kingdom Trust and Centre for Environment for the Handicapped, Dunfermline and London.

—— (1989) 'Museum education and disability', in Hooper-Greenhill, E. (ed.) *Initiatives in Museum Education*, Department of Museum Studies, University of Leicester, Leicester, 22–3.

—— (1991) 'Touch exhibitions in the United Kingdom', in Fondation de France and ICOM, *Museums Without Barriers*, Routledge, London, 122–6.

Peirson-Jones, J. (1991) 'Cultural representation and the creation of dialogue', paper presented to the ICOM/CECA conference at Liverpool Museum on 15 May 1991.

—— (1992) 'The colonial legacy and the community: the Gallery 33 project', in Karp, I., Kreamer, C., and Lavine, S., *Museums and Communities*, Smithsonian Institution Press, Washington and London, 221–41.

Pes, J. (1991) 'Read and understand?: What are the functions of written texts in museums? How can these functions be effectively carried out? A case-study – Lifebox', unpublished paper, Department of Museum Studies, University of Leicester.

Pittman, N. (1991) 'Writing a museum education policy: introductory remarks', *GEM Newsletter*, 43, Autumn, 22–4, Group for Education in Museums, Nottingham.

Plant, A. (1992) 'Expression and engagement', *Journal of Education in Museums*, 13, 12–15.

Pond, M. (1983) 'School history visits and Piagetian theory', *Teaching History*, 37, 3–6.

—— (1984) 'Recreating a trip to York in Victorian times', *Teaching History*, 39, 12–16.

—— (1985) 'The usefulness of school visits – a study', *Journal of Education in Museums*, 6, 32–6.

Porter, G. (1988) 'Putting your house in order', in Lumley, R. (ed.) *The Museum Time Machine*, Comedia/Routledge, London, 102–27.

—— (1991) 'Partial truths', in Kavanagh, G. (ed.) *Museum Languages: Objects and Texts*, Leicester University Press, Leicester, London and New York, 101–17.

Pownall, J. and Hutson, N. (1991) *Science and the Historic Environment*, English Heritage, London.

Prince, D. (1984) 'Approaches to summative evaluation', in Thompson, J. M. A. (ed.) *Manual of Curatorship*, Butterworths, London, 423–34.

—— and Higgins, B. (1992) *The Public View: the Findings of the 1991/92 Study of the Perception and Use of Leicestershire Museums, Arts and Records Service*, Prince Research Consultants Limited for Leicestershire Museums, Arts and Records Service, Leicestershire.

—— and Higgins-McLoughlin, B. (1987) *Museums UK: the Findings of the Museums Data-base Project*, Museums Association, London.

Prochak, M. (1990) 'Multimedia is the message', *Museums Journal*, 90(8), 25–7.

Punt, B. (1989) *Doing it Right: a Workbook for Improving Exhibit Labels*, Brooklyn Children's Museum, New York.

Rees, P. (1990) 'Education, evaluation and exhibitions: an outline of current thought and work on Merseyside', *Journal of Education in Museums*, 11, 9–12.

Report of the National Inquiry into Arts and the Community (1992) *Arts and Communities*, Community Development Foundation, London.

194

Roberts, L. (1990) 'The elusive qualities of "affect"', in Serrell, B. (ed.) *What Research Says about Learning in Science Museums*, Association of Science-Technology Centres, Washington, DC, 19–22.

Robinson, K. (1983) *Museums – Lessons from the USA*, British Tourist Authority, London.

Rosse, Earl of (1963) *Survey of Provincial Museums and Galleries*, Standing Commission on Museums and Galleries, HMSO, London.

Royal Ontario Museum (1976) *Communicating with the Museum Visitor: Guidelines for Planning*, Royal Ontario Museum, Toronto.

Rubenstein, R. (1988) 'The use of focus groups in audience research', *Visitor Studies – 1988*, 180–8.

Runyard, S. (forthcoming) *Museum Marketing Handbook*, Routledge, London.

—— (ed.) (1992) 'MGC News' *Museums Journal*, 92(4), 39.

—— and Anderson, B. (1992), 'MGC News' *Museums Journal*, 92(6), 39.

Schlereth, T. (ed.) (1982) *Material Culture Studies in America*, American Association for State and Local History, Nashville, Tennessee.

Schouten, F. (1983) 'Target groups and displays in museums', *Reinwardt Studies in Museology, 1: Exhibition Design as an Educational Tool*, 3–11.

Screven, C. G. (1969) 'The museum as a responsive learning environment', *Museum News*, 47(10), 7–10.

—— (1976) 'Exhibit evaluation: a goal-referenced approach', *Curator*, 19(4), 271–90.

—— (1986) 'Exhibitions and information centres: some principles and approaches', *Curator*, 29(2), 109–37.

—— (1988) 'Formative evaluation: conceptions and misconceptions', in Bitgood, S., Roper, J. T. Jr and Benefield, A. *Visitor Studies – 1988: Theory, Research and Practice. Proceedings of the First Annual Visitor Studies Conference*, Centre for Social Design, Jacksonville State University, Alabama, 73–81.

—— and Giraudy, D. (1991) 'The Musée Picasso–Antibes Project', *ILVS Review: a Journal of Visitor Behavior*, 2(1), 116–17.

Serrell, B. (1988) *Making Exhibit Labels: a Step-by-step Guide*, American Association for State and Local History, Nashville, Tennessee.

Sharkey, K. (1992) *Marketing Plan*, Museum of Science and Industry, Manchester.

Shelton, A. (1992) 'Constructing the global village', *Museums Journal*, 92(8), 25–8.

Shettel, H. H. (1973) 'Exhibits: art form or educational medium?' *Museum News*, 52(1), 32–41.

Simons, R., Miller, L. and Lengsfelder, P. (1984) *Non-profit Piggy Goes to Market*, Childrens Museum, Denver.

Simpson, M. (1992a) 'Celebration, commemoration, or condemnation?' *Museums Journal*, 92(3), 28–31.

—— (1992b) *Black History – Whose Perspective?*, unpublished paper, University of Warwick.

Smith, N. P. (1991) 'Exhibitions and audiences: catering for a pluralistic public', in Kavanagh, G. (ed.) *Museum Languages: Objects and Texts*, Leicester University Press, Leicester, London and New York, 119–33.

Solinger, J. W. (1989) *Museums and Universities*, National University Continuing Education Association, American Council on Education, and Macmillan Publishing Company, New York; Collier Macmillan Publishers, London.

Southern African Museums Association (1989) *Museum Education and Communication: Guidelines for Policy and Practice*, The Albany Museum, Grahamstown, South Africa, for the Southern African Museums Association.

Spalding, J. (1991) 'Is there life in museums?', in Kavanagh, G. (ed.) *The Museums Profession: Internal and External Relations*, Leicester University Press, Leicester, London and New York, 161–75.

Stansfield, G. and Woodhead, P. (1989) *Keyguide to Information Sources in Museum Studies*, Mansell, London.

Steiner, C. (1991) 'Museum programmes designed for mentally disabled visitors', in Fondation de France and ICOM, *Museums Without Barriers*, Routledge, London, 172–6.

Stevenson, A. and Bryden, M. (1991) 'The National Museums of Scotland's 1990 Discovery Room: an evaluation', *Museum Management and Curatorship*, 10, 24–36.

195

Stevenson, J. (1991) 'The long-term impact of interactive exhibits', *International Journal of Science Education*, 13(5), 521–31.

Stibbons, P. (1991) 'KEY: Resources for schools', *Journal of Education in Museums*, 12, 23–5.

Stoke-on-Trent Museum and Art Gallery (1987) *Palaces of Culture: the Great Museum Exhibition*, Stoke-on-Trent Museum and Art Gallery, Stoke-on-Trent.

Sudely, Lord (1912) 'The public utility of museums', *Museums Journal*, 11(1911–12), 271.

—— (1913) 'The public utility of museums', *The Nineteenth Century*, 74, 1219.

Suina, J. H. (1992) 'Museum multicultural education for young learners' in Museum Education Roundtable, *Patterns in Practice: Selections from the Journal of Museum Education*, Museum Education Roundtable, Washington, DC, 179–84.

Susie Fisher Group (1990) *Bringing History and the Arts to a New Audience: Qualitative Research for the London Borough of Croydon*, Susie Fisher Group, London.

Swank, S. (1992) 'Museums' social contract', in Museum Education Roundtable, *Patterns in Practice: Selections from the Journal of Museum Education*, Museum Education Round-table, Washington, DC, 93–4.

Tilden, F. (1957) *Interpreting our Heritage*, University of North Carolina Press, Chapel Hill.

Tinker, A. (1992) *Elderly People in Modern Society*, Longman, London and New York.

Touche Ross (1989) *Museum Funding and Services – the Visitor's Perspective*, Report of a survey carried out by Touche Ross Management Consultants, London.

Trevelyan, V. (ed.) (1991) *'Dingy Places with Different Kinds of Bits': an Attitudes Survey of London Museums amongst Non-visitors*, London Museums Service, London.

Ulster Museum (1992) *Policy on Education*, Ulster Museum, Belfast.

University of Exeter (1992) *The Wordsworth Museum Visitor Survey 1991: a Report Prepared for the Wordsworth Trust*, Tourism Research Group, Department of Geography, University of Exeter, Exeter.

Visram, R. (1990) 'British history: whose history? Black perspectives on British history', in Baker, F. and Thomas, J. (eds) *Writing the Past in the Present*, St David's College, Lampeter, 163–71.

Walden, I. (1991) 'Qualities and quantities', *Museums Journal*, 91(1), 27–8.

Weil, S. (1990) 'Rethinking the museum', *Museum News*, 69(2), 57–61.

Weisen, M. (1991a) 'Museums and the visually handicapped', in Fondation de France and ICOM, *Museums Without Barriers*, Routledge, London, 83–5.

—— (1991b) 'Art and the visual handicap: a role for the associations for the blind, the museums and art associations, and the official cultural authorities', in Fondation de France and ICOM, *Museums Without Barriers*, Routledge, London, 107–13.

Weiss, R. S. and Boutourline, S. (1963) 'The communicational value of exhibits', *Museum News*, 42(3), 23–7.

Westwood, M. (1989) 'Warwick Castle: safeguarding the future through service', in Uzzell, D. (ed.) *Heritage Interpretation – Volume 2: The Visitor Experience*, Belhaven Press, London, 84–95.

Wilson, G. (1991) 'Planning for visitors', *New Research in Museum Studies*, 2, 89–117.

Wilson, M. (1976) *The Effective Management of Volunteer Programs*, Volunteer Management Associates, Boulder, Colorado.

Windsor, J. (1992) 'A small leap for man; a giant leap for plastic frogs', *The Independent*, 9 May, 41.

Wolf, J. (1991) 'In the realm of the senses', *Times Educational Supplement*, 31 May, 39.

Wolf, R. L. (1980) 'A naturalistic view of evaluation', *Museum News*, 58(6), 39–45.

Wright, J. and Mazel, A. (1987) 'Bastions of ideology: the depiction of precolonial history in the museums of Natal and Kwazulu', *SAMAB*, 17(7 and 8), 301–10.

Wright, P. (1992) 'Discretionary policies', *Museums Journal*, 92(5), 24–5.

Wright, S. (1990) 'Your visitors have something to say', *Evaluating Interpretation – Environmental Interpretation: the Bulletin of the Centre for Environmental Interpretation*, July, 8–10.

—— (1992) 'Susan Wright; Defence of the Realm, Portsmouth', in Hooper-Greenhill, E. (ed.) *Working in Museum and Gallery Education: 10 Career Experiences*, Department of Museum Studies, University of Leicester, Leicester, 18–19.

Index